Strategic Approaches to Regional Development

The existence and persistence of regional disparities between European regions require context-tailored policies to promote structural change. This book explores the congruence between place-based development and regional competitiveness in the EU context.

Drawing on a range of social science disciplines, this book unpicks the complexity of regional transformation processes, aiming to enhance the applicability and transferability of theoretical approaches to innovation and place-based regional development in diverse European territorial settings. The contributors have a particular focus on less-favoured regions and on the application of Smart Specialisation – a strategic approach to innovation-based regional development – to the issues at hand.

The book comes at a critical moment, meeting the growing demand of academics, practitioners and policymakers with an interest in promoting regional economic growth and well-being.

Iryna Kristensen is Senior Research Fellow at the Nordic Centre of Spatial Development (Nordregio) in Stockholm, Sweden.

Alexandre Dubois is a researcher at the Swedish University of Agricultural Sciences in Uppsala, Sweden.

Jukka Teräs is Senior Research Fellow at the Nordic Centre of Spatial Development (Nordregio) in Stockholm, Sweden.

Regions and Cities
Series Editor in Chief
Joan Fitzgerald, *Northeastern University, USA*
Editors
Ron Martin, *University of Cambridge, UK*
Maryann Feldman, *University of North Carolina, USA*
Gernot Grabher, *HafenCity University Hamburg, Germany*
Kieran P. Donaghy, *Cornell University, USA*

In today's globalised, knowledge-driven and networked world, regions and cities have assumed heightened significance as the interconnected nodes of economic, social and cultural production, and as sites of new modes of economic and territorial governance and policy experimentation. This book series brings together incisive and critically engaged international and interdisciplinary research on this resurgence of regions and cities, and should be of interest to geographers, economists, sociologists, political scientists and cultural scholars, as well as to policymakers involved in regional and urban development.

For more information on the Regional Studies Association, visit www.regionalstudies.org.

There is a **30% discount** available to RSA members on books in the ***Regions and Cities*** series, and other subject-related Taylor and Francis books and e-books, including Routledge titles. To order, just e-mail Joanna Swieczkowska, Joanna.Swieczkowska@tandf.co.uk, or phone on +44 (0)20 3377 3369 and declare your RSA membership. You can also visit the series page at www.routledge.com/Regions-and-Cities/book-series/RSA and use the discount code: **RSA0901**.

132. China in the Local and Global Economy
History, Geography, Politics and Sustainability
Steven Brakman, Charles van Marrewijk, Peter Morgan and Nimesh Salike

133. The Entrepreneurial Discovery Process and Regional Development
New Knowledge Emergence, Conversion and Exploitation
Edited by Åge Mariussen, Seija Virkkala, Håkon Finne and Tone Merethe Aasen

134. Strategic Approaches to Regional Development
Smart Experimentation in Less-Favoured Regions
Edited by Iryna Kristensen, Alexandre Dubois and Jukka Teräs

For more information about this series, please visit: www.routledge.com/Regions-and-Cities/book-series/RSA

Strategic Approaches to Regional Development

Smart Experimentation in Less-Favoured Regions

Edited by Iryna Kristensen, Alexandre Dubois and Jukka Teräs

Routledge
Taylor & Francis Group
LONDON AND NEW YORK

First published 2019
by Routledge
2 Park Square, Milton Park, Abingdon, Oxon OX14 4RN, UK

and by Routledge
52 Vanderbilt Avenue, New York, NY 10017, USA

First issued in paperback 2020

Routledge is an imprint of the Taylor & Francis Group, an informa business

British Library Cataloguing-in-Publication Data
A catalogue record for this book is available from the British Library

Library of Congress Cataloging-in-Publication Data
A catalog record has been requested for this book

ISBN 13: 978-0-367-66314-8 (pbk)
ISBN 13: 978-1-138-08435-3 (hbk)

Typeset in Bembo
by Swales & Willis Ltd, Exeter, Devon, UK

Contents

Figures

Tables

Boxes

Graphs

Contributors

Jaime del Castillo is President of INFYDE and was Professor of Applied Economy at the University of the Basque Country (1976–2017). Jaime del Castillo is a well-known expert with more than 25 years of experience at national and international level in the fields of regional development and innovation analysis and strategies, the definition of training and employment policies, and in the feasibility analysis and implementation of intermediate infrastructures such as technological parks, technological centres and incubators. He has participated as a speaker in numerous forums and at various round-tables, and has written several books and scientific articles about these topics. During his long professional career, he has worked as a consultant for several multilateral organisations (EC, World Bank, IBRD, etc.) and for national and regional governments in Europe, Latin America and Asia. He was included by DG REGIO in the list of experts to support RIS3 and the overall Cohesion Policy.

Andrew Copus has been a senior researcher at the James Hutton Institute (Aberdeen) since March 2013. For the previous eight years he was Senior Research Fellow at and the Centre for Remote and Rural Studies, University of the Highlands and Islands. Until February 2018 he had a ten-year association with Nordregio, Stockholm, through a part-time secondment. Andrew is an economic geographer by training, whose research interests relate to the changing rural economy and rural/regional policy. Much of his work has been based upon analysis of small areas or regional secondary data and indicators. He has a long-standing interest in territorial rural development and regional disparities, which through recent projects is presented as 'rural cohesion policy'.

Thomas Dax is Deputy Director of the Federal Institute for Less-Favoured and Mountainous Areas in Vienna (Austria). He is leading work at the institute on the concept and assessment of rural development and mountain regions through national and international studies. He is the Austrian delegate to the Working Group on Rural Policy at the OECD, Paris, and international expert on mountain regions development.

Alexandre Dubois is a researcher at the Swedish University of Agricultural Sciences in Uppsala (Sweden). His current topic of research deals with the role of rural businesses in supporting the transition of local economies in the Nordic countries from an integrated rural development perspective. Prior to this, Alexandre was Senior Research Fellow at Nordregio in Stockholm where he developed an expertise on issues related to territorial development policies in the Nordic countries and the Baltic Sea Region, especially linked to territorial cohesion. He has participated in many international research projects in European programmes (FP7, ESPON) and has worked on commissioned studies for the European Parliament, the European Commission and the Nordic Council of Ministers.

Thomas Ejdemo is currently a PhD-candidate in Entrepreneurship & Innovation at Luleå University of Technology (Sweden). His research focuses on regional economic development and the impacts of specialisation processes. Thomas's previous experience includes research and consulting in the fields of natural resources and regional economics. He has co-authored several applied regional development analyses, commissioned by regional authorities in Norrbotten County.

David Freshwater is the H. B. Price Professor of Agricultural Policy at the University of Kentucky (USA). He has held a number of academic and government positions over his career, including being a senior economist at the Joint Economic Committee of the US Congress and as a consultant to both the Canadian Government and the OECD. With the OECD he has been Head of the Rural Policy Unit and has contributed to most OECD National Rural Policy Reviews as well as to various other OECD studies. His primary interests are policy formation and assessment in rural areas, including agricultural policy, local economic development policy and the role of active labour market policy.

Klaus S. Friesenbichler is a senior economist at the Austrian Institute of Economic Research, where he currently coordinates the research group 'Industrial Economics, Innovation and International Competition'. He was a visiting researcher at the Ratio Institute in Stockholm, the Sheffield Management School in the UK and a World Bank staff member based in Washington, DC. Holding a doctoral degree in Economics, he teaches Development Economics at the Vienna University of Economics and Business. His thematic interests comprise firm and industry performance, and how these are affected by industrial policies.

Kristiina Jokelainen, Senior Expert, works at the Regional Council of Lapland (Finland). Since 2012, she has been involved in the creation and implementation of Lapland's Smart Specialisation strategy and, in particular, leading the regional clusters development as part of the 'Arctic Smartness' Smart Specialisation strategy implementation. In her current position, she applies her experience and knowledge to support Lapland in becoming a strong and the most innovative sparsely populated region in the EU. Previously, Mrs Jokelainen worked in the higher education sector. She has over 20 years of experience working on economic, research and innovation development projects and multi-sector cooperation activities in Finland and in Eastern European, Central Asian and EU countries. During her working career, she has been involved in over a hundred national and international development projects, acquired expertise in the following areas: the development of strategic management; monitoring and evaluation of development processes; integrating multidisciplinary approaches in practice; and seeking new arenas and interfaces for innovation development.

Iryna Kristensen is Senior Research Fellow at the International Research Institute for Regional Development and Planning (Nordregio) in Stockholm, specialising in local and regional economic development and innovation, with national and international experience in this field. Iryna holds a PhD in Economics from Paris Lodron University of Salzburg (Austria), where she studied inter-organisational collaborative practices and their role in shaping the regional innovative systems in both peripheral and urban regions. Iryna is continuously involved in a number of European and Nordic research projects, such as Horizon2020, ESPON, Nordic cooperation programmes. Her current research focuses on questions related to regional development, innovation, green growth and smart specialisation. Iryna has previous experience as a visiting researcher at the Centre for Innovation, Research and Competence in the Learning Economy at Lund University (Sweden).

Henning Kroll studied economic geography at the Universities of Hanover (Germany) and Bristol (UK). From 2003 to 2006 he was employed as a research associate at the Institute of Economic and Cultural Geography at the University of Hanover where he received his PhD in 2005. Since 2006 he has worked at the Fraunhofer Institute for Systems and Innovation Research ISI in Karlsruhe (Germany), and is now a senior researcher in the Competence Center Policy – Industry – Innovation, Business Unit Regional Innovation Systems. His work focuses on the analysis and evaluation of regional innovation policy, smart specialisation, advanced manufacturing in German and European regions, regional innovation and technology indicators, university–industry relations and cluster-based regional development.

Antti Mäenpää is a doctoral student of Regional Studies at the University of Vaasa (Finland). His research is centred around smart specialisation and especially on triple helix measurements (the connections between universities, firms and public administration). His dissertation focuses on the role of public organisations in the smart specialisation process. Antti was part of the team that developed the Ostrobothnian model for smart specialisation as a tool for measuring regional triple helix cooperation.

Daniel Örtqvist is Professor in Entrepreneurship and Innovation at Luleå University of Technology (Sweden) since November 2013 and Deputy

Head of the Department for Business Administration and Social Sciences. Daniel is a member of the board of RegLab, and he is part of the team for developing the regional innovation strategy for Norrbotten. His academic research mainly concerns entrepreneurial identity, the establishment of new ventures and regional development and innovation system research.

Jonatan Paton holds a PhD in Economics from the University of the Basque Country, Bilbao (Spain). He has specialised in various subjects highlighting quantitative economy (statistics and econometrics), microeconomics, geographic economy and the economics of innovation and technical change. He has also studied at the London School of Economics (UK) during 2007 and 2008. He is author and co-author of numerous publications of international reference in the economics of innovation, competitiveness policy and cluster policy. For more than 13 years, he has worked at INFYDE as a consultant and researcher in the field of territorial development and public policies linked to innovation and competitiveness. He is included on a list of experts to support cohesion policy, regional and urban development (OJ 2015/S 053-091748 of 17 March 2015).

Andreas Reinstaller is a senior economist at the Austrian Institute of Economic Research (WIFO) in Vienna (Austria). He holds a master's degree in economics from the Vienna University of Economics (WU Wien) and a PhD from the University of Maastricht (the Netherlands). He joined the Austrian Institute of Economic Research in 2007 and teaches economics and economic policy at the Vienna University of Economics. His main areas of expertise are in the fields of industrial economics, industrial policy, as well as science and innovation policy. In these fields he has managed and contributed to projects for the European Commission, the OECD and Austrian ministries and public bodies, and has served as member of international high-level expert groups. He has published in international journals such as *Research Policy*, the *Journal of Evolutionary Economics, Structural Change and Economic Dynamics*, *Industrial and Corporate Change* and *Applied Economics*.

Jens Sörvik works at Region Skåne with the regional innovation council and the regional innovation strategy. Prior to this he worked at the Swedish Agency for Economic and Regional Growth where he supported Swedish regions develop and implement Smart Specialisation Strategies and the European Commission's Smart Specialisation Platform (S3P) in Seville. The S3P has been set up to support EU Member States and regions in designing and implementing Research and Innovation Strategies for Smart Specialisation (RIS3). At the platform, Jens Sörvik worked as project leader for the collaboration with DG CONNECT on the role of ICT for regional development, but also covered topics such as interregional collaboration, sparsely populated regions, Nordic countries and Baltic sea initiatives. Since 2002, Jens has been working with issues related to innovation management, support and innovation policies, both from an academic perspective as well as hands on in different projects. Jens has done this from different platforms and in different forms, at the Research Policy Institute at Lund University, his own consultancy and Ramböll Management consultants, as well as for an international organisation called IKED.

Jukka Teräs is Senior Research Fellow at Nordregio in Stockholm (Sweden) and holds a Doctor of Science (Technology) degree from the University of Oulu in Finland and an MBA from the Helsinki School of Economics. Jukka has more than 20 years of experience on innovation promotion and regional development in both the public and private sectors. He has gained a special expertise in regional clusters, innovation environments and issues related to non-metropolitan regions. Jukka has experience from several engagements related to the implementation of smart specialisation in European regions. He has also contributed to regional smart specialisation strategy development, e.g. in the Lapland region in northern Finland. Jukka has recent publications on smart specialisation, including in both academic journals and other policy-oriented publications. His primary research interests on smart specialisation focus on non-metropolitan and sparsely populated regions.

Fabian Unterlass is a senior economist at the Austrian Institute of Economic Research (WIFO). He holds masters' degrees in economics, political sciences and history from the University of Vienna. His main research interests are in the fields of resources and waste, the circular economy, as well as green innovation in the context of industrial economics. Since 2006, when he joined the Austrian Institute of Economic Research, he has worked on several national and international projects on behalf of the European Commission, Austrian ministries and other public authorities.

Seija Virkkala is a professor in regional studies at the University of Vaasa (Finland). Her previous research activities covered regional innovation studies, transnational learning, innovation systems in peripheral regions and smart specialisation. She led the team that developed the Ostrobothnian model for smart specialisation as a tool for measuring regional triple helix cooperation.

Johanna Vogel is an economist at Environment Agency Austria, which she joined in July 2015. Her work focuses broadly on the economic aspects of environmental and climate change mitigation policy and on issues related to low-carbon transition, sustainability and greening of the economy. Recent projects have focused on eco-innovation, competitiveness and policy design and evaluation. She uses quantitative and qualitative methods and is involved in research projects as well as consulting work for federal ministries. Before joining EAA, Johanna worked as a project researcher at the Austrian Institute of Economic Research (WIFO). She holds a PhD in economics from the University of Oxford (UK).

Stefan Weingärtner is currently a research assistant at the Austrian Institute of Economic Research (WIFO) in the field of industrial economics, innovation and international competition. Since October 2012, he has been contributing to different projects, including WWWforEurope and the EU Competitiveness Report. Stefan Weingärtner holds a master's degree in economics and development studies from the University of Vienna.

Håkan Ylinenpää is a professor in entrepreneurship and innovation at Luleå University of Technology (Sweden, 2005–2017), research director for the national Centre for Inter-organisational Innovation Research (CiiR, 2011–2017) and, since August 2017, Professor Emeritus at Luleå. He has experience from several engagements and assignments outside the academic world, including serving as a member of the board of directors of the Swedish Agency for Economic and Regional Growth, as external expert for Ingvar Kamprads Family Foundation on entrepreneurship research, as national project coordinator for a European R&D project 'Rural Innovation & Business Systems (RIBS)' funded by the EU (Northern Periphery Program) and as a board member of several private and public companies. His primary research interests focus on entrepreneurial innovation activities and strategies and innovation system research based on cross-sector collaboration.

Foreword

This is a timely book that addresses a long-term puzzle in the academic and policy world: how to understand the lack of development dynamics in many less-favoured regions and the question of what are the relevant policy strategies to provide for growth in such regions.

The book is timely because of an evolving economic globalisation, seen in, amongst others, intensified global production and knowledge and innovation networks, that challenges development potentials in less-favoured regions in particular. The book is also well timed because of the emergence of new dominant regional policy strategies, in particular the EU's Smart Specialisation approach, that advocates place-based and regional adapted policy. Further development of the Smart Specialisation strategy will benefit from critical testing and discussions. Lastly, the topic of the book is still relevant, as some types of regions continue to lag behind in economic development without much sign of a reduction in the gap between less- and well-developed regions. These development trends demand up-to-date knowledge about the mechanisms leading to uneven territorial distribution of economic growth and about relevant policy answers.

Intensified economic globalisation makes the traditional regional economic policy approach that focuses on endogenous development quite irrelevant, and especially so in less-favoured regions. These regions are characterised by organisationally thin regional innovation systems (RISs) that are found in many peripheral regions, while organisationally thick and specialised RISs often describe old industrial regions. Regions with thin RISs suffer from little local knowledge dynamics due to few innovative firms and few knowledge organisations. Regions with specialised RISs may experience lock-in of the industrial development due to dense networks of actors with common world views and who are apt to continue economic and political support for traditional, stagnating industries.

The 'standard policy recipe' for regional economic development, reflected in the Smart Specialisation approach, favours the upgrading of prevailing industrial paths and the creation of new regional industries. This is seen to take place in particular through the combination of existing pieces of regional and, to some extent, extra-regional knowledge and competence. The literature considers technologically related knowledge as a key to the upgrading of existing industries and to the creation of new ones through branching processes (where new industries build on existing knowledge and resources). Combinations of unrelated knowledge have greater potentials to lead to completely new industries for a region.

Such knowledge dynamics are found mostly in large city regions with a range of different industries and knowledge organisations. Thus, they do not portray typical industrial development paths in less-favoured regions, nor do they represent viable economic policy strategies for these. Less-favoured regions often need to link up to extra-regional knowledge organisations and innovative firms to bring in fresh ideas, information and knowledge to thin or specialised RISs. However, capability-building, meaning the strengthening of RISs, should occur together with the acquiring of external knowledge so that regions are better able to utilise the knowledge import.

Understanding development potentials in less-favoured regions, in particular, demands a broad approach to innovation and economic development and to regional economic and innovation policy. Innovation should not be perceived as resulting primarily from scientific activity, as in the linear innovation model. Less-favoured regions that build up excellent research groups risk these operating as so-called 'cathedrals in the desert'; they engage in global academic networks but contribute little to innovation in local industries that may also lack absorptive capacity for scientific knowledge. A broad approach, on the other hand, recognises the importance of experience-based knowledge (know-how) for innovation and economic development, and with that also the significance of applied research and development for firms' innovation processes.

The book addresses the topics of regional innovation, economic development and development strategies in a collection of 14 conceptual, empirical and policy-oriented chapters. The book underlines that policy has to be place-based and adapted to challenges in individual less-favoured regions, but also that one can learn from experimentation of policies that aim to promote innovation and growth in different regions. This makes the book interesting from both an academic and a policy point of view.

Professor Arne Isaksen
Department of Working Life and Innovation,
University of Agder, Norway

Acknowledgements

The editors would like to express their gratitude to all the authors who contributed to this volume. A special thanks to Arne Kempers for his much-appreciated assistance with the layout.

1 Introduction

Unveiling the potential of less-favoured regions in regional policy

Iryna Kristensen, Alexandre Dubois and Jukka Teräs

Introduction

The ongoing globalisation processes have triggered a reconsideration of the relationship between the concepts of space and time in geography. Rodríguez-Pose describes the contemporary configuration of the global economic space as "becoming more 'spiky', peppered with economic agglomerations separated by ever growing economic 'deserts'" (Rodríguez-Pose, 2011, p. 351). The possibility of networking through advanced information and communication technologies creates a flatt*er* world (Rodríguez-Pose and Crescenzi, 2008) that essentially unfolds by creating bridges between the mountain tops (i.e. urban regions). But it also creates a steeper slope to climb for actors in the valleys, i.e. what will later be introduced as less-favoured regions, that strive to be part of these processes. Although the predicaments of the death of distance (Cairncross, 1997) or the annihilation of space (Castells, 1996; Massey, 1999) never materialised as potently as imagined a few decades ago, it is fair to acknowledge that urban economies have indeed become increasingly powerful in the global economy, often casting a shadow on their respective national economies, and that the processes of socio-economic marginalisation have heightened on the periphery of these centres.

Barca et al. (2012) refers to two sides of the space concept: on the one hand, space is rather 'slippery', marked by continuously intensified mobility of goods and people; on the other hand, however, it is rather 'sticky' and 'thick' due to an increasing resource concentration in large agglomerations. This reasoning presents a dilemma to policymakers as it implies that change and development processes are "non-linear, complex and continually emergent, popping up in unexpected ways from a variety of actors" (Shucksmith, 2009). This changing perception of space and geography, combined with the existence of regional disparities between European regions as well as the relative failure of public selective intervention, calls for a reconsideration of regional policy. The former generation of regional economic development approaches, largely based on neoclassical economic thinking (e.g. Solow, 1956), focused predominantly on external factors that may predict economic growth without sufficient consideration of the presence of knowledge asymmetries and the importance of region-specific assets.

The development and dissemination of good practices have become key components in the policy process at the transnational level, promoting policy transfer and learning (Bulkeley and Betsill, 2005); yet different policy concepts take root in different ways across the European territory (Böhme and Waterhout, 2008; Stead, 2012). Following the "best practices" logic of equal applicability of European Union (EU) policies in diverse regional settings, many policymakers tend to fall for the fallacy to 'imitate success stories' and eventually fail because differentiating factors such as local governance systems, administrative cultures and professional capacities are not sufficiently taken into consideration (Stead, 2012, p. 107). Barca refers to it as the "best practice syndrome" (Barca, 2009, p.114) developed by European authorities in an attempt to promote a one-size-fits-all blueprint of territorial governance arrangements, based on successes observed in a few regions.

Looking beyond endogenous development

Endogenous approaches to socio-economic development have increasingly paid attention to the interplay between local and extra-local interrelations and the role of endogenous forces and processes in facilitating territorial development (Lowe et al., 1995; Ray, 1998). The logic of such approaches lies in the ability of a territory "to think in terms of cultivating its own development repertoire" (Ray, 1999); this is understood as entailing "the idea of local ownership of resources and the sense of choice [. . .] in how to employ those resources [. . .] in the pursuit of local objectives" (Ray, 1999). In other words, "the well-being of a local economy can best be animated by basing development action on the resources – physical, human and intangible – that are indigenous to that locality" (Ray, 1998), which should be sustained and enriched by combining internal and external modes of cooperation (Mattes, 2012).

This growing importance of localities and their interaction for economic growth has marked a shift in regional policymaking towards strategic mobilisation of diverse territorial assets for future growth and competitiveness (Barca et al., 2012). Increased interdependencies between various regional actors, which extend beyond locally based and territorially rooted interactions, have grown to become a significant precondition for enhancing existing or discovering new competitive advantages necessary for economic growth. In this light, the EU promotes smart specialisation strategies (S3) as an attractive approach to support economic transformation and differentiation based on local resources and comparative strengths. The S3 perception is now gradually being adopted by policymakers at all levels of government; however, although the concept has gathered significant momentum during the past few years, its applicability (as well as the long-term effects of its application) to diverse territorial settings remains debatable. Former practices have shown that, given the extent of territorial diversity, "no single model of how to implement local development or of what strategies or actions to adopt" (OECD, 2001) may be applicable to all regions, nor would it be desirable as a matter of fact. This is particularly true for the so-called less-favoured regions as their innovation capabilities deviate in many respects from those regions branded as "success stories" (Tödtling and Trippl, 2005). Due to varying contextual factors, whatever good practices developed "elsewhere" would not add much to policy learning without careful consideration of what constitutes "local circumstances" (Stead, 2012, p. 111).

Against this backdrop, the overarching objective of this book is to contribute to the ongoing debate on the congruence between place-based development and regional competitiveness in the context of Europe's less-favoured regions. Throughout the book, it is shown that the added value of experimentation and testing activities, not least in relation to the ongoing implementation of S3, is about helping regions "to develop their own sources of economic dynamism" (Benner, 2014). The book aims to provide an outlook on the complexity of regional transformation processes taking place in less-favoured regions and enhance the applicability and transferability of theoretical approaches to innovation and place-based regional development in diverse European territorial settings.

What do we mean by 'less-favoured regions'?

'Less-favoured regions' (LFRs) is an umbrella term that comprises an amalgam of very diverse regional settings. Although there is no clear-cut definition of what makes a region less favoured, this assessment is often made by supra-regional tiers of government on the basis that these regions are faced with a certain disadvantage that may hamper their future development prospects. Here, an attempt is made to roughly identify three main types of these disadvantages: sectoral, locational and institutional.

Certain regions have an economic profile or sectoral specialisation that is deemed 'out of tune' with the contemporary, global economic development processes. For instance, rural regions that still have a strong profile of commodity production, such as agriculture, forestry, fisheries or mining, are considered as not having the proper 'tools' for competing globally in an economy that is overly focused on knowledge and service industries. Poor endowment in R&D capabilities in these regions hampers the ability for regional actors to benefit from knowledge spillovers. Likewise, regions with a strong legacy of manufacturing industries that used to hold a prominent place in their respective countries' development during the Industrial Revolution are considered backward and unfit as sites for future economic growth. They were considered remnants of another (industrial) age and became increasingly conceived as 'shadow areas' of urban–urban connectivity (Richardson, 2000, p. 58). The demotion of these regions from engines of growth to regions in transition has lasted for decades, with dire social consequences such as long-term structural unemployment. These regions can be found in old industrial nations, for instance the UK (Liverpool region, Wales), France (Nord-Pas-de-Calais), Belgium (Wallonia).

A second type of disadvantage is what Copus (2001) defined as 'locational disadvantage'. Locational disadvantage refers to the way the geographical context of a region, whether linked to physical features or human development, affects the ability of these regions to compete 'fairly' with other regions. In the economic geography literature, this has often been referred to in terms of the centre–periphery paradigm. In that respect, 'peripherality' is considered a spatial theory that links geographical features, such as population distribution or physical distance, to the economic development processes (Anderson, 2000). Copus (2001) identified a number of different factors that contribute to the creation of such locational disadvantage: causal, e.g. increased transportation costs or lack of critical mass for firms and services; contingent, e.g. high cost of service provision to persons and businesses and low rates of entrepreneurship and innovation; and associated, e.g. dependence on primary industries, poorly developed local and interregional infrastructure. However, there now is a better understanding that there is no causal relationship between being peripheral in geographical terms and lagging behind in economic terms, as those can be fertile grounds for competitive and innovative firms (Virkkala, 2007). In addition, recent studies of social exclusion and poverty have shown that even the most 'central' regions are subject to pockets of socio-economic marginalisation that create a much more intricate patchwork of inner peripheries throughout the European territory (Madanipour et al. 2015, Copus et al., 2017).

Although the first two types are fairly old in the context of EU Cohesion Policy (ECP), a more recent typology of LFRs shares significant similarities with the former one. Indeed, the EU enlargement to embrace Central and Eastern European countries in 2004 has radically changed the landscape of what can be considered as an LFR. Suddenly, a large number of regions, including highly urbanised ones, affected by low levels of development, with high unemployment and low GDP compared to European standards, had to be catered for in cohesion policy. The focus on supporting the catching up of lagging regions and countries was a trigger for the 'competitiveness turn' of ECP in the mid-2000s.

These different types of disadvantages highlight different mechanisms that may contribute to the detachment of these regions from contemporary growth processes. Tödtling and Trippl (2005) deemed that their resulting innovation capabilities may be "assigned to specific types of problem regions, such as peripheral regions (organisational thinness), old industrial areas (lock-in) and some metropolitan regions (fragmentation)".

Broadening the scope of smart specialisation thinking

Regional policy is a central means for implementing the Europe 2020 strategy, the EU's ten-year jobs and growth strategy that was launched in 2010 to create the conditions for smart, sustainable and inclusive growth (European Commission, 2010). In its current approach, regional innovation policy tries to emphasise the role played by geography in promoting economic development (McCann and Ortega-Argilés, 2013). The concept of smart specialisation, which was originally developed to address the gap between Europe and other global competitors (namely, the USA and Japan) in R&D investment (Foray and van Ark, 2007), is currently the cornerstone of the EU's bottom-up approach to regional innovation. Much of the literature focuses on investigating practical cases of the implementation of smart specialisation. However, some alternative approaches have already been proposed to refine the current smart specialisation concept, e.g. Benner's proposal of the concept of 'smart experimentation' (Benner, 2014).

However, and as shown throughout this book, the scope of territorial innovation initiatives taking place in LFRs is much wider than just smart specialisation implementation. Instead, the analysis of smart specialisation should be enriched by covering additional methods and approaches to promote innovation and growth –beyond the scope of the policy instrument. Moreover, the search for good methods for, approaches to and practices in regional innovation should also be extended to regions outside the EU.

This book thus proposes to highlight the learning processes emerging from the experimentation with various methods and approaches to promote innovation and growth in LFRs, both inside and outside Europe. Although many of the experiences showcased stem from the implementation of smart specialisation strategies, it includes a more comprehensive set of methods for and approaches to regional innovation policy.

Less-favoured regions and the making of EU Cohesion Policy

The fate and development of LFRs has long been the main focus of EU Cohesion Policy. However, the discourse and perception of the potentials and challenges inherent in these regions' development has evolved along with the changing institutional context of EU policymaking. Indeed, although the design and implementation of ECP may have changed over time, its main historical ambition has remained "to promote economic convergence by assisting less favoured regions, namely, by means of investments funded by EU Structural and Cohesion Funds" (Medeiros, 2017).

The first reference to LFRs was made in the founding Treaty of Rome in 1957. At that time, the challenge posed by the development of LFRs was associated with the goal of economic cohesion at the national level ("strengthen the unity of their economies") and the ambition to reduce the growing disparities by "mitigating the backwardness of the less favoured regions" (Faludi, 2004; Faludi, 2011). Early on, the agenda promoting regional development in LFRs was thus paired with the greater 'cause' of the recovery from the aftermath of WWII on European post-war economies.

In the 1986 Single European Act, the focus on economic cohesion was augmented by a reference to social cohesion, although this changed little how issues related to the development of LFRs were apprehended. LFRs were addressed in terms of backwardness. The accession to the EU of Austria, Finland and Sweden in 1995, relatively rich countries compared to the EU average, but with extensive mountainous and sparsely populated areas, changed the perception of the characteristics of LFRs away from mere economic backwardness to more complex territorial development factors such as topography and remoteness to decision centres. The accession to the EU of Central and Eastern European countries in 2004 shifted the perception of LFRs back to economic backwardness, as these countries were much poorer and much more unstable institutionally. In that regard, cohesion policy aimed at closing the gap between poor and rich European countries *and* regions at the same time (Margaras, 2016).

The Treaty of Amsterdam in 1997 then further specified the 'objects' of cohesion policy, i.e. its main beneficiary regions: least-favoured regions, rural areas, areas affected by industrial transition and regions that suffer from severe and permanent natural or demographic handicaps such as the northernmost regions with very low population density and island, cross-border and mountain regions (Faludi, 2011).

A major policy development from this era was the shift from a redistributive to a growth-oriented paradigm of cohesion policy. The rationale for this shift was laid down in the Green Paper on Territorial Cohesion. This new paradigm aims at supporting the 'harmonious development' of all places, and the role of public policy is to help these territories to make best use of their assets (European Commission, 2008). A new development was also that cohesion policy was not solely targeted at LFRs in their multiple shapes, but at *any* European region, including the largest urban regions. One emerging element was the intra-regional dimension of territorial cohesion: even the most competitive regions are faced with 'pockets' of social marginalisation that hamper their development and may slow down the ability of the EU to meet its ambitious goals set out in the Europe 2020 agenda.

The shift towards an understanding of LFRs through territorial cohesion was somehow reflected in Article 174 of the Treaty on the Functioning of the EU in the late 2000s. Although the TFEU still emphasised that "the Union shall aim at reducing disparities between the levels of development of the various regions and the backwardness of the least favoured regions", it also acknowledged that

> among the regions concerned, particular attention shall be paid to rural areas, areas affected by industrial transition, and regions which suffer from severe and permanent natural or demographic handicaps such as northernmost regions with very low population density and island, cross border and mountainous regions.

The argument was then made that "some of these regions may thus require additional assistance" (Margaras, 2016).

What's next?

The efficacy of ECP as a policy tool for actually achieving its proclaimed ambitions has been debated over the years. Many lagging or low-growth regions (including several southern European regions) have still lower GDP than the EU average, despite benefitting for decades from EU structural funds (Margaras, 2016). Rather than being an agent of cohesion, ECP has been 'accused' of favouring, directly or indirectly, the most well-off and socio-economically dynamic regions, such as capital cities and urbanised regions (Medeiros, 2017).

Notwithstanding the ECP's emblematic significance, and although it represents a substantial part of the EU budget, the agenda of other major EU sectoral policies such as transport, innovation or competition are designed to sustain agglomeration economies in an era of globalisation, and thus tend to 'favour' these already well-off regions, not through redistribution of funds but rather by unleashing the flows of capital and investments, both intra- and extra-European, towards these regions. In that regard, LFRs can be said to have been systemically *disfavoured* by major EU sectoral policies, and ECP has tried, and failed, to compensate for these shortcomings. In that regard, Kinossian (2017) pinpointed that

> the disputed universality of growth-oriented policies for less favoured and peripheral regions leads to further questions regarding the meaning of development beyond the growth paradigm, and the nature of policy intervention under conditions of structural economic problems, low population density, population decline, geographical remoteness and poor institutional capacity.

A possible improvement in that area is through improved governance practices turning investments into sound territorial development as "their capacity to accommodate investment and new jobs (as a conventional measure of development) is lower than in core regions" (Kinossian, 2017). Landabaso (2014) identified that "the key obstacle to innovation promotion in less favoured regions is good governance in the form of strong connections between innovation actors, including local, regional and national institutions, working towards common and not competing aims". Tighter collaboration between regional actors in a Triple Helix fashion is thus perceived as a necessary step to enforce institutional change in those regions.

It is this diversity of regional contexts that this book intends to reflect. However, for analytical purposes, it is important to acknowledge that these various types of regional contexts, although simplistically and collectively labelled as 'less favoured' actually bear differentiated opportunities and challenges to territorial development. Beyond the individual success of innovation initiatives in LFRs, the specificity of the challenges for LFRs and the opportunities of 'smart experimentation' for these regions are wider-ranging, as they lay the ground for regional development 'success' and cohesion across Europe. This links to societal issues (e.g. migration and attractiveness of regions) are wider-ranging than their mere economic impacts.

It is in that spirit that each contribution to this book delves deeper into one particular 'form' of less favoured-ness in order to improve our knowledge about the innovation and learning processes, but also the shortcomings, found in these places.

An overview of the book

The book is structured around 12 thematic chapters that have been written independently of each other. Hence the reader may choose the order in which they engage with the material. In each chapter, authors were free to apply their own definition and understanding of what a 'less-favoured region' is. Each chapter addresses the issue of development trajectories through the lens of specific themes and socio-economic processes. The work contained in this book thus reflects not only the diversity of LFRs but also the wealth of research tracks that may be pursued and undertaken in order to fully grasp the complexity of regional development processes, policies and practices in those regions.

Chapter 2, "Fostering growth in less favoured regions: adapting the concept of Smart Specialization to rural economic development" (David Freshwater) focuses on rural regions of the OECD countries. In the current policy environment, large metropolitan regions are seen as the main drivers of national economic growth, while rural regions are often seen as less favoured. Yet, some rural regions perform well in terms of GDP per capita, a common measure of productivity. These high-performing 'low-density economies' rely on different growth mechanisms than do large metropolitan regions. This makes recognising these differences and incorporating them into regional development policy crucial if nations are to achieve more balanced growth that utilises the potential of both rural and urban regions. Smart specialisation policy offers a framework for doing this, but it requires a broader approach to fostering both innovation and entrepreneurship than has been commonly adopted.

Chapter 3, "Smart specialisation in economically and institutionally less favoured regions" (Henning Kroll) outlines possible options concerning which strategies could still be found to fertilise the definition of effective smart specialisation strategies in, by and for less favoured regions. In this context, suitable coalitions of actors are discussed. When first devised, the smart specialisation agenda aimed at providing a generalisable, place-based approach to all European regions, while at the same time pointing out that a focus on critical mass would be crucial for supporting centres of excellence for specific domains that could help reposition Europe's economy amongst international competition. The ability for all regions to develop novel applications of existing technologies and the congruence between S3 and the territorial capacities in production, craft and agriculture were acknowledged but did not find a prominent place in the European Commission's guidelines and – subsequently – the regional strategies themselves. Overall, challenges can be seen in two broad areas: first, with respect to the regions' real economies. Many regions simply do not have the capacity and networks among either their industrial or their public research sector needed to constitute regional innovation systems of even an adaptive nature. Second, institutional and administrative capacity in many lagging regions is significantly low. Therefore, it is hard to trigger 'entrepreneurial discovery processes', as foreseen in the concept, much less to keep it alive in mutual collaboration between administratively rigid governments and weak business sectors that lack both trust and experience.

Chapter 4, "Development of mountainous regions: smart specialization approaches as a means to overcoming peripheralization" (Thomas Dax) addresses the potential of smart specialization and innovation strategy to provide a fresh perspective on the complexity of mountain development and strengthen spatial inter-linkages and related learning processes. While no short-term improvements can be expected, this novel approach might impact on the foundations for local development action in the long term. This perspective aims at enhancing local participation and envisages overcoming the bias towards urban areas in past policies by addressing local assets and natural resource use, the specific social dimensions and the increasing needs for interrelations and cultural changes in remote mountain regions.

Chapter 5, "Smart specialisation at the edge of Europe: case study of sparsely populated regions in the Arctic" (Jukka Teräs, Kristiina Jokelainen, Thomas Ejdemo and Daniel Örtqvist) studies the application of the smart specialisation concept in the peripheral regions of northern Finland and northern Sweden, in order to develop a better understanding of the possibilities and potential limitations in using the smart specialisation concept in more peripheral regions. The study highlights that peripheral and sparsely populated regions in the Nordic Arctic possess knowledge and innovation potential that many other peripheral regions do not have, despite challenges related to critical mass and long distances. The regional adaptation of the smart specialisation concept so far differs rather significantly between the case study regions. Lapland may be considered as being one of the early adopters of the concept, also adopted European-wide, whereas in Norrbotten smart specialisation has until recently been seen more as an embedded element of the existing regional development strategies. Due to the freshness of the smart specialisation concept, it is too early to judge the long-term impact of smart specialisation application in the Nordic Arctic region. In any case, our study indicates that sparsely populated regions have the potential to use the smart specialisation concept as a complementary instrument to their existing regional development instruments.

Chapter 6, "The wisdom of the fathers? Regional/rural development policy and structures for the Highlands and Islands of Scotland (1965–2015) through the lens of Smart Specialisation" (Andrew Copus) seeks to apply the principles of smart specialisation as a framework for ex-post-evaluation of the fifty-year history of development agency activity in the Highlands and Islands of Scotland. The intention is to demonstrate that even if the terminology was unknown, smart specialisation principles have been an implicit 'golden thread' through several generations of regional development activities of the Highlands and Islands Development Board (HIDB) and its successor, Highlands and Islands Enterprise (HIE). The HIDB/HIE narrative is placed within the broader rural/regional policy context, both before and after the granting of devolved powers to the Scottish Government, including an account and assessment of the evolution of community development and various forms of local development strategy. The chapter also considers how recent initiatives to implement smart specialisation strategies at a national level can be of benefit to the Highlands and

Islands as a region. This review and analysis is based largely upon desk research, with policy and 'grey literature' playing an important role, supplemented by structured interviews with a range of stakeholders.

Chapter 7, "The role of biorefineries in the revitalisation of (old) industrial and rural regions" (Alexandre Dubois and Iryna Kristensen) proposes to investigate how and to what extent biorefineries move forward a place-based development agenda in (old) industrial rural regions. Contemporary rural regions are complex spatial-social systems that host both medium-sized towns and a set of resource-based local economies surrounding them. Previous rounds of RIS in rural regions have privileged the development of these regional cores, at the expense of the hinterland, as the focus on nature-based industries was considered as being backward-looking. The rise of the bioeconomy, and especially the increased importance of bioenergy as a sustainable source of renewable energy, has revealed that nature-based industries have the potential to conciliate science-based advancements with more traditional economic activities anchored in rural economies.

Chapter 8, "Models of institutional governance for smart specialisation: a comparative study of Asturias and the Basque Country" (Jaime del Castillo and Jonatan Paton) analyses conceptually and operatively the drivers of economic transformation in two old industrial regions of southern Europe and the ways in which they manage to overcome it through a mix of policy measures and context conditions. Since both regions are well known for their experiences in industrial policymaking, the objective is to link the current smart specialisation understanding to those processes that guided the transformation of these regions since the beginning of the 1980s, highlighting the elements that generated a different territorial development path, though the initial starting points had some similarities.

Chapter 9, "Digital Innovation Hubs as enablers of Smart Specialisation in Sparsely Populated Areas" (Jens Sörvik) explores the role of Digital Innovation Hubs (DIHs) in Smart Specialisation (S3) processes in Sparsely Populated Areas (SPAs) and outlines issues based on the experiences of cluster initiatives and regional strategies in northern Swedish SPAs. The chapter argues that DIHs can play an important role in S3, both by providing horizontal digitalisation support and in the development of priority areas. Distributed innovation support solutions can be a way of overcoming issues of large distances and critical mass in these regions. DIH networks can connect actors regionally and also to important knowledge sources from outside of the region.

Chapter 10, "Diversification patterns at the regional level and their relationship to regional knowledge capabilities: differences between advanced and less favoured regions" (Andreas Reinstaller and Fabian Unterlass) analyses the relationship between regional capabilities to generate and apply knowledge and changes in industrial specialisation in advanced and less-favoured regions. The results suggest that local technological search and learning reinforce existing specialisation patterns, whereas educational investments weaken path dependence. They reduce the importance of local capabilities to generate comparative advantages and allow tapping into new technologies or industries fostering diversification. Regions with higher educational attainment levels tend also to be more specialised in high-end markets. The educational system therefore plays a key role in diversification processes and should be a constitutive element of S3 policies.

Chapter 11, "The role of proximity in less-favoured regions: smart experimentation between triple helix actors" (Antti Mäenpää and Seija Virkkala) argues that focusing on proximities and distances between stakeholders can stimulate the regional entrepreneurial discovery process. The chapter analyses the innovation network based on triple helix theory and the proximity approach. Results from a Finnish case study show that geographical proximity facilitates social proximity slightly. Moreover, the cognitive proximity between companies and regional universities is lower than that between companies and extra-regional universities, which indicates that the companies complement any shortfalls in knowledge production from regional universities for extra-regional cooperation. The entrepreneurial discovery process is a process of searching for new business areas, but it is also a process fostering the optimal proximity between actors. Regional developers could actively seek optimal proximity, which is a precondition for smart experimentation.

Chapter 12, "Relatedness, diversification and economic performance at the regional level: differences between advantaged and less favoured regions" (Johanna Vogel and Stefan Weingärtner) examines empirically the effect of regional diversification patterns on economic performance in relation to the regional level of economic development in the European Union. It does so using data for a panel of EU regions covering the period from 2008 to 2011. The aim is to investigate whether 'related' and 'unrelated' diversification (variety) affect economically advantaged and less favoured regions differently, and thus to provide insights for the EU's smart specialisation approach to cohesion policy. The findings highlight the growth-enhancing impact of diversification into unrelated areas of activity in production and knowledge (unrelated variety) for economically less favoured regions.

Chapter 13, "Regional structural policies and industrial evolution: evidence from three European case study regions" (Klaus S. Friesenbichler) addresses the question of why some less-favoured regions escaped their structural problems, while others did not. It provides case study evidence on three EU regions that have faced structural challenges at some point in recent history: Styria in Austria, Bucharest Ilfov in Romania and Valencia in Spain. Both regional economic policies and the evolution of the industry structures are discussed against an evolutionary economics background, focusing on path dependence, diversification processes and human capital formation. The findings suggest a series of conclusions for smart specialisation policies aimed at escaping structural lock-ins.

Chapter 14, "A concluding note: future prospects of entrepreneurship and innovation policy" (Håkan Ylinenpää, Iryna Kristensen, Alexandre Dubois and Jukka Teräs) examines potential future avenues for regenerating the debate on place-based development from both a policy and a research perspective.

It begins by reviewing the evolution over the years of the dominant paradigms in regional innovation thinking. From this point on, the chapter acknowledges the need for 'next generation' regional development models to better integrate the socio-economic factors and territorial context that appear to be determinant in unlocking growth and producing knowledge- and bio-based economies in *all* regions, be they metropolitan, rural, mountainous, insular or sparsely populated.

References

Anderson, A. R. (2000). Paradox in the periphery: an entrepreneurial reconstruction? *Entrepreneurship & Regional Development 12*(2): 91–109.

Barca, F. (2009). *An Agenda for Reformed Cohesion Policy: A Place-based Approach to Meeting European Union Challenges and Expectations*. Independent report prepared at the request of Danuta Hubner, Commissioner for Regional Policy. Brussels: European Commission.

Barca, F., McCann, P., & Rodríguez-Pose, A. (2012). The case for regional development intervention: place-based versus place-neutral approaches. *Journal of Regional Science 52*(1): 134–152.

Benner, M. (2014). From smart specialisation to smart experimentation. *Zeitschrift für Wirtschaftsgeographie 58*(1): 33–49. doi:10.1515/zfw.2014.0003

Böhme, K., & Waterhout, B. (2008). The Europeanization of planning. Faludi (Ed.) *European Spatial Research and Planning*. Lincoln Institute for Land Policy, Cambridge (MA), pp. 225–248.

Bulkeley, H., & Betsill, M. (2005). Rethinking sustainable cities: multilevel governance and the 'urban' politics of climate change. *Environmental Politics 14*(1): 42–63.

Cairncross, F. (1997). *The Death of Distance: How the Communications Revolution Will Change Our Lives*. Boston: Harvard Business School Press.

Castells, M. (1996). *The Information Age: Economy, Society, and Culture. Volume I: The Rise of the Network Society*. Oxford, UK: Blackwell.

Copus, A. K. (2001). From core-periphery to polycentric development: concepts of spatial and aspatial peripherality. *European Planning Studies 9*(4): 539–552.

Copus, A., Mantino, F., & Noguera, J. (2017). Inner peripheries: an oxymoron or a real challenge for territorial cohesion? *Italian Journal of Planning Practice* 7(1): 24–49.

European Commission (2008). *Green paper on territorial cohesion – turning territorial diversity into strength*. Communication from the Commission to the Council, the European Parliament, the Committee of the Regions and the European Economic and Social Committee (616 final). Brussels: European Commission.

European Commission (2010). *EUROPE 2020 A strategy for smart, sustainable and inclusive growth*. Communication from the Commission (2020 final). Brussels: European Commission.

Faludi, A. (2004). Spatial planning traditions in Europe: their role in the ESDP process. *International Planning Studies 9*(2–3): 155–172.

Faludi, A. (2011). Cohesion, coherence, cooperation: EU policy beyond hard territoriality. In Richardson, H. W., Bae, C. H. C. and Choe, S. C. (Eds.), *Reshaping Regional Policy*. Cheltenham, UK: Edward Elgar, pp. 83–101.

Foray, D., & van Ark, B. (2007). Smart specialisation in a truly integrated research area is the key to attracting more R&D to Europe. *Knowledge for Growth. European Issues and Policy Challenges 1*: 26–28.

Kinossian, N. (2017). Planning strategies and practices in non-core regions: a critical response. *European Planning Studies 26*(2): 365–375.

Landabaso, M. (2014). Guest editorial on research and innovation strategies for smart specialisation in Europe: theory and practice of new innovation policy approaches. *European Journal of Innovation Management 17*(4): 378–389.

Lowe, P., Murdoch, J., & Ward, N. (1995). Networks in rural development: beyond exogenous and endogenous models. In: Van der Ploeg, J. D. & van Dijk, G. (Eds.), *Beyond Modernization: The Impact of Endogenous Rural Development*, (pp. 87–105). Assen, the Netherlands: Van Gorcum.

McCann, P., & Ortega-Argilés, R. (2013). Modern regional innovation policy. *Cambridge Journal of Regions, Economy and Society 6*(2): 187–216.

Madanipour, A., Shucksmith, M., & Talbot, H. (2015). Concepts of poverty and social exclusion in Europe. *Local Economy 30*(7): 721–741.

Margaras, V. (2016). *Challenges for EU cohesion policy: issues in the forthcoming post-2020 reform*. Brussels: European Parliamentary Research Service.

Massey, D. (1999). Imagining globalization: power-geometries of time-space. In Brah, A., Hickman, M. and Ghaill, M. M.a. (Eds.) *Global Futures* (pp. 27–44). Basingstoke, UK: Palgrave Macmillan.

Mattes, J. (2012). Dimensions of proximity and knowledge bases: innovation between spatial and non-spatial factors. *Regional Studies 46*(8): 1085–1099.

Medeiros, E. (2017). From smart growth to European spatial planning: a new paradigm for EU cohesion policy post-2020. *European Planning Studies 25*(10): 1856–1875.

OECD (2001). *Best Practices in Local Development*. Paris: OECD.

Ray, C. (1998). Endogenous development in the era of reflexive modernity. *Journal of Rural Studies 15*(3): 257–267.

Ray, C. (1999). Towards a meta-framework of endogenous development: repertoires, paths, democracy and rights. *Sociologia Ruralis 39*(4): 522–537.

Richardson, T. (2000). Discourses of rurality in EU spatial policy: the European spatial development perspective. *Sociologia Ruralis 40*(1): 53–71.

Rodríguez-Pose, A. (2011). Economists as geographers and geographers as something else: on the changing conception of distance in geography and economics. *Journal of Economic Geography 11*(2): 347–356.

Rodríguez-Pose, A. and Crescenzi, R. (2008). Research and development, spillovers, innovation systems, and the genesis of regional growth in Europe. *Regional Studies 42*(1): 51–67.

Shucksmith, M. (2009). Disintegrated rural development? Neo-endogenous rural development, planning and place-shaping in diffused power contexts. *Sociologia Ruralis 50*(1): 1–14.

Solow, R. M. (1956). A contribution to the theory of economic growth. *The Quarterly Journal of Economics 70*(1): 65–94.

Stead, D. (2012). Best practices and policy transfer in spatial planning. *Planning Practice & Research 27*(1): 103–116.

Tödtling, F., & Trippl, M. (2005). One size fits all?: towards a differentiated regional innovation policy approach. *Research Policy 34*(8): 1203–1219.

Virkkala, S. (2007). Innovation and networking in peripheral areas – a case study of emergence and change in rural manufacturing. *European Planning Studies 15*(4): 511–529.

Part I

Shifting perspectives

Reframing regional innovation processes in less-favoured regions

2 Fostering growth in less favoured regions

Adapting the concept of smart specialization to rural economic development

David Freshwater

Introduction

OECD countries increasingly recognize that strong national growth requires strong regional growth, but also that regions within countries perform at very different levels. Reducing these differences in performance requires place-sensitive regional policy that can target both key impediments to, and opportunities for, region-specific growth mechanisms (Barca, McCann & Rodríguez-Pose, 2012; Mendez, 2013). However, the rural regions of OECD countries, particularly those more remote from large metropolitan regions, are often considered to be "less favoured" and less capable of contributing to growth. Their development challenge is seen as stemming from a variety of causes, such as: weak connectivity to the larger national economy and society, geographic impediments in the form of a harsh climate or challenging topography, an ongoing reliance on older and declining industries and technologies, weak social and political institutions and poor demographic prospects that are associated with an aging and shrinking population that is further challenged by an inability to attract new migrants.

Because rural areas in OECD countries account for a shrinking share of national populations and produce a smaller share of GDP, it has become common to conclude they are synonymous with economic and social decline and that public policy should focus on enhancing urban growth opportunities (Jacobs, 1969; World Bank, 2009; Katz, 2010). Moreover, changes in the underlying nature of developed country economies, with advanced producer services and technologically sophisticated manufacturing leading growth, also seem to favour large metropolitan areas. In addition, both the New Economic Geography literature and the macroeconomic literature on endogenous economic growth also lead to an emphasis on larger cities as drivers of economic prosperity (Jonas & Ward, 2007; Bettancourt & West, 2010).

Further, standard models of regional economic growth stress the importance of endogenous growth that is driven by investments in science-based innovation and by agglomeration economies, as emphasized by the literature on learning regions (Etzkowitz & Klofsten, 2005; Morgan, 2007). These models formed the initial basis for smart specialization strategies. Such models leave no space for rural economic progress because it is not consistent with their logic of how growth occurs. However, another stream of research has developed that recognizes that smart specialization is really a variation on place-based policy, in that it is an argument for regions to identify those sectors and firms where they have either a current or a potential comparative or absolute advantage (Tödtling & Trippl, 2005, Charles, Gross & Bachtler, 2012).

Recently, the OECD has identified two distinct regional growth mechanisms, as outlined in Figure 2.1 (OECD, 2016). The first is the well-recognized, metropolitan growth model that underpins the New Economic Geography, urban economics and much of regional economics. The second, the Low-Density Economy (LDE) is drawn from analysis of rural regions in OECD countries and reflects the characteristics of successful rural regions. It suggests that the economic dynamics of rural regions differ fundamentally from those of urban regions. Crucially, rural regions rely on the export of a small number of tradable goods and services to support a small, truncated local economy. In these regions, the majority of firms are small and medium-sized enterprises (SMEs), but there can also be branch plants of large multinational corporations. While these regions are geographically far from large

Metropolitan: High-Density Economies	**Rural: Low-Density Economies**
• Advanced producer services and sophisticated manufacturing drive local growth – endogenous process	• Natural resource extraction and resourced-based tourism drive local growth – exogenous process
• Large home market absorbs a large share of firm output reducing the need for exports	• Small home market makes exports essential to achieve firm minimum efficient scale and grow
• Large local population and local labor market	• Small local population and local labor market
• Workforce provides virtually all skills firms need	• Workforce offers a truncated set of skills, with advanced skills absent
• Most goods and services are available locally	• Many goods and services are not available locally
• Competition among firms encourages innovation and customer service, and limits profits	• Local firms face limited competition – protected by distance and limited size of local market
• Full range of firm sizes with complex interactions among firms	• Mainly very small and a few medium-sized firms that have weak linkages
• Numerous strong financial institutions offer a wide range of debt and equity products at competitive rates	• Limited financial institutions that offer weak support for business – low loan limits and almost no equity finance
• Strong internal formal R&D capacity with firm, government and university research centers	• No formal R&D capacity in region. Any innovation is imported or comes from informal acts by entrepreneurs
• Able to exploit both Marshallian and Jacobs agglomeration effects	• Agglomeration effects are mostly not available

Figure 2.1 Stylized characteristics of rural and metropolitan economies

metropolitan regions, they are well connected, both by physical transport networks and by communications media. Finally, they are typically characterized by the availability of a high-quality natural resource base that underpins a major part of the regional economy.

LDEs have distinct economic opportunities and constraints because their economies are structurally different than those of metropolitan regions. This means that policies to support regional economic development, including smart specialization, have to be capable of fostering innovation and entrepreneurs in different ways in different contexts (Bradford & Bramwell, 2016). When defined narrowly, smart specialization is only applicable to those metropolitan regions that have the capacity to support science-driven innovation (Wolfe, 2016). But, a broader definition of smart specialization that accepts that innovation occurs in many ways and that growth can be based on more than advanced manufacturing and producer services allows rural regions that rely on LDEs to grow by adding innovation that supports traditional economic functions, allowing them to continue to remain the base of the regional economy (Camagni & Capello, 2013; Isaksen & Karlsen, 2016).

The next section of this chapter identifies a set of growth mechanisms that underpin both models of economic growth. Each of these processes is individually well recognized in economic theory. The contribution of this chapter comes from jointly connecting them to the different growth dynamics of metropolitan and rural regions. This is followed by a discussion of how smart specialization policy can be easily reframed into a broader place-based strategy for enhancing growth that encompasses both high-density and low-density economies. The chapter concludes with observations and conclusions on rural growth opportunities and on the types of policies that can support these efforts.

Sources of regional economic growth

Crucially, if different types of regions within a nation experience differences in economic performance, the explanation for the differences cannot come from standard macroeconomic or stage of growth models, since all regions in a given country experience these effects in the same way. Instead, explanations must be grounded in underlying differences among regions, which implies a spatially sensitive framework. With both fast- and slow-growing metropolitan and rural regions, the explanation also cannot be a simple dual economy model, where urban regions alone lead growth. Further, urban and rural regions within a country each exhibit large degrees of variability, so the explanation must also account for these differences. Consequently, differences in geography, differences in opportunities and differences in socio-economic conditions lead to differences in regional structure that in turn require different policies to reflect different determinants of regional growth.

In his book *Economics Rules*, Dani Rodrik argues that any economic theory is only useful in specific contexts and that no model provides clear guidance in all circumstances (Rodrik, 2016, pp. 43 and 81). This leads him to suggest that when providing policy advice, economists should first conduct diagnostics of specific economies to determine their characteristics and only then determine which models are appropriate for use in framing policy recommendations (pp. 52–54). Because urban and rural regions differ considerably, different economic models will be appropriate in developing regional policy. Where different growth mechanisms are active in different types of regions, then public policy has to adapt to these differing circumstances if it is to be effective.

Differences in underlying conditions lead in turn to different mechanisms driving or impeding economic growth. Joel Mokyr has identified four basic growth mechanisms in his work (Mokyr, 1990, 2003, 2005, 2016). Each is well recognized in the economic growth literature, but Mokyr's insight is to see the forces as interacting in different ways in different places and at different times. He emphasizes the role of innovation as the main driver of growth over long periods of time, with capital deepening but trade effects and supportive institutions playing lesser roles, but roles that can be intermittently vital. Given the focus of this chapter on regional growth, and particularly on distinguishing between growth processes in urban and rural regions, three additional mechanisms can be identified. These are the geographic location and natural resource endowment of a region and two forms of agglomeration – the advantage accruing to firms in an industry from colocation first identified by Marshall (1920) and the benefits of urbanization that come from locating in a large city, as identified by Jacobs (1969).

These seven mechanisms in various combinations play more or less important roles in specific types of regions, and through their interactions lead to different rates and patterns of growth. For example, first nature geography almost always has a central role in the growth path of rural regions, especially those that are far from urban places. Similarly, agglomeration and urbanization effects play a central role in the growth of metropolitan regions, but are not relevant in rural regions. Regions that grow either have, or create, favourable combinations of conditions that support a varying set of the seven drivers in ways that reinforce their individual effects in a positive way.

Lagging regions are unable to do this. In particular, lagging Less Favoured Rural Regions typically have particularly weak aspects of first nature geography, which limits their opportunities to take advantage of a main driver of rural growth. But they can also have other structural weaknesses, including poor social capital or weak entrepreneurs, that can also limit the role of other growth mechanisms. Collectively, the seven basic models of economic growth provide a way to understand how different types of regions can grow. The implications of this for public policy, including efforts to stimulate innovation, are that different policy approaches may be required in rural regions than in urban regions, even though the broad policy goals for each type of region are the same. Figure 2.2 briefly describes how the seven drivers operate in metropolitan and low-density economies, while a more complete description follows below.

Mechanism Originator	High-Density Economy	Low-Density Economy
Adam Smith (expanded trade)	Large home market allows specialization and internal trade, while good transport networks can allow exports	A small home market requires a high level of exports for any firm to benefit from worker specialization and scale effects
Robert Solow (capital deepening)	Ready access to machinery manufacturers, either local or external, and good access to financial intermediaries allow ongoing mechanization	New machinery has to be imported and may be difficult to source and finance due to remoteness and weak local financial institutions
Josef Schumpeter (innovation)	Local formal R&D capacity leads to innovation and there are good opportunities to access R&D capacity in other regions	Innovation has to be brought in or adapted from other regions, or developed informally by local entrepreneurs
Douglas North (role of institutions)	Both government and non-government institutions are: numerous, well-funded and professional. The multiplicity of institutions can make coordination complex	Local governments are small, often staffed by volunteers, and have limited resources. Informal institutions play a large role and can have the largest capability
Alfred Weber (role of geography)	The built environment is more important than the natural environment in shaping growth, but there is ready access to most natural resources	The quality and diversity of the natural resource endowment is a major determinant of growth potential. Exploiting natural resources is the basic means to initiate and expand growth
Alfred Marshall (industrial districts)	The complex local economy with multiple firms in most industries allows opportunities for Marshallian agglomeration effects	Examples of Marshallian agglomeration exist in rural areas, but they are in niche markets that are hard to emulate
Jane Jacobs (large city advantages)	Only metropolitan regions can provide urbanization benefits	Not possible

Figure 2.2 Applicability of the various growth mechanisms to metropolitan and rural regions

Basic mechanisms of economic growth

Smithian growth

The essential aspect of the Smithian growth process is the benefit from trade, in the form of allowing labour specialization and opportunities to capture scale economies associated with expanding production to serve larger markets. Metropolitan regions have large home markets and benefit from localized scale economies, which can make this internal trade the dominant source of growth. Conversely, because LDEs are inherently small and truncated, they offer few local opportunities for Smithian growth. Within an LDE, only a few firms in a few sectors are the main economic drivers for the local economy, and these firms rely on export markets for their success.

To be competitive in distant markets, exporting firms have to be large enough to capture economies of scale. They must also be able to transport their output to these external markets in a timely manner and at a reasonable cost. Similarly, they must also be able to access inputs that are not available locally. This makes the regional economy highly dependent on a good transport infrastructure. Because the communities in which they are located are small, with a limited number of workers, there can only be a few exporting firms that are large enough to achieve a minimum efficient scale.

In rural areas, natural resource industries and first stage processing of their output are striking examples of the Smithian growth process. In mining, forestry and energy, and in many forms of agriculture, there are significant economies of scale at the establishment level that have led to steady increases in the minimum efficient size of firms and to high rates of labour productivity. Where these firms are successful, they can become the dominant employers in a community and may be large enough to be owned by a multinational corporation. These large firms are mainly in commodity-type industries, where competiveness hinges on achieving low unit costs of production, leading to the steady growth in output of the most efficient firms.

On the other hand, there are many circumstances where firms in rural areas are not able to take advantage of the Smithian growth process. For some firms, the local area is the only potential market, either because of high transport costs or because of truly localized demand. In this instance, the advantages of a larger market do not exist. In the context of the export-base model, the non-basic or local firms meet these conditions. This does not imply that these firms are not useful to the local economy, but it does suggest that they make an indirect contribution to growth.

Solow growth

The essential aspect of Solow growth is a capital-deepening process, where labour is replaced by equipment, which in turn leads to an increase in labour productivity measured by output per worker. Capital deepening contributes to lowering the unit cost of production as cheaper or more productive capital replaces more expensive labour, thereby increasing competitiveness. A secondary benefit is that new investment can allow the firm to adopt better technology, which increases competitiveness. Inherent in capital deepening is the idea of investment. Firms spend a large amount of money now to obtain machinery and equipment that yields a higher future profit stream. Investing typically requires that the firm has access to financial markets to provide funds, either as debt or equity capital. In urban areas, large and liquid capital markets are common, but in rural areas such markets may not exist, and firms can be capital-constrained, which limits their ability to make needed investments.

Capital-intensive large firms in LDEs, for example, mines, oil drilling and pulp mills, are largely branch plants of large national or international firms that have access to a variety of deep financial markets located in urban centres. However, local SMEs that constitute the majority of firms in a rural region lack access to major financial markets and must rely on local sources of funds. Lacking well-developed financial markets that extend into rural regions, SMEs can only invest in capital deepening through retained earnings or owner equity, which limits growth.

In LDEs, Solow growth mechanisms are most apparent in the large firms that dominate resource extraction and processing. The forestry industry in recent decades has seen a huge decline in the use of labour, both in tree harvesting processes, where logging machines have replaced workers with saws, and in timber processing and in pulp and paper mills where automation has eliminated jobs. Fewer, but better-skilled, workers are now required, and this has had an important implication for job prospects for males with low formal qualifications. While in the past, young men with little interest in pursuing advanced education had a career path in the resource industries, this is largely no longer the case and can contribute to high rates of youth unemployment. On the other hand, Solow processes need not only apply to large firms. Capital deepening can make small firms more competitive. For example, the modern fishing industry is dominated by small firms, but boats have become far more sophisticated in terms of fish-finding technology, and also in terms of actual fish-harvesting technology. This allows small crews to catch far more fish than much larger crews could in the past.

Schumpeterian growth

Joseph Schumpeter developed a theory of economic growth that is driven by a steady process of technological change that leads to better products and better processes (Schumpeter, 1934). The ideas of Schumpeter underpin smart specialization strategies that seek to identify ways to increase the rate of innovation in a region. A key aspect of technology-driven growth is its public good nature – once an idea is created, there is no additional cost for others to adopt it. Further, in principle, technological change allows economic growth to continue unabated as long as technology continues to improve. The key question for Schumpeterian growth is where do these new ideas come from?

The prevailing belief today is that innovation is an urban phenomenon and that LDEs have little potential to innovate (Shearmur, 2017). Even were this true, it does not mean that rural areas do not benefit from adopting and adapting urban innovations. Many innovations have applications in rural areas that may be relatively more significant than their use in urban areas. For example, while the internet is useful in urban locations because it allows another access path to information that was already reasonable accessible, it can be crucial for rural areas because it is essentially the only medium for gaining timely access to new ideas and knowledge. Similarly, there is a significant body of research and development performed in urban locations, but with an intended market in rural areas. Once again, the natural resource industries provide an example. Most agricultural research occurs at major universities, government research centres and corporate laboratories, virtually all of which are in urban places, but the research is almost universally applied in rural areas. The same is true of new technologies in mining and forestry. The conclusion is that if the global market for a particular form of innovation that is specific to rural regions is large enough, it will pay urban regions to search for appropriate new technologies.

While LDEs have access to innovations that are generated in urban areas, important new technologies have been created in rural areas (Freshwater & Wojan, 2014; OECD, 2014). Often, these come from a very different process than the formal, science-based innovation systems that are the standard model of how innovation occurs. This form of innovation is based on a different approach where individuals have a particular problem for which there is no satisfactory solution that can be purchased on the market. This leads them to develop their own solution, and, in doing so, to innovate. In most cases, these innovations mainly benefit the locality because they are not widely adopted. Nevertheless, they can add some new income and improve the viability of local firms. However, in other cases, rural innovations can turn out to be disruptive and spread globally.

Northian growth

This process of growth stems from the ideas of Douglas North that the institutions in which an economy is embedded influence economic performance. Nations and regions with formal and informal institutions that encourage taking advantage of economic opportunity experience stronger economic growth than those with weak institutions. Formal institutions include: clear property rights, the rule of law, well-functioning financial markets, the absence of corruption and a stable political system. Informal institutions include: strong social capital, social cohesion and the general belief that economic outcomes are largely equitable.

Assessing the role of institutions in economic growth takes place at various levels. International relations among countries play an important role in shaping trade opportunities and the opportunities that firms and individuals have beyond their national boundaries. Similarly, national institutions provide a macroeconomic context in which different regions operate, including monetary policy, fiscal policy and various national sectoral policies. Finally, at the regional or local level, there are community-based institutions that are specific to particular places.

Urban regions have specific institutional characteristics that have been associated with growth. These include: deep financial markets, competition, the benefits of agglomeration effects, the presence of cultural amenities and high rates of diversity. These attributes are largely seen as providing an environment that supports economic growth. Many of these attributes are not present in rural regions. The simple conclusion has often been that the absence of the framework or context that is most commonly associated with economic growth implies that economic growth in LDEs is improbable.

More appropriately, it should be asked whether there are alternative rural institutional frameworks that can also support growth. This requires examining rural areas where growth has taken place and seeing whether patterns can be found. In a rural context, a different milieu can provide an institutional context that supports growth. Because interpersonal contacts are frequent and complex in a small community, trust can play an important role in structuring relationships. Market exchanges and formal contracts may be less relied upon than personal commitments. Similarly, there may be a greater reliance on reciprocity, non-profit firms and voluntary organizations to provide goods and services than is the case in more urbanized regions where governments and market exchange play a larger role. However, if the sense of community breaks down, there can be adverse consequences for local institutions in rural regions, because both markets and formal government approaches can be hard to introduce.

Weberian growth

Alfred Weber established much of the early work in location theory that focused on how the geographic location of material inputs and markets, and associated transport costs, affected firms' location decisions. Weber's analysis shows that a firm's location choice is influenced by: the production costs it faces at a location, the transport costs associated with moving site-specific inputs to the location and the cost of shipping output to markets. The essence of the analysis is that geographic differences in endowments of resources, differences in access to transport networks and the spatial distribution of markets all play a role in location choices. The more complex the mix of inputs and markets and the larger the number of transport options, the more complex the location decision becomes.

Weber's framework suggests that rural regions with a valuable site-specific natural resource can have an absolute advantage in its production and can capture resource rents from extraction, but they may also have the opportunity to add significant additional value if they can introduce processing functions. However, where the resource is not locally owned and little or no local processing occurs, the regional benefits from the resource can be little more than some direct employment with profits flowing to urban investors. Distance from markets and weak transport infrastructure can also reduce the benefits from resource utilization to an LDE. Typically, returns to the resource provider are net of transport costs, and where transport costs are high, the residual profit can be small or negative.

Marshallian growth

Alfred Marshall first formalized in the 1890s the benefits to firms in the same or related sectors from locating in close proximity (Marshall, 1920). His idea of an "industrial district" is associated with three types of externality effects: access to a deep pool of specialized labour that makes it easy for the firm to adjust employment as needed, access to a range of specialized firms that supply specific goods and services to firms in that industry, and the opportunity for formal and informal interaction with peers that provides access to formal and tacit information about the industry.

While there are examples of small highly specialized clusters of firms in a specific type of business being found in rural areas, this is the exception. The agglomeration benefits of colocation are mainly found in larger urban areas. First, large urban areas have a large number of workers, which allows the possibility of a group of workers obtaining specialized skills for a particular industry and of them finding sufficient local employment to obtain and improve these skills over time. Second, a larger urban place is generally necessary for the range of specialized firms that support the cluster of firms in an industry to develop. Third, the opportunity for peer learning requires that there be more than a handful of firms collocated in order for meaningful interaction to occur.

Agglomeration benefits based on a large home market underpin most models of urban growth where the external benefits of colocation allow increasing returns to scale. The larger the urban place, the greater the opportunity for more agglomeration effects across a range of industries. Large metropolitan regions have both a broader variety of industries and more firms in any given industry, and both of these factors make the Marshallian growth mechanism more effective. By contrast, LDEs can at best have only a few firms in one or two industries, because the local labour force is small and has only a narrow range of skills.

Jacobian growth

Jane Jacobs, the influential urbanist, saw large cities as driving national growth (Jacobs, 1969). Part of her argument rested on the opportunities for Marshallian growth, but she also introduced the idea of urbanization economies that are not specific to a particular industry but are broadly available to all firms and residents in a metropolis. With increased size, a city can offer a broader range of amenities to its residents, making it more attractive. For example, although medium-sized cities have commercial air services, larger cities have more airlines and flights to more destinations, which increases the value of an airport to all firms and residents. Similarly, larger cities have professional sports teams, more variety in their cultural offerings (art galleries, museums, theatres) and educational institutions (universities and colleges) and more corporate head offices. These last two elements are particularly important for science-based innovation, which is mainly found at large research universities and corporate research centres that are typically located near headquarters.

The result is that large cities provide benefits that no other size of region can provide, enabling them to take advantage of a unique growth mechanism. By contrast, LDEs have no ability to access Jacobian growth processes. Rural regions in relatively close proximity to an urban agglomeration usually have some ability to "borrow" some the Jacobean benefits if they have good transport links to the urban place, particularly if those benefits are used infrequently.

Assessing growth mechanisms in LDEs

Only Jacob's urbanization growth driver is not applicable to LDEs, but several other drivers also have a limited role. Marshallian agglomeration effects are hard to identify, as are science-based characterizations of innovation activity. On the other hand, successful rural regions take advantage of: Smith-type trade benefits, Solow capital deepening, first nature geography benefits associated with Weber, and have a sound set of institutions as described by North. The more restricted set of growth drivers available to rural regions is an inherent element of being an LDE. This means that efforts to stimulate growth in rural regions have to focus on those drivers that can be most readily improved.

Trade-based growth is essential for an LDE because it relies on a small number of exports to fund the purchase of the vast number of goods and services that cannot be produced locally. LDEs can only become competitive in a few industries, and these tend to have a strong connection to the particular resource endowment found in the region. But success in exporting also requires the ability to invest in capital deepening to match the productivity level of competing regions, as well as investments in transportation and communication networks that can help overcome the cost of distance (Weber & Freshwater, 2016).

Crucially, the institutional framework within LDEs is significantly different than is the case for larger regions. Many national institutions are not present in rural regions or operate at a different scale – for example, education and health care. Local government provides fewer services and has fewer professional staff, and elected officials work on a part-time, and often voluntary, basis. Markets and government play a smaller role in local society than is the case in larger population regions, while non-profits are more prevalent. But many of these non-profit institutions are informal in nature, with no official status, and appear and disappear as conditions change. Agreements are often not formalized through contracts, and personal relationships govern behaviour. In prosperous rural regions, society has managed to develop innovative ways to put in place and operate a sound set of institutions that can provide a foundation for economic activity, while in lagging rural regions, there is typically a high degree of institutional weakness.

In the modern economy, whether metropolitan or rural, the ability to innovate is vital. Not only are new products, services and processes a key element in economic competitiveness, but a perceived inability to innovate can lead to reduced access to public and private investment in the region. Because rural regions are not well suited to the formal science-based research and development activity that underpins the majority of most current innovations, they are often seen as lacking the capacity to develop and grow through innovation. Yet innovation occurs in many rural regions despite the absence of formal R&D capacity (North & Smallbone, 2000; Isaksen & Karlsen, 2016). This suggests that innovation in rural regions follows a different path, just as does the development of effective institutions.

The role of innovation in LDEs is important but, as indicated in Figure 2.2, quite different from that in metropolitan regions. A high rate of innovation can be found in some industries in some LDEs, but not in all. Regions with high-value natural resources tend to experience the benefits from a high rate of technological change. Most, but not all, of the new technology comes from formal R&D efforts that take place in an urban setting, but with firms in LDEs as the target users. Agriculture is the single best example of an industry that is largely located in an LDE setting but which has experienced a fast rate of technological progress, largely driven by formal R&D that takes place in metropolitan areas. Yet there are also examples of successful small-scale rural innovations. Some have large consequences, such as the Danish wind turbine manufacturer Vestas that originated as a farmer cooperative effort to generate electricity for on-farm use, and is now one of the global leaders in wind turbine manufacturing. Others remain more local in impact, such as the Austrian cooperative effort to produce low-cost solar water heaters that could be assembled by users, and which over time became the largest provider in Austria (Ornetzeder & Rohracher, 2006). Conversely, many sectors and LDE regions experience low rates of innovation that reduce the potential for economic growth.

How might these seven drivers be jointly applied to the economic development situation facing rural less favoured regions? In the medium-term, regions have limited ability to alter either the endowment of natural geography they possess (Weber) or the institutions found within the region (North), although in the longer term it may be possible to improve both. Similarly, neither form of agglomeration (Marshall nor Jacobs) has a strong role in rural regions. This leaves the focus on linking trade (Smith), investment (Solow) and innovation (Schumpeter) as the best approach to strengthen regional productivity and growth. In particular, there can be strong complementarities among these three drivers. Enhancing trade is the base for regional growth, because the local market is too small to absorb increased output. But expanding trade flows typically requires the introduction of new products and processes that can add new exports or increase the competitiveness of existing firms. Adopting these innovations requires investments in new machinery and in expanding markets. All three drivers are required for a dynamic growth process, as is largely recognized in the smart specialization literature with its emphasis on innovation that when adopted leads to enhanced competitiveness.

Growth processes and smart specialization in LDEs

As the OECD notes:

> Although initially relatively simple as a concept – the concentration of public resources in knowledge investments on particular activities in order to strengthen comparative advantage in existing or new areas – the conceptual and policy implications of smart specialization are far more complex.
> (OECD, 2013, p. 11)

Essentially smart specialization requires that both sectors and the projects of specific entrepreneurs be identified as having the potential to drive regional growth. This might seem to be a considerably greater challenge than is involved in traditional industrial policy where more is known about both the sectors and the firms involved. A considerable burden rests on the regional public officials who carry out this task, who must in essence forecast market trends and assess the ability of the region to compete.

A broader concept of smart specialization that stresses efforts to improve productivity in those sectors where a region has either an existing or potential competitive advantage can be readily applied to rural regions. Rural regions, because they are LDEs, are inherently driven to focus on a small number of sectors where they must be efficient producers and marketers to survive. In rural areas, the vast majority of firms are SMEs where an entrepreneurial focus is a major factor in ensuring firm viability. OECD analysis shows that rural regions with a strong focus on tradables are more prosperous, which further supports the importance of an export-oriented economy (including tourism and other services that are provided to external customers) (OECD, 2016).

For rural regions, the archetypal drivers of growth are: the ability to trade on a larger market, which requires both good transportation infrastructure and connectivity that provides access to potential customers; the ability to adopt modern technologies that allow investments in equipment and other technologies to increase worker productivity; the means to improve workforce skills to achieve a better match with employer needs; a strong set of local institutions that provides a framework for the collaborative actions of firms and organizations that support economy and social development; and, in most cases, a natural resource base that is of high enough quality to provide a foundation for the local economy.

Entrepreneurship plays a larger role in firm formation and employment in rural areas than it does in metropolitan regions, because small and medium-sized firms are more dominant. However, the challenge of fostering innovative entrepreneurs may be more difficult. One more favourable aspect of rural areas is that the limited size and scope of the local economy may make it harder for an individual or firm to purchase an acceptable solution to a problem they are facing. Similarly, a local entrepreneur may be able to develop their product or process from a prototype stage to something that is more refined without fear of competition from an imitator because the local market is isolated. But, on the other hand, latent entrepreneurs in rural areas can lack role models, face great challenges in getting even rudimentary support for starting a business, and operate in an environment where it is difficult to identify both suppliers and potential buyers for their products.

Beyond these conditions there is the question of the role of innovation. Smart specialization continues to have a connotation of Schumpeterian growth, where new products or processes create disruptive change that conveys advantages to those who develop them. Yet, the standard metrics for innovation remain: patents filed, relative presence of high-technology sectors, formal investments in research and development activity and the presence of research-oriented organizations like research universities or firm research centres (Fagerberg, 2006; Morgan, 2007). From this perspective, rural regions are unlikely sites for innovation to influence growth. But from a broader perspective on innovation, it is possible to see how it can play a role in rural regional growth.

Perhaps the strongest argument for adopting smart specialization as a regional development policy is its focus on expanding knowledge, which has clear public good aspects. This is reinforced by the common occurrence that ideas appearing to have limited value for the originator can be repurposed by another to create a successful innovation. This possibility of significant spillover effects from investments in creating new knowledge can increase the public return from support for smart specialization. In particular, the benefits from General Purpose Technologies (GPTs) that underpin specific products or processes can benefit multiple regions (OECD, 2013, p. 13). For rural regions, the challenge is to develop a strong enough understanding of GPTs that new rural applications can be identified and acted upon. For example, the internet and browsers provide a remote rural bed and breakfast facility with the same potential web presence as a large urban hotel.

While the core ideas of smart specialization – a focus on core and emerging regional strengths and efforts to improve productivity in these strengths – are challenging for rural regions, they are also imperative. Without a large home market and the opportunity for dense local networks, rural regions must be export-oriented to be economically viable. This makes them reliant on a small set of growth drivers – opportunities to expand trade volumes and value, the ability to invest in capital deepening to increase productivity, exploiting core natural resources and developing a sound set of local institutions. Innovation is complementary to each of these drivers. It can allow reduced transport costs and provide better market intelligence that expand trade. It can create the new technologies that underpin capital deepening. It can help identify new resource endowments and improve the technologies for managing them. And, it can provide new options for managing the core public institutions of rural communities, the local organizations and government services that provide the social foundation on which the local economy rests.

Innovations in a rural region can occur in three possible ways. The first is through a formal R&D process that takes place in metropolitan areas but with rural regions as the target location for implementation. Agricultural biotechnology is the classic example, with large biotechnology firms conducting research on pesticides and pesticide-tolerant seed varieties in urban laboratories but with farms as the target customer. Similarly, multinational heavy equipment manufacturers produce a large range of machinery, much of which is employed in rural places. A second way that rural regions innovate is through emulation, by taking an innovation developed elsewhere and adapting it to a new rural use. In this case, the innovation is a new application of a product or process that the original innovators did not foresee. Open innovation systems rely on this process, where ideas developed in one setting find a new opportunity in another context. For example, fracking reflects the combination of two initially distinct technologies – horizontal drilling and the injection of fluids to hydraulically fracture rock that were developed independently. Finally, there is the potential for local entrepreneurs to innovate to resolve a problem they currently face for which there is not a locally available solution. This idea of "user innovation," or "Doing-Using-Interacting" as it is termed by Isaksen and Karlsen, is relatively more common in rural regions where markets are thinner and formal R&D processes are less common. (Freshwater & Wojan, 2014; Isaksen & Karlsen, 2016).

In many places, the largest problem facing the expansion of innovative rural entrepreneurs is the limited exposure of the local populations to a broad range of ideas, information and activities. In an urban context, the high level of diversity provides this exposure and is an aspect of the urbanization benefits identified by Jane Jacobs. This exposure can trigger both completely new ideas as well as suggest opportunities for emulation or adaptations to meet an unserved rural opportunity. Factors that can mitigate this problem can include: an emphasis on exposing students to a broader global environment, efforts to attract new immigrants who can provide a different perspective, providing information and technology support services that can assist both start-ups and incumbent firms, and promoting exchange programmes that expose the local population to different places and bring people from other places to the community.

Finally, a potential benefit of adopting a smart specialization approach to rural economic development is that it offers a way to think about improving synergies among the particular set of growth mechanisms that are available in a specific rural region. Smart specialization is inherently an argument for identifying and strengthening sectors where there is an opportunity for stronger comparative advantage. However, while the main emphasis should remain on innovation and entrepreneurship, there is also a need to acknowledge other growth drivers so they can support the innovation process, such as increasing connectivity to improve trade or building stronger local institutions.

Discussion

National governments are increasingly concerned with improving rates of economic growth, and this has led to a renewed interest in regional policy.

In this process, rural regions have often been seen as weak candidates for national investments in economic development. However, the ongoing existence of high-productivity rural regions that lack the main attributes that are believed to drive metropolitan growth creates the need for an alternative regional growth model to complement the existing urban-oriented approach. Rural regions that are inherently less favoured under standard models of regional growth grow by taking advantage of natural resource endowments that continue to play a foundation role in the modern economy (Ronningen, 2016). These LDEs make an individually small, but collectively significant, contribution to national economic growth.

Because there are multiple pathways to growth that vary by type of place, there is an inherent need for spatially sensitive regional policy. This can be as simple as, recognizing in standard industrial policy that different parts of particular sectors are suited to different types of place, or as complex as smart specialization policy, which emphasizes a forward-looking approach to competitive advantage. While smart specialization had its origins as a national strategy without a spatial element, it was adopted as the basis for regional development policy by the European Union in 2010 (Foray, David & Hall, 2011). Over time, the importance of this form of place-specific regional policy has become clearer, but there is still a too-narrow focus on locally generated science-driven innovation implemented through entrepreneurs that ignores the opportunity for other innovation mechanisms.

Rural regions are clearly attuned both to the need for specialization in sectors where they have a strong competitive advantage, because they are export dependent, and to the important role of entrepreneur-led growth because local SMEs are the dominant source of income and employment in the region. The remaining gap between rural reality and the concept of smart specialization is the focus on locally developed knowledge-based innovation. In rural regions, innovation is more likely to come from some other source. It could be emulation, where firms copy innovations from elsewhere but place them within the local context. It could be innovation that is developed for rural industries but in national or corporate laboratories located in metropolitan regions. Or, it could be innovation that comes from informal efforts by local firms or individuals to solve problems for which there is no acceptable solution on the market. None of these processes seems to fit closely with the sense that a formal R&D effort underpins the entrepreneurial innovation process.

There is clear evidence that significant amounts of innovation occur in rural areas (North & Smallbone, 2000; Baumol, 2010; OECD, 2014; Atterton, 2016). This evidence also suggests that, just as LDEs rely on a different growth process than do metropolitan regions, so too do they rely on a different innovation approach. This means that while the essential element of a smart specialization strategy, a focus on building competitive advantage by increasing productivity, applies in both types of regions, in rural regions, innovation comes mainly from imported technologies and from relatively informal innovations by new entrepreneurs and by owners of small and medium-sized firms.

The essence of an effective place-based policy is that it focuses on achieving the same types of outcomes without worrying too much about the mechanics of how they are produced. If rural regions are to become more productive and make a full contribution to national economic goals, they will require support from national governments, just as metropolitan regions do. Smart specialization policy can, with only minor adjustments to move beyond its current focus on linking formal R&D to innovative firms in advanced technology sectors, help increase productivity in rural regions. This mostly requires supporting a broader perspective on how innovation is conceived to make smart specialization policy more compatible with broader rural development approaches that collectively can reduce the challenges that rural regions inherently face in terms of: remoteness, low density and limited opportunities to achieve economies of scale.

Acknowledgement

I owe a great debt to colleagues at the OECD Rural Policy Unit who helped me with the evolution of the ideas in this chapter. The words and figures in this chapter are my own, but they have been improved over the last decade by my experiences in rural areas of OECD member countries.

References

Atterton, J. (2016). Invigorating the New Rural Economy: Entrepreneurship and Innovation. In M. Shucksmith & D. Brown (Eds.), *Routledge International Handbook of Rural Studies*. London: Routledge.

Barca, F., McCann, P. & Rodríguez-Pose, A. (2012). The Case for Regional Intervention: Place-Based versus Place-Neutral Approaches. *Journal of Regional Studies, 52*(1), 134–152.

Baumol, W. (2010). *The Microtheory of Innovative Entrepreneurship*. Princeton, NJ: Princeton University Press.

Bettancourt, L. & West, G. (2010). A Unified Theory of Urban Living. *Nature 467*, 912–913.

Bradford, N. & Bramwell, A. (2016). Regional Economic Development: Institutions, Innovation and Policy. In R. Shearmur, C. Carrincazeaux and D. Dolereux (Eds.), *Handbook on the Geographies of Innovation*. Cheltenham, UK: Edward Elgar.

Camagni, R. & Capello, R. (2013). Regional Innovation Patterns and the EU Regional Policy Reform: Toward Smart Innovation Policies. *Growth and Change, 44*(2), 355–389.

Charles, D., Gross, F. & Bachtler, J. (2012). *Smart Specialization and Cohesion Policy: A Strategy for All Regions?* IQ-Net Thematic Paper No. 30(2), Tampere, Finland: European Policies Research Centre.

Etzkowitz, H. & Klofsten, M. (2005). The Innovating Region: Towards a Theory of Knowledge-Based Regional Development. *R&D Management, 35*(3), 243–255.

Fagerberg, J. (2006). Innovation: A Guide to the Literature. In J. Fagerburg & D. Mowery (Eds.), *The Oxford Handbook of Innovation*. Oxford, UK: Oxford University Press.

Foray, D., David, P. & Hall, H. (2011). *Smart Specialization: From Academic Idea to Political Instrument, the Surprising Career of a Concept and the Difficulties*

Involved in Its Implementation. MTEI-Working Paper 2011–001. Lausanne, Switzerland: Management of Technology & Entrepeneurship Institute, Ecole Polytechnique Federale de Lausanne. Retrieved from: https://infoscience.epfl.ch/record/170252/

Freshwater, D. & Wojan, T. (2014). *User Entrepreneurship: Defining and Identifying Explicit Types of Innovation*. Working Paper 492, Lexington, KY: Department of Agricultural Economics, University of Kentucky. Retrieved from: https://ageconsearch.umn.edu/record/229301/files/RuralInov.pdf

Isaksen, A. & Karlsen, J. (2016). Innovation in Peripheral Regions. In R. Shearmur, C. Carrincazeaux & D. Dolereux (Eds.), *Handbook on the Geographies of Innovation*. Cheltenham, UK: Edward Elgar.

Jacobs, J. (1969). *The Economy of Cities*. New York: Random House.

Jonas, A. & Ward, K. (2007). Introduction to a Debate on City-Regions: New Geographies of Governance, Democracy and Social Reproduction. *International Journal of Urban and Regional Research*, *31*(1), 169–178.

Katz, B. (2010). Obama's Metro Presidency. *City and Community*, *9*(1), 23–31.

Marshall, A. (1920). *Principles of Economics* (eighth edn.). London: Macmillan.

Mendez, C. (2013). The Post-2103 Reform of EU Cohesion Policy and the Place-Based Narrative. *Journal of European Public Policy*, *20*(5), 639–659.

Mokyr, J. (1990). *Twenty-Five Centuries of Technological Change*. London: Routledge.

Mokyr, J. (2003). Thinking About Technology and Institutions. *Macalester International*, *13*(1), 33–66.

Mokyr, J. (2005). Long-Term Economic Growth and the History of Technology. In K. Arrow and M. Intrilligator (Eds.), *Handbook of Economic Growth, Vol. 1, Part B*. Amsterdam: Elsevier.

Mokyr, J. (2016). *A Culture of Growth: The Origins of the Modern Economy*. Princeton, NJ: Princeton University Press.

Morgan, K. (2007). The Learning Region: Institutions, Innovation and Regional Renewal. *Regional Studies*, *41*(5), 147–159.

North, D. & Smallbone, D. (2000). Innovative Activity in SMEs and Rural Economic Development: Some Evidence from England. *European Planning Studies*, *8*(1), 87–106.

OECD (2013). *Innovation-Driven Growth in Regions: The Role of Smart Specialization*. Paris: OECD Publishing.

OECD (2014). *OECD Rural Policy Reviews: Innovation and Modernizing the Rural Economy*. Paris: OECD Publishing.

OECD (2016). *Regional Outlook 2016: Productive Regions for Inclusive Growth*. Paris: OECD Publishing.

Ornetzeder, M. & Rohracher, H. (2006). User-led Innovations and Participation Processes: Lessons from Sustainable Energy Technologies. *Energy Policy*, *34*(2), 138–150.

Rodrik, D. (2016). *Economics Rules: The Rights and Wrongs of the Dismal Science*. New York: W.W. Norton.

Ronningen, K. (2016). Environment and Resources: New and Old Questions for Rural Landscapes. In M. Shucksmith & D. Brown (Eds.), *Routledge International Handbook of Rural Studies*. London: Routledge.

Schumpeter, J. (1934). *The Theory of Economic Development* (translated by R. Opie). Cambridge, MA: Harvard University Press.

Shearmur, R. (2017). Urban Bias in Innovation Studies. In H. Bathelt, P. Cohandel, S. Henn & L. Simon (Eds.), *The Elgar Companion to Innovations and Knowledge Creation: A Multi-disciplinary Approach*. Cheltenham, UK: Edward Elgar.

Tödtling, F. & Trippl, M. (2005). Towards a Differentiated Regional Innovation Policy Approach. *Research Policy 34*(8), 1203–1219.

Weber, B. & Freshwater, D. (2016). The Death of Distance? Networks, the Cost of Distance and Rural-Urban Networks. In M. Shucksmith. & D. Brown (Eds.), *Routledge International Handbook of Rural Studies*. London: Routledge.

Wolfe, D. (2016). Innovation and Creativity in City-Regions. In R. Shearmur, C. Carrincazeaux & D. Dolereux (Eds.), *Handbook on the Geographies of Innovation*. Cheltenham, UK: Edward Elgar.

World Bank (2009). *The World Development Report: Reshaping Economic Geography*, Washington, DC: World Bank.

3 Smart specialisation in economically and institutionally less favoured regions

Henning Kroll

Introduction

When first devised, the Smart Specialisation (S3) agenda aimed at providing a generalisable, place-based approach to all European regions, while at the same time pointing out that a focus on critical mass would be crucial to support centres of excellence for specific domains that could help reposition Europe's economy amongst international competition. From the outset, S3 policy implementation thus entered a field of tension between leading-edge industrial and place-based cohesion policy.

While it was pointed out by Foray and others that the application of technologies available from elsewhere should play a central role in the design of smart specialisation strategies for regions with limited capacity for technology generation, this paradigm shift was in practice hardly implemented. Also, less immediately, technology-oriented territorial capacities in production, craft and agriculture that were not directly covered by the European Commission's specifications did not, in many cases, receive much additional attention in entreprenerial discovery processes and – subsequently – the resulting smart specialisation strategies.

Overall, challenges can be seen in two broad areas. First, with respect to the regions' real economies. Many simply do not possess the needed capacities in and networks among either their industrial or their public research sector to constitute regional innovation systems of even an adaptive nature. Second, institutional and administrative capacity in many less favoured regions is sufficiently low that 'entrepreneurial discovery processes' as foreseen in the concept are hard to trigger and, even more so, to keep alive between administratively rigid governments and weak business sectors that lack both trust and experience in mutual collaboration.

In line with the objectives of this book, this chapter understands 'less favoured' regions as those that are facing more challenging starting conditions than others in initiating local processes of smart specialisation. Intentionally, it will not apply any specific classifications from spatial planning, such as peripheral/central or urban/rural, which subsume regions with in fact very different starting conditions under similar headings. Instead, this chapter builds on the conceptual premises of smart specialisation by distinguishing between those in which dynamic processes of entrepreneurial discovery are naturally given and those that are in a 'less favoured' position, as this is not currently the case. A good measurable proxy of this is their currently achieved state of economic development, which will in the following be used as a distinguishing feature.

In light of these challenges, this contribution will outline which possible options could still be found to fertilise the definition of effective smart specialisation strategies in, by and for less favoured regions. In this context, suitable coalitions of actors will be discussed. The remainder of this paper will be organised as follows: the chapter starts with a conceptual introduction to the role of technology application and preconditions for entrepreneurial discovery that are specifically relevant for smart specialisation in less favoured regions. Subsequently, it provides survey-based evidence for the actual inclusion of these in existing smart specialisation strategies. Concluding, it discusses the implications of central aspects' current presence or absence for future processes of smart specialisation in lagging regions.

Conceptual background

Technology application as a central tenet of the smart specialisation approach

Based on a technology-oriented line of argument, the original smart specialisation discourse sought to establish how economic development in the so-called 'real economy' (i.e. the industrial not the financial services sector; Landabaso, 2012, 2014) could be put on a more dynamic track. The key line of argument for smart specialisation put forward that it was in fact less the sectoral structure of an economy and more the overall productivity level in industry that should be the object of concern (O'Mahony & van Ark, 2003; Wilson, 2009; Foray et al., 2009; Foray, 2014). To improve productivity, it was argued, multiple-purpose technologies needed to be conceived and existing ones implemented on a broader scale (Rodrik, 2004; Enkel & Gassmann, 2010; Foray, 2012; Landabaso, 2012).

In principle, the initial discussion suggested that while capacities for technology development should be concentrated, creating critical mass (Foray et al., 2009), an equally important objective would be to motivate more regions to consider additional domains of applications (Boschma, 2014). Against this background, the by now close to proverbial "processes of entrepreneurial discovery" (Foray et al., 2009, 2011, 2012) were to transfer a business sector notion to the sphere of public–private negotiations and actions (Foray et al., 2009) – the search for viable and strategically promising domains for investment (Hausman & Rodrik, 2003). That is, strategically promising domains should be identified at the interface of technology and industry, with an at least as prominent a view to the use as to the development of technologies (Coffano & Foray, 2014).

While many rightly consider the process of smart specialisation as building upon, or at least strongly related to, the concept of "constructing regional advantage"

(CRA) (Asheim et al. 2011), it at the same time transcends it in relevant ways. Correctly, Morgan (2016) points out that the emphasis that the CRA model still places on collocation as a dynamic force is not necessarily placed at the centre of smart specialisation in the same way. Quite to the contrary, smart specialisation places an emphasis on leveraging the potential of connecting localised critical mass in technology generation with distributed capacities in technology usage through a combination of local and non-local exchanges (Bathelt et al., 2004). Moreover, it suggests that it is the forging of additional cross-sectoral as well as cross-regional ties through which the emergence of new domains or new niches in technological space (Markard & Truffer, 2008) will eventually be prompted.

Once the concept was taken up as a policy agenda, however, the role of technology development reaffirmed its position in the discourse, while the original idea of technology exploitation in different locations moved somewhat into the background (Foray, 2014; Kroll, 2015). Gradually, the emphasis on *technology as a means* (as initially conceived) to the end of – regionally and sectorally – broad-based economic development was replaced by an emphasis on *technology per se* (Capello & Kroll, 2016; Kroll, forthcoming). While an emphasis on place-based and regionally adapted strategies was upheld, even extended to the consideration of societal challenges (Foray et al., 2012), it met with a traditional science-push mindset at the regional level that had been conditioned for years and was difficult to alter (Kroll, 2015). Latest, when the legal requirement to develop smart specialisation-based strategies was formulated as concerning support for technology and innovation only (European Union, 2013), a gate was opened for those adamant to pursue their known paradigm of technology-oriented support policy (Capello & Kroll, 2016).

Preconditions for effective entrepreneurial discovery with tangible impact

A further point that merits consideration is that while processes of consultation and the brokering of interests are comparatively easy to organise, processes that make an actual difference to priority setting in the 'real economy' are not (Henderson, 2000), in particular, not in locationally and institutionally less favoured regions. Over the past two to three decades, regional science and economic geography have established a broad body of literature emphasising the fact that not all regions harbour complete 'regional innovation systems' in the sense originally outlined by Cooke (1992, 1996). In practice, however, many regional innovation systems are incomplete due to a fragmentation of actors, a lack of connectivity and institutional thinness (Landabaso, 1997; Tödtling & Trippl, 2005; Capello & Kroll, 2016). Hence, there is quite often no diverse business sector that simply needs to be reconnected, and no functionally coherent population of enterprises at all. In these situations, the smart specialisation discourse has advocated that the government or public organisations need to step in to play the role of dynamic facilitators and entrepreneurial agents (Foray et al. 2012; Landabaso, 2012). However, less than optimal governance practices (Farole et al., 2011; Rodríguez-Pose & Di Cataldo, 2015;

Rodríguez-Pose & Garcilazo, 2015), the delegation of strategy development to inappropriate levels of government (Reid et al., 2012) and lingering traditions of top-down planning (Nauwelaers & Reid, 2002; Kroll, 2015) make it less than trivial to achieve truly transformative dialogues in practice (Capello & Kroll, 2016). Far from being limited to Eastern European Member States, this problem has been encountered in many regions since the beginning of 'Regional Experimentalism' in the 1990s (Henderson, 2000; Iacobucci, 2014).

Against the background of both the deviation from the concept's initial orientation and its so far limited consideration of framework conditions, the role that smart specialisation policies could play for less favoured and peripheral regions remains conceptually underexplored (Cooke, 2012). To some extent, evidently, strategic discussions in such regions need to focus to a greater extent on promising applications of technology and the piloting of new solutions under the regions' specific framework conditions than they should in the technological development hubs of Central Europe (Foray et al., 2009, 2012; Kroll et al., 2016). While they can perfectly well develop and validate business models based on the use of novel technologies, greenfield investments in technology generation will hardly be effective. Furthermore, fragmented systems will have to connect to the outside world more strongly than others. If application or piloting is to be on the agenda, ties with external technology providers need to be established. At the same time, the limited number of local enterprises that can make an excellent contribution to international technology and product development in some areas need to connect to customers and networks outside of the region. Finally, preconditions to run effective entrepreneurial discovery processes involving relevant stakeholders from both the public and the private sectors need to be established in administrative practice and political commitment (Rodríguez-Pose, 2013; Kroll, 2015; Capello & Kroll, 2016).

As long as the local institutional and governance system remains effective (Kroll, 2015) and political commitment exists (Kroll, forthcoming), the mere fact of being peripheral and sparsely populated need not impact negatively on a region's capacity for (relative) economic development. At the same time, an absence of governance capacity (Kroll, 2015) or political commitment (Kroll, forthcoming) can limit more central and relatively well-developed regions' ability to set up suitable and effective entrepreneurial processes of discovery. Consequently, a correlation between being in a less favoured economic position and being less able to initiate effective entrepreneurial processes of discovery cannot per se be considered given. Other factors like governance capacity and political commitment can intervene to cause deviations either way.

Finally, many less favoured regions feature specific advantages in the interregional sharing of tasks based on natural resources or touristic potential (Woods, 2013) that, while not technology-oriented per se, could still constitute relevant areas of application. Moreover, a high level of local social capital (Dubois & Roto, 2012) may improve their ability to orchestrate local processes of inclusive strategy development – a claim that, in principle, is supported by repeated findings on the conducive role and successful societal embedding of mid-range universities in such contexts (Kroll et al., 2015). Evidently, such strategies would have to focus on different objectives than are common and useful in leading regions (Nuur & Laestadius, 2010), i.e. on capacity building, market diffusion and providing lead application and piloting environments instead of technological developed. Beyond making these choices out of need, as mentioned above, it can thus equally be argued that they are better, more effective choices, both with a view to local productivity and with a view to suitably position less favoured regions in the international sharing of tasks in the European innovation system.

Research questions

In consequence, therefore, theory and existing empirical studies clearly suggest which general avenues would have to be pursued more strongly in less favoured, peripheral regions. Also, there is anecdotal evidence that the consultation processes triggered by the ex-ante conditionality have in many areas not yet fully translated into discussions and negotiations on actual joint actions. What is less known, however, is the status quo of such processes in less favoured regions and the factors that might limit the adoption of relevant practices and the development of regionally adapted "processes of entrepreneurial discovery".

The following section will give a closer examination of the relevance of the S3 agenda in less favoured and peripheral regions from the perspective of the entrepreneurial discovery process and regional institutional capacity. Against this background, the following research questions can be put forward: first, how is the relevance of the research and innovation strategies for smart specialisation (RIS3) agenda perceived in less favoured and peripheral regions and are there differences with how it is perceived in other places? Second, is there any evidence of specific particularities of processes of entrepreneurial discovery in less favoured regions (concerning application orientation, interregional orientation and the role of universities or public research organisations). Third, do the potentials that local policymakers in less favoured regions see in entrepreneurial processes of discovery differ from those in others?

Data

This chapter will draw on the annual Fraunhofer ISI survey of managing authorities and other policymakers in charge of smart specialisation strategy development. The first round of this survey was conducted in 2013, ahead of the completion of many regions' formal strategies (Kroll et al., 2014). While in the first round, a focus was placed on the region's general assessment of the European Commission's policy agenda, later rounds focused more specifically on issues of policy implementation, monitoring and interregional collaboration. At the time of writing, the most recent round, launched in May 2016, focused on the continuation and substance of entrepreneurial discovery processes.

As described in detail in Kroll (2015), the survey seeks to address responsible policymakers rather than external observers. For that purpose, a database of addressees was built from information available on European Commission as well as regional administrations' websites. Every year, this list is updated and cleaned before the survey is conducted. In 2016, the survey was sent out to more than 1,000 contacts, of which 113 answered completely and 66 partially – yielding a response rate of 15% at the level of individuals, yet a much higher one at the level of administrations. Overall, the survey covers more than 50% of all managing authorities and provides answers from almost all Member States. More than half of the respondents in 2016 had participated in earlier rounds, creating a core with panel characteristics.

With respect to the issue of being less favoured, the only point of reference that the survey provides is the question of economic development, or, more precisely, gross regional income per inhabitant. Further information on peripherality is not included in the dataset. While, in the 2015 survey, respondents were directly asked to identify their areas of reference as either former Convergence or Regional Competitiveness and Employment regions, this was not done in the 2016 round. However, a question that addressed the relevance of European Structural and Investment Funding for regional innovation policy can be used as a proxy – as a high relevance of such means for a region typically results from a below-average level of economic development. For the purpose of the analysis below, regions whose innovation policy depends by more than 20% on ESIF sources were classified as 'less favoured'.

Empirical findings: the relevance of the S3 agenda in less favoured regions

Research question 1: perceived relevance of the RIS3 agenda

In the most general terms, no substantive difference can be identified between less and more developed regions when it comes to the general assessment of the RIS3 process. Overall, this picture had already been the same a year earlier – even though nuances have changes. Whereas, in 2015, less favoured regions outperformed more developed ones with a view to very favourable assessments, this balance has now tilted in favour of the more developed areas. However, the combined shares of favourable and very favourable assessments are by and large still very similar.

Moreover, the 2015 survey had revealed that, different from what intuition would suggest, the added value was fairly similar in various areas, ranging from the creation of new competences in the administration, the sustained (rather than one-off) involvement of additional stakeholders, to factual changes in the policy mix. Only with a view to optimism that the RIS3 process will yield further outcomes in the years to come were very positive attitudes limited to more developed regions – while generally positive ones were once more equally widespread. Finally, no substantive differences could be identified with a view to the extent to which working groups and expert panels convened during the RIS3 process of entrepreneurial discovery continue to exist and operate.

In summary, less favoured regions do not generally harbour a different attitude to the RIS3 process than more advanced ones. Partially, this may be due to different learning experiences from which they, in sum, equally benefit (cf. Kroll, 2015).

Research question 2.1: application orientation of entrepreneurial discovery

Contrary to assumptions, a first general analysis finds that, in less favoured regions, an on average slightly stronger focus is placed on technologies than on societal challenges. Overall, approaches based on technology application to address societal challenges – that are in general rare enough – are slightly more common in more developed regions, whereas approaches that are exclusively focused on technologies are slightly more common in less favoured regions.

Partially, this may be due to the fact that the overall range of actors active in less favoured regions' processes of entrepreneurial discovery are not substantially different from those in leading regions (cf. Figure 3.1). They, too, remain dominated by public sector research organisations. While, encouragingly, stakeholders from civil society are somewhat more prevalently involved in the processes, their overall role remains too insignificant to prompt a substantial reorientation. Moreover, less encouraging signals can be detected – such as a

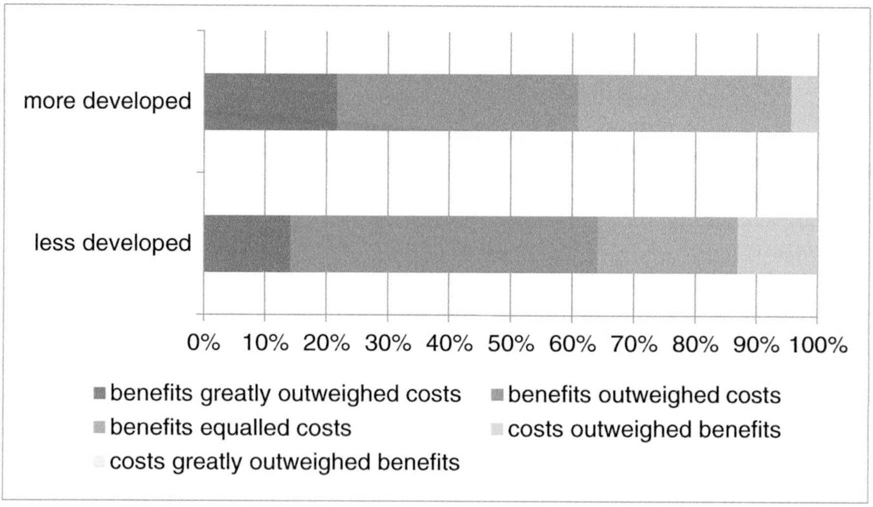

Figure 3.1 General assessment of the RIS3 process (2016 survey round)

Source: own analysis

weaker presence of intermediaries and a stronger presence of large domestic firms. On a positive note, the role of local small and medium-sized enterprises (SMEs) and start-ups seems to be somewhat higher in less favoured regions' processes of strategy definition.

Research question 2.2: interregional orientation of entrepreneurial discovery

With a view to this chapter's most central point of inquiry, the 2015 survey's findings confirm the conceptual proposition that many regions – no matter how developed – face clear market opportunities for locally developed R&D outside their boundaries, while at the same time in particular lesser-developed regions whose decision makers indicate that more local innovation opportunities could be leveraged once their linkage with external knowledge providers is improved. In 2016, this finding was once more confirmed with slightly, even if not fundamentally, higher shares of less favoured regions stating that they see potential in interregional cooperation. Empirically, then, the case for interregional smart specialisation is clearly confirmed. Quite in contrast to this, however, interregional linkages are not considered as very prominent aspects in most RIS3 strategies. Given that more than two thirds of either type of region see at least some benefit in strengthening their interregional linkages in at least one direction, it must be considered surprising that a mere third articulates this strongly in their RIS3 strategies. With a view to peripheral regions, it seems particularly noteworthy that their political perspective beyond the boundaries of their nations seems much less pronounced than in leading ones. Of those considering external knowledge input most fruitful, a mere 5% chose to articulate this strongly in their RIS3 strategies.

Somewhat consequently, the 2015 survey found that, in less favoured regions, obstacles for international collaboration across national borders are perceived as higher. Additionally, the 2016 survey revealed that while such regions are more likely to be part of Macro-Regions or INTERREG Collaborations, their willingness to collaborate strategically across borders, even in the absence of funding, is markedly less pronounced. Furthermore, the 2016 survey's findings suggest that – other than sometimes attributed to them in innovation theory – local universities in less favoured regions less commonly and less effectively perform functions of 'antennas' or interregional interfaces. All that notwithstanding, policymakers tend to take a 'glass half full' approach towards to the potential effects of newly launched RIS3 strategy processes in this respect. While the difference is not fundamental, a notable larger share of respondents from less favoured regions expressed at least moderate optimism that the entrepreneurial discovery process (EDP) will lead to more cooperation with research organisations, firms and other bodies from outside the region (Figure 3.2).

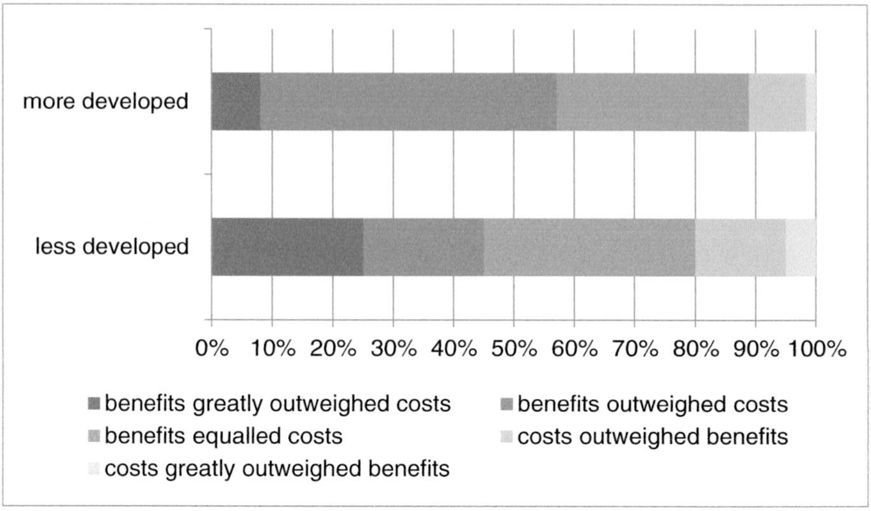

Figure 3.2 General assessment of the RIS3 process (2015 survey round)
Source: own analysis

Research question 2.3: 'entrepreneurial role' of public research and universities

With a view to the question of whether participants in the process of entrepreneurial discovery assume different roles, depending on the environment they are located in, a positive finding, first identified in the 2015 survey, is that the role of businesses, i.e. those who know the actual needs of the local market best, is, if anything, slightly more pronounced in less favoured regions. From a different perspective, the 2016 survey supported this impression by finding that the capacity of RIS3 processes to leverage private funding was, on average, not notably lower in less favoured regions than in leading ones. While the share of processes considered 'not at all' capable of achieving this effect is indeed higher, it seems more adequate to interpret this as a higher tendency of processes going wrong in less favoured regions (in line with the findings of Kroll, 2015) than of such processes being in principle unfit to operate under such conditions.

As suggested by theory and earlier empirical studies, moreover, universities were clearly, even if not drastically, more commonly found to act as active, politically well-embedded co-developers of local RIS3 strategies. At the same time, it was found that, while it was indeed less common to find peripherally located universities to act in no way at all in an entrepreneurial manner, it was equally less common for them to do so 'very strongly'. In fact, entrepreneurial engagement appears to, on average, be slightly more prevalent among centrally located universities (Figure 3.3).

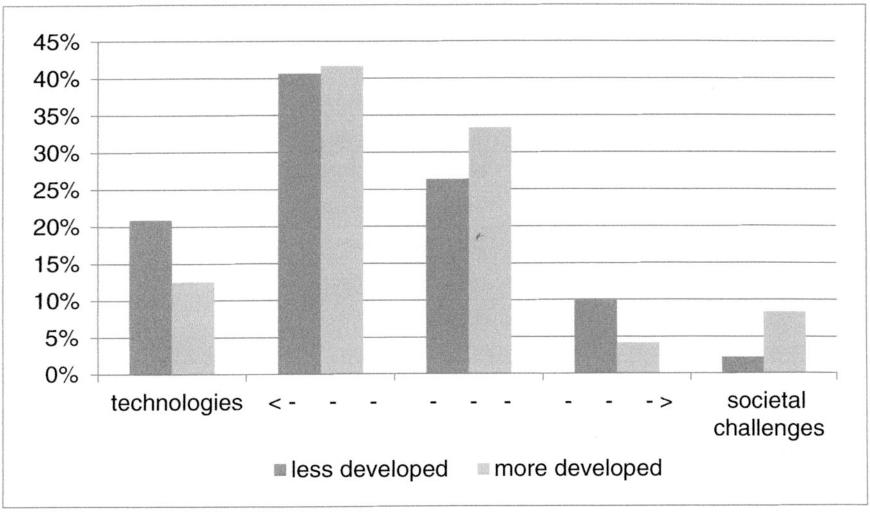

Figure 3.3 Overall focus of regional innovation strategy and process (2016 survey round)

Source: own analysis

Research question 3: potentials seen in entrepreneurial discovery

With a view to the effect of RIS3 processes in less favoured regions, no fundamental differences can be identified, with the exception of the fact that such regions are slightly more likely to emphasise the otherwise underrepresented area of industrial modernisation, which, with a view to their starting conditions, can be read as a positive sign of local adaptation.

Furthermore, the share of less favoured regions in which RIS3 results are considered particularly guiding for investments in public–private partnerships for innovation or decisions on new, large-scale projects – two areas in which RIS3 efforts can be considered to be particularly pertinent in regions with larger budgets – is on average indeed higher than in more developed regions. While respondents from more developed regions may be the majority among those who see such effects 'very strongly', respondents from less developed regions are much more strongly represented among those who see 'some impact' of RIS3 results. On average, therefore, RIS3 processes occurring in them can be considered as more effective with regard to large-scale investment.

Hence, the on-average similar assessment of the role of RIS3 processes (cf. research question 1) and the on-a-global-scale similar areas in which they are considered to achieve effects (Figure 3.4) can be considered as evidence of similar global ambitions pursued in a manner adapted to regional framework conditions and budgetary room for manoeuvre. As the analysis consistently shows for other accounts, the effects perceived with a view to the "de facto allocation of

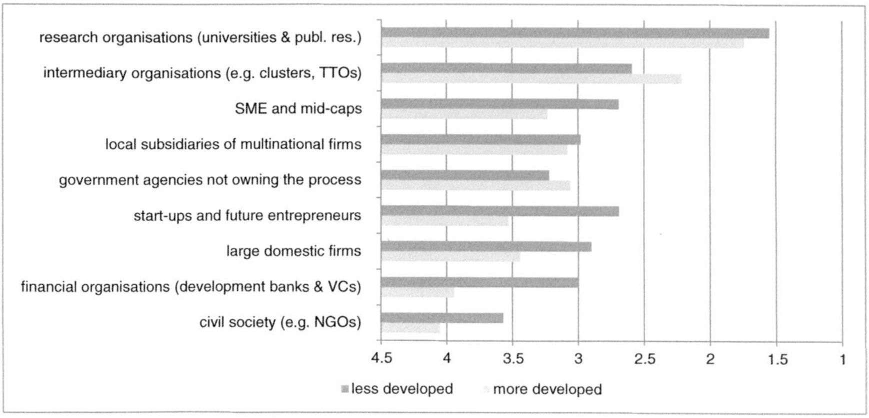

Figure 3.4 Dominant actors in the process of defining the innovation strategy (2016 survey round)

Source: own analysis

funding from as such not technology specific support programmes", "the set-up of entirely new intermediary organisations (e.g. clusters)" is higher in leading regions that merely adapt existing support systems than it is in less favoured ones, where those are still absent.

Discussion

Initially, smart specialisation set out with the ambitious objective of reviving European regional policy in concept and implementation that was bound to meet with a number of structural and mental path dependencies. For weaker regions, and in particular peripheral ones, the new concept came with the specific challenge of rethinking their positioning and support activities in a larger concept that was never likely to be comprehensively adopted right away.

Against this background, the results of the two RIS3 surveys carried out in 2015 and 2016 leave mixed impressions. On the one hand, findings on external opportunities for regional providers as well as business opportunities inside the regions for external providers underline that there is practical substance to Foray et al.'s (2009) original idea of smart specialisation as a tool to activate pan-European networking between complementary potentials, with some regions focusing on providing technologies and others on actively using them in a place-based manner – which, in turn, can propel the innovation process. Apparently, the main basis of the policy proposition did not originate from single economists' thinking. Instead, policymakers from both more and less favoured regions recognise their mutual dependency and the potential benefits of interregional cooperation. At the same time, the actual degree of adaptation of regional strategies to their environment remains comparatively limited, at least insofar as this can be established by coarsely differentiating between two groups of 'less favoured' and 'more developed' regions.

On a positive note, their assessment of the RIS3 process is close to equally positive, underwriting Kroll's (2015) assumption that different types of regions may profit in their own specific ways. By and large, there is no general aspect of smart specialisation policy that would be reported as entirely inapplicable to less favoured areas. For example, both evidence-based analyses and participatory approaches to policymaking can, *per se*, be relevant under different starting conditions. So far, very few stakeholders from less favoured regions have been known to have given up hope for gradual change even under inclement circumstances. Quite to the contrary, a number of voluntary local RIS3 initiatives have sprung up in countries with otherwise less favourable conditions. In line with this anecdotal evidence, as well as the propositions of the conceptual section, both RIS3 processes and perceived outcomes have been found to suggest some extent of situational fit to starting conditions. In summary, stakeholders from less favoured regions do not seem to, in principle, consider RIS3 processes as something with less potential under their framework conditions.

From a different perspective, however, it could be argued that the overall low degree of variety observed in respondents' assessment of the design, nature and effectiveness of RIS3 strategies does not adequately reflect the level of diversity and disparity that characterises the regions addressed by them. While the intrinsically place-based nature of the approach justifies that its overall assessment does not differ between regional types, the same fundamental orientation would suggest that more evidence is found with respect to emphases on different steps of the process, the involvement of different target groups or the emergence of different types of coalitions. While a dichotomising classification may suppress some elements of variety – and, in fact, some of the figures could be read as reflecting mutually overlapping patterns – the overall lack of distinctiveness between actor behaviour in regions faring well and those still working to address fundamental issues appears striking. Moreover, many less favoured regions continue to report substantial obstacles with a view to transnational cooperation, and were it not for INTERREG or the Macro-Regions, nothing much would arguably happen at all. In that light, a notion of a European Innovation Union in which less favoured and peripheral regions are seamlessly integrated in transnational networks must appear distant on the horizon.

With a view to the conceptual background and the political thrust of the smart specialisation agenda that was outlined above, the survey data thus, on the one hand, confirm the justification of the case, as well as the first seeds of its taking effect in practice. At the same time, however, they caution that many obstacles will still have to be overcome before a genuinely new paradigm can emerge. Currently, less favoured, peripheral regions have a way to go to establish their own distinct approach to the design of smart specialisation strategies.

Conclusions

As stated in the discussion, smart specialisation was a new notion of policymaking setting out to replace, or at least amend, established routines of policymaking at various levels and in various ways. It requires local coalitions committed to promoting international orientation and cross-sectoral thinking where parochialism and sectoral policies had been the norm. Against this background, all place-based particularity in less favoured regions programme design should be considered welcome, as long as it helps to dynamise socio-economic development in the region and to tackle societal challenge.

That said, it is evident that the smart specialisation approach, in particular when it comes to connecting less favoured, peripheral regions to Europe's core hubs of development through ways other than financial or human capital transfer, runs counter to many established and, for different reasons by some also, appreciated practices. However, this connectivity is crucial, in particular in environments where collaboration between neighbouring, equally disadvantaged regions offers limited leverage – or at best one consolidated side of larger collaboration arrangements. In principle, smart specialisation is about developing new active ways of technology application to address place-based challenges. While this chapter underlines that the opportunity to collaborate with distant technology providers is important precisely because of this, it equally finds that perseverance and gradual pursuit will be needed to achieve progress, even more so than with regard to the already relatively well-developed system of interregional collaboration between neighbouring regions.

For less favoured and peripheral regions, the new approach harbours substantial potential that they have yet to fully uncover. Until today, the obvious merits of truly place-based, challenge-oriented approaches remain to be fully acknowledged in far too many regions. Put at jeopardy of losing support in their local electorate as well as national relevance, policymakers in peripheral regions are facing difficulties in promoting those processes and specialisations that are based on truly 'local' capacities yet potentially less fashionable.

In short, progress in the design of place-based smart specialisation strategies for less favoured and peripheral regions will have to come from a mixture of far-sighted leadership, open-minded communication and coalitions that ensure an involvement of those businesses and representatives of civil society that actually matter for local development. Other than policymakers, businesses and NGOs do not have to answer to a specific local electorate. Instead, such organisations often display a natural openness in collaborating with external stakeholders, as long as those are relevant partners in the pursuit of their own interests, which, at an aggregate level, also benefit the region.

As in more dynamic regions, the key to genuinely smart specialisation strategies for the periphery may thus well lie in strategically involving those who have a limited profile in local politics but good knowledge about local capabilities – and a natural interest in catalysing this knowledge through the involvement of external actors. As either capacity will, on its own, remain fruitless, developing the regional–transregional interface in local coalitions and collaborations will be among the key tasks of less favoured regions' policymakers in the years to come.

Acknowledgements

The author acknowledges support from the European Commission's Directorate General for Regional and Urban Policy, which financially supported the analysis of the Smart Specialisation Survey in 2016. He also acknowledges support from his colleague Hendrik Berghäuser.

References

Asheim, B., Boschma, R., Cooke, P. (2011). Constructing regional advantage: platform policies based on related variety and differentiated knowledge bases, *Regional Studies*, *45*(7), 893–904.

Bathelt, H., Malmberg, A., Maskell, P. (2004). Clusters and knowledge: local buzz, global pipelines and the process of knowledge creation, *Progress in Human Geography*, *28*(1), 31–56.

Boschma, R. (2014). Constructing regional advantage and smart specialisation: comparison of two European policy concepts, *Scienze Regionali, Italian Journal of Regional Science*, *13*(1), 51–68.

Capello, R., Kroll, H. (2016). From theory to practice in smart specialization strategy: emerging limits and possible future trajectories, *European Planning Studies*, *24*, 1393–1406. DOI:10.1080/09654313.2016.1156058.

Coffano, M., Foray, D. (2014). The centrality of entrepreneurial discovery in building and implementing a smart specialisation strategy, *Scienze Regionali, Italian Journal of Regional Science*, *13*(1), 33–50.

Cooke, P. (1992). Regional innovation systems: competitive regulation in the new Europe, *Geoforum*, *23*(1992), 365–382.

Cooke, P. (1996). The new wave of regional innovation networks: analysis, characteristics and strategy, *Small Business Economics*, *8*, 159–171.

Cooke, P. (2012). *Complex Adaptive Innovation Systems: Relatedness and Transversality in the Evolving Region (Regions and Cities)*. London: Routledge.

Dubois, A., Roto, J. (2012). *Making the best of Europe's Sparsely Populated Areas, On making geographic specificity a driver for territorial development in Europe* (Nordregio Working Paper 15. Available at https://www.diva-portal.org/smash/get/diva2:700300/FULLTEXT01.pdf (accessed 8 September 2016).

Enkel, E., Gassmann, O. (2010). Creative imitation: exploring the case of cross-industry innovation, *R&D Management*, *40*(3), 256–270.

European Union (2013). Regulation (EU) No 1303/2013 of the European Parliament and of the Council laying down common provisions on the ERDF, the ESF, the Cohesion Fund, the EAFRD and the EMFF and laying down general provisions on the ERDF, the ESF, the Cohesion Fund, the EAFRD and the EMFF and repealing Council Regulation (EC) No 1083/2006.

Farole, T., Rodríguez-Pose, A., Storper, M. (2011). Cohesion policy in the European Union: growth, geography, institutions, *Journal of Common Market Studies*, *49*(5), 1089–1111.

Foray, D. (2012). Smart Specialisation and the New Industrial Policy Agenda, Innovation for Growth, i4 g Policy Brief No. *8*. Brussels: European Commission.

Foray, D. (2014). *Smart Specialisation, Opportunities and Challenges for Regional Innovations Policy*. London: Routledge.

Foray, D., David, P.A., Hall, B.H. (2009). Smart Specialisation – The Concept, Knowledge Economists Policy Brief n° 9, June. Brussels: European Commission. Available at http://ec.europa.eu/invest-in-research/pdf/download_en/kfg_policy_brief_no9.pdf (accessed 8 September 2016).

Foray, D., David, P.A., Hall, B.H. (2011). Smart Specialization – From Academic Idea to Political Instrument/the Surprising Career of a Concept and the Difficulties Involved in Its Implementation MTEI-WORKING-PAPER-2011-001. Lausanne: École Polytechnique Federale de Lausanne.

Foray, D., Goddard, J., Goenaga Beldarrain, X., Landabaso, M., McCann, P., Morgan, K., Nauwelaers, C., Ortega-Artilés, R. (2012). Guide to Research and Innovation Strategies for Smart Specialisation (RIS3). European Commission, RIS3 Platform. Available at: http://ec.europa.eu/regional_policy/sources/docgener/presenta/smart_specialisation/smart_ris3_2012.pdf (accessed 15 May 2017).

Hausman, R., Rodrik, D. (2003). Economic development as self-discovery, *Journal of Development Economics*, *72*(2), 603–633.

Henderson, D. (2000). EU regional innovation strategies, regional experimentalism in practice?, *European Urban and Regional Studies*, 7(4), 347–358. DOI: 10.1177/096977640000700404

Iacobucci, D. (2014). Designing and implementing a smart specialisation strategy at regional level: some open questions, *Scienze Regionali, Italian Journal of Regional Science*, *13*(1), 107–126.

Kroll, H. (2015). Efforts to implement smart specialization in practice – leading unlike horses to the water, *European Planning Studies*, *23*(10), 2079–2098. DOI: 10.1080/09654313.2014.1003036.

Kroll, H. (forthcoming). Smart specialisation policy in an economically well-developed, multi-level governance system. In Radosevic, S., Andreescu, L., Wade, I., Roman, A. (Eds.) *Advances in the Theory of Smart Specialization*. Amsterdam: Elsevier.

Kroll, H., Dornbusch, F., Schnabl, E. (2015). Universities' regional involvement in Germany: how academics' objectives and opportunity shape choices of activity, *Regional Studies*, *50*(9), 1595–1610. DOI: 10.1080/00343404.2015.1051016

Kroll, H., Gabriel, M., Braun, A., Muller, E., Neuhäusler, P., Schnabl, E., Zenker, A. (2016). A Conceptual Analysis of Foundations, Trends and Relevant Potentials in the Field of Frugal Innovation (in Europe). Interim report for the project 'study on frugal innovation and reengineering of traditional techniques'. Brussels.

Kroll, H., Muller, E., Schnabl, E., Zenker, A. (2014). *From Smart Concept to Challenging Practice: How European Regions Deal with the Commission's Request for Novel Innovation Strategies*, Working Papers Firms and Regions No. R2/2014. Karlsruhe: Fraunhofer ISI.

Landabaso, M. (1997). The promotion of innovation in regional policy: proposals for a regional innovation strategy, *Entrepreneurship and Regional Development*, *9*(1), 1–24.

Landabaso, M. (2012). What public policies can and cannot do for regional development. In Cooke, P., Parrilli, M., Curbelo, J. (Eds.) *Innovation, Global Challenge and Territorial Resilience* (pp. 364–381). Cheltenham, UK: Edward Elgar.

Landabaso, M. (2014). Time for the real economy: the need for new forms of public entrepreneurship, *Scienze Regionali, Italian Journal of Regional Science*, *13*(1), 127–140.

Markard, J., Truffer, B. (2008). Technological innovation systems and the multi-level perspective: towards an integrated framework, *Research Policy, 37*(4), 596–615.

Morgan, K. (2016). Collective entrepreneurship: the Basque model of innovation, *European Planning Studies, 24*(8), 1544–1560.

Nauwelaers, C., Reid, A. (2002). Learning innovation policy in a market-based context: process, issues and challenges for EU candidate-countries, *Journal of International Relations and Development, 5*(4), 357–379.

Nuur, C., Laestadius, S. (2010). Development in peripheral regions: case studies in Sweden, *European Urban and Regional Studies, 17*(3), 293–307.

O'Mahony, M., van Ark, B. (Eds.) (2003). *EU Productivity and Competitiveness: An Industry Perspective. Can Europe Resume the Catching-Up Process?* Luxemburg: European Commission.

Reid, A., Komninos, N., Sanchez, J., Tsanakas, P. (2012). *RIS3 National Assessment: Greece. Smart Specialisation as a Means to Foster Economic Renewal.* Report to the European Commission, DG Regional Policy. Brussels: European Commission.

Rodríguez-Pose, A. (2013). Do institutions matter for regional development? *Regional Studies, 47*(7), 1034–1047.

Rodríguez-Pose, A., & Di Cataldo M. (2015). Quality of government and innovative performance in the regions of Europe. *Journal of Economic Geography, 15*(4,1), 673–706. https://doi.org/10.1093/jeg/lbu023

Rodríguez-Pose, A., & Garcilazo, E. (2015). Quality of government and the returns of investment: examining the impact of cohesion expenditure in Europe. *Regional Studies, 49*(8), 1274–1290.

Rodrik, D. (2004). Industrial Policy for the Twenty-first Century, CEPR Discussion Paper Series No. 4767. London: Centre for Economic Policy Research.

Tödtling, F., & Trippl, M. 2005, One size fits all?: towards a differentiated regional innovation policy approach. *Research Policy, 34*(8), 1203–1219.

Wilson, D.J. (2009). IT and beyond: the contribution of heterogeneous capital to productivity, *Journal of Business and Economic Statistics, 27*(1), 52–70.

Woods, M. (2013). Regions engaging globalization: a typology of regional responses in rural Europe, *Journal of Rural and Community Development, 8*(3), 113–126.

4 Development of mountainous regions

Smart specialization approaches as a means to overcoming peripheralization

Thomas Dax

Introduction: why do we need an invigorated impetus for mountain regions?

This chapter focuses on the prospects of mountain regions and the potential of Smart Specialization (S3) to harness place-specific assets and development options. The delineation of mountain areas as highlighted by comparative analysis of European mountains (Price, 2010) usually cuts across regional borders. In this regard, the pertinence of mountain contexts in regional strategies is often blurred by internal divergence. The early decades of EU regional policy were characterized by the notion of "Less-Favoured Areas" (LFA), initially in close relationship to farming and forestry production difficulties and the need to overcome 'permanent disadvantages' (Cooper et al., 2006). In view of its prime orientation to establish policies to cope with 'severe and permanent natural handicap' (Art. 174 of Treaty on the Functioning of the European Union, 2007) the respective agricultural policy measure recently was relabelled as an instrument for 'Areas of Natural Constraints'. The respective compensation measures represent mainly just a cure for symptoms and hardly enable structural changes and innovative approaches for mountain regions to be adopted.

In terms of objectives to achieving social and territorial cohesion in Europe, policies are increasingly taking into account specific place-based development opportunities, bearing in mind ecological vulnerability and threats to biodiversity provision, and particular challenges for agriculture and forestry. Indeed, for a long time, policy strategies have sought increased coherence to achieve frameworks for land use management systems and regional economic development that enhance environmental and social beneficial outcomes. This assessment follows a reconsideration of the various strengths and weaknesses and visible opportunities for mountain regions (and other regions with specific geographic features) that increasingly build upon the unique natural and cultural heritage of specific regions. However, "(i)t is not straightforward . . . for mountainous regions to be able to 'exploit' their particular 'assets', particularly given their distinct territorial contexts and combinations of different socio-economic, demographic and environmental challenges" (Gløersen et al., 2016).

This perspective has been framed over the last few decades following the integration of the mountain development discourse into the discussion of global sustainable development through implementing Agenda 21 strategies adopted at the UN Conference on Environment and Development in Rio de Janeiro in 1992. Since then, research and policy concerns for mountain development have intensified, and the complexity of the particular eco-social systems of mountain areas has been increasingly explored (Dax, 2017). The theoretical framework thus elaborated has underscored a vision of land management in mountain contexts being inherently linked to the preservation of ecosystem services and, more generally, public goods. The actual difficulty in providing these public goods is due to the highly localized structures of natural resources and services and, on the other hand, the rising interrelation of mountain features to global change (Debarbieux & Price, 2008). Relevant policies are only gradually taking up these considerations and very often remain in their sectoral line of argument, be it the shaping of mountain agriculture (EC, 2009) or the establishment of regional policies directed at mountain specificities (Analysis for Economic Decisions, 2012).

The process was supported by a strong increase in new institutional arrangements (Debarbieux et al., 2015) combining a territorial and environmental focus and enlarged networks of stakeholders, particularly in mountain regions with dense internal institutional structures and enhanced knowledge linkages, exemplified by Central and Western European mountain ranges like the Alps, the Carpathians and the Pyrenees. However, lack of appropriate institutional settings and fragmentation of actors are persistent for many peripheral mountain regions and represent substantial obstacles to regional development. It is the features of natural handicaps in particular and the characteristics of less-favoured regions (LFR) that imply an enlarged interest in mountain regions for innovative regional policy approaches. While the conceptual discussion of S3 (Kroll, 2017) discerns limited chances for remote regions to apply that approach, particularly due to concerns about the 'lack of critical mass' and the focus on the crucial role of relatedness, an increasing number of studies focus on the prerequisites and opportunities for remote rural areas to participate in those strategies. Case study presentations, even in a context of peripheral, sparsely populated regions, underscore the adaptability of the concept for those spatial structures (Dubois et al., 2017). Some of the arguments brought to the fore resemble, astonishingly, those of the era of 'neo-endogenous regional development' in which concepts of nurturing local assets were blended with aspects of cross-fertilization and networking with external drivers, providing incentives and knowledge development for LFR. As such, the recent smart specialization approaches succeed in highlighting the scope of innovation potential and the different nature of innovation activities in rural areas, underpinning the high impact of 'social innovation' features of these processes (Rosa Pires et al., 2014). In respect of the way in which it differs from technological innovation, Phills, Deiglmeier and Miller (2008, p. 36) define social innovation as "(a) novel solution to a social problem that is more effective, efficient, sustainable, or just than existing solutions and for which the value created accrues primarily to society as a whole rather than private individuals". It therefore involves new forms of organization that lead to "a change of attitude, behaviour or perceptions" (Neumeier, 2012, p. 55) and collaborative action that improves the lives of those involved. The LEADER[1] programme developed one of the most influential sets of activities in rural development to address this spirit of mobilizing the countryside, by focusing on endogenous potential and activating local stakeholders across all sectors. Local initiatives stimulated by Local Action Groups of the LEADER programme include agricultural diversification and value-chain development, new approaches in tourism development, cross-sectoral collaboration, social and cultural initiatives and trans-regional cooperation.

The emerging concept of S3 opens up new options and reinvigorates important aspects of regional development. As the new approach reaffirms opportunities for regional development (OECD, 1999), it enhances a visionary strategy that focuses on participation, relationships and social transformation as against a non-reflective belief in solutions derived from technological adaptations. However, in public discourse, often the 'smart' part of the strategy is equated with technology alone and misses the need for social concerns. This chapter aims to increase understanding of the need for transformations that address, in a comprehensive manner, not just smart growth assumptions, but extend to issues of societal transitions, including the reassessment of regional performance by placing well-being considerations at the centre of interest of local actors (Dax & Fischer, 2017).

Challenges arising from mountain contexts

Taking account of the local conditions is extremely important in mountain contexts, where challenges and opportunities for economic activities and social development may vary significantly at a fine scale. Indeed, the relationships between societies and nature are changing at an increased pace, and mountain regions are probably first in line to face this challenge. The research call for proposals on "Mountains as Sentinels of Change", issued by the Belmont Forum, which is a group of the world's major funders of global environmental change research, aimed "to deliver knowledge needed for action to mitigate and adapt detrimental environmental change and extreme hazardous events - and to Future Earth research themes" (Belmont Forum, 2015, p. 2). This is a strong indication of the relevance of fundamental changes in this area, which underpins the task of realizing global changes through observing physical, social and cultural trends in mountain areas as driving forces of regional development. Implications for the physical environment that are discernible in all mountain ranges of the world are due to fundamental shifts in resource use and have significant repercussions for the opportunities available to humans in mountains and lowlands. Strong interdependence is a defining background for any regional development strategy and crucially shapes the options for future activities. It is a highly demanding task to conceive S3 for these type of regions. Following from the specific conditions and local trends, a set of influences on the various dimensions of sustainable development have to be recognized as influential triggers. In particular, preconditions for further development include both technical improvements (infrastructure), protection and adaptive measures for the environment (ecological performance and climate change) as well as an enhanced recognition of community development (governance and institutional development) and social changes (social capital and social innovation). This wide range of crucial spheres of influence creates an interesting test bed for S3 experimentation in transforming mountain regions.

As mountain areas cover 36 per cent of Europe's land area and cross many national borders, a trans-border analysis is highly important for this spatial category. Moreover, mountain regions heavily influence, and are heavily influenced by, lowland areas – both nearby and distant – and thus activities within and development processes due to influences from those areas are of even greater relevance to European spatial changes. Also, internal differentiation is highly important as mountain regions not only embrace remote, low-density areas but significant urban agglomerations as well. Rural–urban interlinkages hold a particular potential for addressing innovation strategies that make synergistic use of the complementary features and functions of different types of spaces (within and beyond mountain regions). Due to topographically restricted accessibility in many cases, a fine-tuned differentiation of local characteristics applies and leads to a particularly high level of regional diversity (Dax, 2015a, 2015b).

The challenges associated with mountain regions and the differentiation required due to the diversity of mountain ranges across Europe imply an assessment of socio-demographic changes, economic activities and ecosystem services at a fine geographical level. Several European studies (Nordregio, 2004; EEA, 2010; Gløersen et al., 2016) underpin a differentiated view and reveal the wide scope in the socio-economic performance of mountain areas. They indicate a number of common features, which include in particular the following key points:

- Data provision at the fine geographical scale has improved substantially over recent decades; still, there is an urgent need for spatially disaggregated data collection and synthesis analysis-driven mountain definitions and differentiation.
- In the past, mountains have been characterized as presenting 'barriers' and hostile environments for economic development and innovation. There was an overemphasis on 'hard infrastructure' interventions to improve accessibility. Recently, technological development, at least in theory, enables significant convergence towards a 'space*less*' digital world.
- For centuries, large parts of Europe's mountains have been perceived as areas that needed protection schemes to ensure continued provision of ecosystem services. More recently, with accelerating changes in land management systems, threats to biodiversity and specific exposure to climate change. and

environmental functions in general, have led to an understanding of the high environmental sensitivity of these areas.

- With an enhanced understanding of nature–human interlinkages, socio-economic development acquires the role of a pivotal driver of future development. Integrated approaches to providing greater insight into the interactions between human populations and their environments thus represent the core of spatial strategies.
- Population development, economic activities and regional performance in mountain regions are highly diverse, but, at any rate, cannot be limited to decline and negative trends. The increased valuation of "rural amenities" (OECD, 1999) has led to shifts in economic and population trends, converting regions of decline into areas attracting population in-flows and new economic activities and lifestyles. Nevertheless, a large part of mountain regions, particularly those characterized by peripheral locations and low accessibility, still face problems of out-migration, weak economic performance and even marginalization trends.
- Increasingly, analysis and local practice initiatives suggest that the specific potentials and opportunities of mountain areas have to be considered as much as the traditionally well-known challenges.
- The elaboration of place-based sustainable development strategies, based on Cohesion Policy and other policy areas, with an impact on spatial development could address the inherent challenges and promote their economic and social development by referring to the particular opportunities for local and regional development.
- However, more integrated approaches require not just an enhanced strategy process, but also useful frameworks for inter-sectoral policy coordination and multilevel governance arrangements.

Mirroring the traditional connotation of mountains with topographical obstacles, the persistence of topographical preconditions and features of natural constraints recall the core of development challenges for LFR. While production difficulties for farming and forestry in mountain areas are obvious, specific obstacles arise also for other economic activities and service provision due to remoteness, fragmentation of governance and lack of knowledge exchange. This differentiated view contrasts with the line of argument by analysts of the 'death of distance' (Cairncross, 1997). Those concepts of "progressive convergence towards 'global' cultural models, and, above all, the frictionless availability of information and knowledge determine an ever-decreasing influence of both physical distance and the underlying contextual conditions upon economic interactions" (Rodríguez-Pose & Crescenzi, 2008, p. 384). However, this dynamic in the global economic geography is not leading to similar development levels across space but rather "large cities emerge as real winners, as they provide the right environment to allow economic agents to thrive. So . . . the flat world is full of high peaks" (Rodríguez-Pose & Crescenzi 2008, p. 385).

S3 are put forward for all types of regions, and therefore the applicability to mountain contexts is to be scrutinized. Regarding the peculiar challenges of mountain areas, the mere adoption of S3 seems an over-simplistic approach that would prove to be a victim of the views of liberalization, heavily believing in the 'flattening of the world'. However, location in mountain regions is not a disadvantage per se since some middle-range urban centres are some of the most innovative places in Europe (e.g. Grenoble, Lausanne, Bolzano etc.). Increasingly, the main issue is how the success of these centres in mountain regions can affect the development opportunities and attractiveness of the more rural hinterlands. Good practice with regard to innovative strategies in mountain regions reveals that the unique strengths and assets of mountains lie not in copying 'leading' economic regions, but in positioning their divergence from lowlands and harnessing internal diversity and variance at the fine geographical scale. While this is widely seen as weakness in terms of limiting 'critical mass' in a restricted geographical area, it can be appreciated as an attractive hallmark when compared with trends of 'standardization' of uniform spatial and cultural developments in other areas. Furthermore, with an increased weight for sustainable development and reference to global challenges, a transition towards a new framework of policy objectives emerges that targets prosperity beyond growth (Bina, 2013). This shift is addressed in an increasing number of initiatives and discourses at various levels in all parts of the world. Mountains could provide an important type of 'gateway area' for the tremendous efforts needed in the upcoming social transformation processes.

Achievements and lack of mountain development policies

The discourse on the effects of technological changes and the 'integration' of 'all spaces' into a globalized network has been epitomized by the picture of creating a 'flat world'. However, it seems that, despite these announcements, location factors still matter and peripherality and proximity are crucial aspects of the dynamics of spatial restructuring (Rodríguez-Pose & Crescenzi, 2008). Conventional explanations of peripheral disadvantage referred to spatial disparities in economic activity, with a strong emphasis on issues of (physical) accessibility, the role of agglomerative economies and processes of 'cumulative causation'. Copus (2004) started to address additional aspects of peripherality, analyzing the rising influence of 'aspatial' features for differentiating rural economies. A similar extension of theoretical consideration is valid for the analysis of the need for close interlinkages and the emerging forms of non-physical proximity (Torre & Wallet, 2014). Both these concepts, peripherality and proximity, provide important insights into the relevance of S3 for mountain regions, implying the need for addressing interregional exchange not just towards adjacent areas, but between different scales of distance and actor groups.

This is specifically addressed by recent regional innovation strategies that have gained importance also in mountain regions, particularly since societal demand for core 'mountain' amenities is increasing. The precondition of long-term efforts to initiate change processes and achieve an effective turn in the development process and revert 'spiralling-down' trajectories was a new insight in the discussion of the 1970s/1980s when the 'endogenous development' paradigm was first framed (Stöhr, 1985). This was particularly relevant for peripheral locations and mountain areas in Western Europe. Much of the discourse of the Highlands and Islands Development Board (HIDB) in Scotland during that period relates to reflecting that approach and indicating the temporal aspects and dynamics involved with any regional development aspiration (see Chapter 6 of this book on the early experience of the emerging local development strategy in Scotland). Similar to the driving patterns and socio-economic shifts addressed by institutional development in the case of peripheral areas, as in the socio-political development of Scotland, a significant conversion in social dynamics, institutional and organizational settings and local governance was the prerequisite to realizing innovative approaches in the mountain regions of Austria (Dax, 2001) and many other less-favoured regional contexts of Europe as well.

The development approaches compiled at that period were heavily based on a refocusing of local assets, enhanced endogeneity, the strengths derived from developing regional learning structures and a reliance on natural resource assets. Concepts related above all to the natural environment and the search for sustainable development, resilient lifestyles and healthy environments. Decision makers increasingly highlighted these aspects as core influences of rural policies (e.g. OECD, 1999), which later added to the complexity of understanding regional development processes. Particularly for LFR, and including specifically mountain regions, knowledge network improvements were seen as indispensable, but not a sufficient condition for addressing place-specificity. In seeking to establish a comprehensive research framework appropriate to the needs of those areas, ideas were extended from Triple to Quadruple to Quintuple Helix ideas, which were aimed at integrating the core aspect of natural resource preservation and strong sustainability approaches into the framework for analyzing adapted regional development efforts (Carayannis & Campbell, 2010).

While resource reliance and sustainable development were the prime focus for many actors and for a long period, this approach largely overlooked in its initial phase the dependence on interlinkages and interdependencies. The 'relational turn' in regional development analysis in the 2000s (Bathelt & Glückler, 2011) rectified that over-optimistic focus on local resources and development forces and rearranged the perception of influential drivers. Copus, Shucksmith, Dax and Meredith (2011) revealed that territorial interrelations and aspects of 'aspatial' proximity are of increasing relevance for rural areas, which is often neglected due to incumbent stereotypes of the very restricted scope and evidence-base of narratives of the development options of rural areas.

A third crucial aspect for mountain areas is the institutional basis that is regarded as one of the main building blocks for implementation of effective policies. An important strand of analysis has dealt with the role of institutions in regional development and, inspired by Amin and Thrift (1994), argued that "institutional thickness" provides crucial arguments for the understanding of non-economic factors influencing regional development. With the increased search for capturing the complexity of the driving forces of spatial dynamics, the discussion of the relevance of institutions intensified in recent years (Rodríguez-Pose, 2013) and the original concept was extended: recognizing the shortcomings of the concept, Zukauskaite, Trippl and Plechero (2017) added aspects for the differentiation of contexts and processes to the conceptual discussion of institutional and organizational thickness. They also addressed issues of assessing, supporting and hindering developments, achieving effective processes and taking account of different structures across regions.

The plethora of new concepts should, however, not remain 'buzz words' of minor relevance, but deploy effects on the spot and beyond. Indeed, in mountain regions throughout the world, an increasing number of local initiatives addressing specific parts of this complex environment is being elaborated. Empirical cases reveal proactive strategies in those mountain ranges with a long-term commitment to policy support targeted at a diversified mountain economy.

Examples of the impact of social innovation in marginal areas (Burlando et al. 2017) and of the opportunities afforded by digital technology for mountain regions (DANTE, 2014) are particularly widespread in the Alps, but extend also to initiatives in the mountain areas of Nordic European countries (see Chapter 5 of this book, Teräs et al., 2018) and in the Carpathians and the Pyrenees. The autonomous region of the Aosta Valley represents a specifically interesting case, depicting the potential of S3 in addressing mountain-specific answers to the concept (see Box 4.1).

Box 4.1 Aosta Valley's S3 strategy: placing mountains at the centre of the regional innovation system

The Aosta Valley is an exemplary case of an Alpine region that selected a long-term vision to focus "on the region and its unique asset, the mountains, with the aim of exploiting indigenous resources and tackling geographical challenges" (Rollandin 2016, p. 47). S3 is based on a vision of the mountain is being central, and its evocative brand is attributed to three interconnected pillars, epitomized by the terms "excellent", "smart" and "sustainable mountain" (Regione Autonoma Valle d'Aosta, 2014, pp. 59ff.). The strategy combines a reflection on the long-term development of the regional profile, with the specific assets linked to mountains, and addresses branches like innovative manufacturing, tourism specialization, public digital services and urban–rural networking, as well as "green economy" features and ecosystem development activities.

The objective of the strategy is to overcome the weaknesses of local development by further enhancing the culture of partnership and trans-regional cooperation (between the Italian region and the French regions). It stimulates user-oriented innovation, e.g. through the regional innovation project Alcotra, which identified smart energy and energy efficiency, as well as intelligent automotive mobility, transport and territorial monitoring as priority actions.

The comprehensive selection of impact indicators (Regione Autonoma Valle d'Aosta, 2014, p. 100) expands to all socio-economic aspects and includes, for example (objectives for development 2013–2023, in %):

Economy:

Value added in productive sector of industry: from 11.0 to 14.0

Export rate (with regard to regional GDP): from 13.4 to 20.0

Education:

Graduations from science and technology: from 2.4 to 4.0

Rate of school dropouts: from 19.8 to 17.0

Research – innovation:

Share of R&D investment (compared to regional GDP): from 0.57 to 1.0

Enterprises with innovative products/processes: from 29.3 to 35.0

Digital society:

Enterprises with broadband access: from 90 to 100

Employed persons (in enterprises of more than 10 employed people) utilizing computers connected to the Internet: 31.7 to 60

Source: Regione Autonoma Valle d'Aosta, 2014

The S3 approach is implemented throughout the European regions in very diverse ways (Polverari, 2017) and in addressing the specificities of the mountain context, in general, to a limited extent. In particular, a number of Italian regions refer to mountain contexts as an asset in their development strategies. Besides the case of the Val d'Aosta (highlighted in Box 4.1), the presentation of the concept of "Smart Valley" in Lombardia's Valtellina region is an inspiring case of seeking "intelligent diffusion systems". It includes priorities for mobility, construction and landscape, sustainable tourism, renewable energy, regeneration, education and digitalization, and poverty-reduction activities (Punto.Ponte, 2017). Significant other project examples, highlighting specific aspects of the concept or providing regional practice examples, are scrutinized very often through trans-regional projects (supported, for example, by the Alpine Space programme and others). All over European mountain areas, examples that make use of opportunities can be summarized in the following manner:

- the increasing demand for healthy environments (e.g. Conci et al., 2015) and quality development (e.g. Regulation (EU) No. 1151/2012 of the European Parliament and of the Council on quality schemes for agricultural products and foodstuffs, establishing in Art. 31 the basis for a European label for "mountain products")
- intensified discussion on resource use, addressing the potential of the bio-economy and the eco-economy (e.g. Bösze and Meyer, 2014), but also the integration of regional value chains into global chains, as well as aspirations to enhance wood processing, local energy provision and pathways towards a 'circular economy')
- spatial changes in settlement patterns and mobility, particularly affecting the sensible environment of mountain areas, and
- changes in tourism demand, seeking to strengthen approaches to sustainable and nature-based tourism that respects the environmental sensitivity of mountain regions (Gløersen et al., 2016).

A review of innovative mountain initiatives and approaches to fostering multi-sector development underscores the increasing visibility of the opportunities in these spatial contexts, but also emphasizes the need for a comprehensive understanding, the conceptualization of strategies and a coherent policy framework (Euromontana, 2013). The priorities for future mountain development have to reflect the place-based assets and particular potentials for mountain action: this implies initiatives to centre on issues of (mountain) specificity, focus on strategies to raise product labelling of regional origin and high quality, and enhance regional value chains, reinforce natural resource focus and public goods provision, for example, by including landscape development and awareness and knowledge of actors, as well as the use of technological developments and digital opportunities to overcome peripheralization. Within all these aspects, the potential for innovation within mountain areas is to be nurtured, with important innovation fields in mountain businesses realized for "life sciences, bio-economy (including agriculture and forestry), energy, materials, e-services, tourism, health ageing and specific technological innovation in natural resource development" (see Euromontana, 2013, p. 15).

Many of these development activities have been inspired by the long-term engagement of area-based partnerships and various financial instruments promoting economic development. Support remains, however, scattered, and hardly applies a comprehensive local and/or national strategy, enhancing the positive contributions of mountain areas in the national (European) context. In this regard, EU Cohesion Policy could play a more active role in place-based mountain development (Copus and De Lima, 2015). Moreover, as there is a significant gap in realizing mountain support activities, the transferability of approaches to good practice is a specific challenge for mountain action.

Potential for smart strategies to overcome 'lock-in' situations

In reviewing actions for mountain development, it becomes obvious that, in the context of LFR, globalization and sustainable development issues are of particular influence. Within large-scale spatial dynamics, mountains face significant obstacles due to low accessibility of agglomerations and economic centres, lack of 'critical mass' and gaps in competitiveness. Although the various components of 'proximity' are a potential improvement for mountain areas, and increase the suitability of innovative approaches in these areas, mountain regions have to find instruments to increase their connectivity and relationships to other places (Boschma, 2005). Policies addressing these challenges are primarily sector-specific and, in few cases, conceived with the aim of coping with mountain challenges (ADE, 2012; Gløersen et al. 2016). A comprehensive assessment of the various policy contributions is hardly available and, in general, of limited impact due to fragmentation of actors, divergent perspectives about effective pathways by stakeholders and "leakages" of implementation following action at different scales (Dax, 2014b). While there is no doubt that technological innovation remains important, the examples of many mountain regions' strategies reveal the core relevance of amenities linked to local natural resources, the "symbolic" dimension of production and the high impact of aesthetic quality (Schirpke et al., 2016), as well as integration into current communication styles (Peyrache-Gadeau et al., 2017). The effectiveness of these activities is based on the empowerment of local people targeted at social change that is responding to key local needs (Dro and Therace, 2011). As pilot programmes in the past repeatedly underpinned the complex issues of project initialization and showed that meaningful social transformation is the result of long-term and intensive cooperative efforts by actors at diverse (geographical) scales, participation issues will not achieve immediate results. This important prerequisite for S3 processes is at the heart of major concerns for evaluating "new" programmes, i.e. the difficulty of discerning "early positive signals" (Kyriakou, 2017), which is, however, indispensable to providing impetus and momentum for effective uptake of innovative ideas and policy approaches.

The main aspects with regard to the role of S3 for mountain development include therefore: (i) a core position for governance issues (beyond simple multi-governance frameworks) and institutional development that pays attention to the interface of human–nature relationships in mountain environments; (ii) a specific focus on the need for innovative action, particularly based on 'progress' in socially innovative activities, and by an enhanced understanding of the complex environment (supported by qualitative assessment methods); (iii) a spatially integrated view of the challenges and opportunities of small-scale mountain areas, related to their interlinkages to other spaces and internal and external networks; and (iv) an enhanced understanding of mountains as places disposing of significant assets (amenity development), and not only/primarily deficits and failures in economic terms.

Conclusions

Such a change in perspective on the potentials and options available for mountains (Dax, 2014a) might be advanced significantly by framing 'smart specialization' processes in an innovative strategy for regional development of mountain areas. These would address, specifically, social innovation as a crucial precondition for successful place-based transformations (Rosa Pires et al., 2014) and highlight specific supporting features for implementation in LFR. Crucial aspects in this regard have to highlight the geographical specificity and dynamics of institutional and organizational change, which are not cast in stone. Given the short period of implementation of the S3 approaches, no widespread success stories are to be expected in such a short timeframe. On the contrary, it would be opposite to the key assumptions and features of the approach to imply swift and standardized answers (Kroll, 2015, p. 2095). It seems much more appropriate to choose a distinct stance as opposed to approaches of central agglomerations and regions with favourable disposition for broadening the (economic) scope of activities. Distinctiveness in this regard means, in particular, that the decisions about objectives and strategies are not simply transferred or templates 'copied' from more accessible, highly competitive central regions, but that mountain regions deliberately have to choose alternative pathways. This reflects also the insight of high variance in regional development performance and the search for a transformative process of S3 (Wostner, 2017). As shown above, smart specialization cannot just focus on a 'more effective' application and realization of new technologies and digitalization in all areas, but needs to differentiate (Dubois et al., 2017) the specific outlines, goals and societal relevance due to the characteristics of the diverse regions. As Asheim (2013) points out, due to strong path-dependency, the S3 approach can be interpreted as "old wine in new bottles". An increased conceptual clarity on social development (including transformation), future societal challenges and objectives (transcending the incumbent 'growth' paradigm), place-specific opportunities (mountain specificity) and potential contributions to 'sustainable' pathways seem therefore to be core features, which have to receive higher priority in S3 considerations.

As shown for sparsely populated areas, such regions have to be conceived as not only lagging behind other areas but disposing also of opportunities to create innovative environments. Future strategies adopting this approach would have to build on networking capability with external-regional knowledge and make use of abundant natural resources (Teräs et al., 2015). While the need for stronger coherence of diverse policies has long been expressed in many policy reviews, the novelty of smart specialization and innovation strategy is a more realistic trajectory of institutional and social change, which, however, needs a much longer timeframe to become effective. No short-term improvements can be expected, but impact on the foundations for local development action has to be sought in the long term. The altered perspective of the approach is primarily oriented not at a 'technical' adaptation but requires a "new paradigm of rural innovation" (Jean, 2014), fostering local participation and enabling learning environments that involve rural people to address mountain specificity. In this regard, the approach has the potential to enable fields of 'experimentation' that have been eliminated over past decades but need to be explored again. S3 also envisages overcoming the bias towards urban areas of previous policies and addressing the specific social dimensions and the need for interrelations and cultural change in mountain regions.

Note

1 LEADER is an acronym for the French term 'Liaison entre actions de développement de l'économie rurale' (liaison between actions for the development of the rural economy).

References

Amin, A. & Thrift, N. (1994). Living in the global. In: A. Amin and N. Thrift (Eds.) *Globalization, institutions, and regional development in Europe* (pp.1–19). Oxford: Oxford University Press.

Analysis for Economic Decisions – ADE (2012). Study on the relevance and the effectiveness of ERDF and Cohesion Fund support to Regions with Specific Geographical Features – Islands, Mountainous and Sparsely Populated areas. Report for the European Commission, Louvain-la-Neuve. Retrieved October 2018 from http://ec.europa.eu/regional_policy/sources/docgener/evaluation/pdf/eval2007/geographical_final1.pdf.

Asheim, B. (2013). Smart specialization: old wine in new bottles or new wine in old bottles? Presentation at the ERSA Conference, 28 August, Palermo.

Bathelt, H. & Glückler, J. (2011). *The relational economy: geographies of knowledge and learning*. Oxford: Oxford University Press.

Belmont Forum (2015). Collaborative Research Action on "Mountains as sentinels of Change", Call for Proposals, Implementation Plan 2015.

Bina, O. (2013). The green economy and sustainable development: an uneasy balance? *Environment and Planning C: Government and Policy*, *31*(6), 1023–1047. doi:10.1068/c1310j

Boschma, R.A. (2005). Proximity and innovation: a critical assessment. *Regional Studies*, *39*(1), 61–74.

Bösze, S. & Meyer, H. (Eds.) (2014). Regional Development Opportunities of Protected Areas and Natural Assets in the Carpathians. Work Package 4. Integrated Management of Biological and Landscape Diversity for Sustainable Regional Development and Ecological Connectivity in the Carpathians. WWF Danube-Carpathian Programme, Vienna, Austria.

Burlando, C., Secco, L., Pisani, E. & Da Re, R. (2017). What Methods to Evaluate Social Innovation in Mountain Areas? EU-Project H2020 "Social Innovation in Marginalised Rural Areas" (SIMRA), paper presented at the conference "Mountain regions, territories of innovation" LabEx ITEM, Cité des Territoires, University of Grenoble-Alpes, Grenoble, 11–13 January.

Cairncross, F. (1997). *The death of distance: how the communications revolution is changing our lives.* Cambridge, MA: Harvard Business School Press.

Carayannis, E.G. & Campbell, D.F.J. (2010). Triple helix, quadruple helix and quintuple helix and how do knowledge, innovation and the environment relate to each other? A proposed framework for a trans-disciplinary analysis of sustainable development and social ecology, *International Journal of Social Ecology and Sustainable Development, 1*(1), 41–69. DOI: 10.4018/jsesd.2010010105

Conci, M., Mion, L., Morganti, E. & Nollo, G. (2015). Smart Trentino: an inclusive territory for the wellbeing of all, *Urbani izziv*, thematic issue, No. *1*, 25–31.

Cooper, T., Baldock, D., Rayment, M., Kuhmonen, T., Terluin, I., Swales, V., Poux, X., Zakeossian, D. & Farmer, M. (2006). *An evaluation of the valuation of the less favoured area measure in the 25 Member States of the European Union.* London: The Institute for European Environmental Policy.

Copus, A., Shucksmith, M., Dax, T. & Meredith, D. (2011). Cohesion policy for rural areas after 2013: a rationale derived from the EDORA project (European Development Opportunities in Rural Areas) ESPON 2013 Project 2013/1/2. *Studies in Agricultural Economics, 113*(2), 121–132. http://dx.doi.org/10.7896/j.1113

Copus, A.K. (2004). Aspatial Peripherality, Innovation and the Rural economy (AsPIRE), Final Report. FP5-project No. QLK5-2000-00783. SAC, Aberdeen.

Copus, A.K. & De Lima, P. (Eds.) (2015). *Territorial cohesion in rural Europe. The relational turn in rural development.* Regions and Cities 76. London: Routledge.

DANTE (2014). Final meeting report. EU-project "Digital agenda for new tourism approach in European rural and mountain areas", Brussels.

Dax, T. (2001). Endogenous development in Austria's mountain regions: from a source of irritation to a mainstream movement, *Mountain Research and Development, 21*(3), 231–235. Retrieved October 2018 from http://www.bioone.org/doi/abs/10.1659/0276-4741%282001%29021%5B0231%3AEDIAMR%5D2.0.CO%3B2.

Dax, T. (2014a). A new rationale for rural cohesion policy: overcoming spatial stereotypes by addressing inter-relations and opportunities, Chapter 3. In: OECD (Ed.) *Innovation and modernising the rural economy* (pp. 79–93). Paris: OECD Publishing.

Dax, T. (2014b). Drawing on mountain policy experiences in the Alps: how to shape common strategies? Workshop 3-1. In: Giorgi, A., Borsdorf, A., Köck, G. & Scheurer, T. (Eds.) *Forum alpinum '14, Alpine resources; use, valorization and management from local to macro-regional scale (pp. 81–84),* Conference Proceedings, 17–19 September, Darfo Boario Terme.

Dax, T. (2015a). Beteiligungsprozesse im ländlichen Raum gestalten. In: *BBE Europa-Nachrichten, Newsletter für Engagement und Partizipation in Europa* 5/2015, Berlin. Retrieved October 2018 from http://www.b-b-e.de/fileadmin/inhalte/aktuelles/2015/05/enl05_gastbeitrag_dax.pdf.

Dax, T. (2015b). Why are local initiatives so important in mountain regions? *Mountain Views, Chronicles of the Consortium for Integrated Climate Research in Western Mountains,*

CIRMOUNT, *9*(2), 44–46. Retrieved October 2018 from http://www.fs.fed.us/psw/cirmount/publications/pdf/Mtn_Views_dec_15.pdf.

Dax, T. (2017). *Mountain development in Europe: research priorities and trends*, Doctoral Thesis. University of Natural Resources and Life Sciences Vienna, Department of Economics and Social Sciences, Vienna.

Dax, T. & Fischer, M. (2017). An alternative policy approach to rural development in regions facing population decline, *European Planning Studies*, *26*(2), 297–315. DOI: 10.1080/0965313.2017.1361596

Debarbieux, B. & Price, M.F. (2008). Representing mountains: from local and national to global common good, *Geopolitics*, *13*(1), 148–168.

Debarbieux, B., Price, M.F. & Balsiger, J. (2015). The institutionalization of mountain regions in Europe, *Regional Studies*, *49*(7), 1193–1207.

Dro, I. & Therace, A. (Eds.) (2011). *Empowering people, driving change. Social innovation in the European Union*. Luxembourg: Publications Office of the European Union.

Dubois, A., Kristensen, I. & Teräs, J. (2017). Outsmarting geography: implementing territorial innovation strategies in sparsely populated regions. *European Planning Studies*, *25*(8), 1316–1333. DOI:10.1080/09654313.2017.1320355

EC (2009). Peak performance: new insights into mountain farming in the European Union, SEC(2009) 1724 final, Commission staff working document. Brussels: European Commission.

EEA (2010). *Europe's ecological backbone: recognizing the true value of our mountains*. EEA Report No. 6/2010. Copenhagen: European Environment Agency.

Euromontana (2013). Toward Mountains 2020: capitalising on Euromontana work to inspire programming.Brussels.

Gløersen, E., Price, M.F., Borec, A., Dax, T. & Giordano, B. (2016). *Research for REGI Committee: cohesion in mountainous regions of the EU*. European Parliament, DG for Internal Policies, Policies Department B: Structural and Cohesion Policies, Regional Development, IP/B/REGI/IC/2015_175. Brussels: European Parliament. Retrieved October 2018 from http://www.europarl.europa.eu/RegData/etudes/STUD/2016/573420/IPOL_STU%282016%29573420_EN.pdf.

Jean, B. (2014). A new paradigm of rural innovation: learning from and within rural people and communities. In: OECD (Ed.), *Innovation and modernising the rural economy* (pp. 113–126). Paris: OECD Publishing.

Kroll, H. (2015). Efforts to implement smart specialization in practice: leading unlike horses to the water. *European Planning Studies*, *23*(10), 2079–2098. http://dx.doi.org/10.1080/09654313.201.1003036

Kroll, H. (2017). The Challenge of Smart Specialisation in Less Favoured Regions. Working Paper Firms and Regions No. R1/2017, Fraunhofer Institute, Karlsruhe.

Kyriakou, D. (2017). Smart specialisation concepts and significance of early positive signals. *European Structural and Investment Funds Journal (EStIF)*, *5*(1), 4–11.

Neumeier, S. (2012). Why do social innovations in rural development matter and should they be considered more seriously in rural development research? – Proposal for a stronger focus on social innovations in rural development research. In: *Sociologia Ruralis*, *52*(1), 48–69. DOI: 10.1111/j.1467-9523.2011.00553.x

Nordregio (2004). *Mountain areas in Europe: analysis of mountain areas in EU member states, acceding and other European countries*. Study prepared for the EU Commission DG Regio, Nordregio Report 2004:*1*, Stockholm.

OECD (1999). *Cultivating rural amenities: an economic development perspective*. Paris: OECD Publishing.

Peyrache-Gadeau, V., Rutter, S. & Bélicard, J. (2017). Innovation in sustainable tourism projects in Alpine resorts. In: Kebir, L., Crevoisier, O., Costa, P. &

Peyrache-Gadeau, V. (Eds.) *Sustainable innovation and regional development, rethinking innovative milieus* (pp. 170–188), Cheltenham, UK: Edward Elgar Publishing.

Phills, J.A., Deiglmeier, K. & Miller, D.T. (2008). Rediscovering social innovation. *Stanford Social Innovation Review, 6*(4), 34–43.

Polverari, L. (2017). Smart specialisation in 2014–2020 ESI Funds Programmes: not just a narrative, *European Structural and Investment Funds Journal (EStIF), 5*(1), 20–31.

Price, M.F. (2010). *Europe's ecological backbone: recognizing the true value of our mountains*. Copenhagen: European Environment Agency (EEA) Report No. 6/2010.

Punto.Ponte (2017). E' tempo di parlare di SMART VALLEY [It is time to speak of SMART VALLEY]. Online blog. Sondrio. Retrieved October 2018 from https://puntoponte.wordpress.com/2014/12/07/e-tempo-di-parlare-di-smart-valley-in-valtellina/.

Regione Autonoma Valle d'Aosta (2014). Smart Specialisation Strategy in Valle d'Aosta.

Rodríguez-Pose, A. (2013). Do institutions matter for regional development? *Regional Studies, 47*(7), 1034–1047. doi:10.1080/00343404.2012.748978.

Rodríguez-Pose, A. & Crescenzi, R. (2008). Mountains in a flat world: why proximity still matters for the location of economic activity. *Cambridge Journal of Regions, Economy and Society, 1*(3), 371–388. doi: 10.1093/cjres/rsn011

Rollandin, A. (2016). Aosta Valley: A pioneer in pre-commercial public procurement and open innovation. In: Committee of the Regions (Ed.), Regional Innovation Ecosystems, Learning from the EU's Cities and Regions, CoR guide (pp. 47–52). Brussels: European Union. Retrieved October 2018 from https://www.google.com/url?sa=t&rct=j&q=&esrc=s&source=web&cd=1&cad=rja&uact=8&ved=2ahUKEwjQo6GN0o_eAhUGiCwKHW_QAW8QFjAAegQICRAC&url=http%3A%2F%2Fs3platform.jrc.ec.europa.eu%2Fdocuments%2F20182%2F84453%2FRegional%2BInnovation%2BEcosystems%2F48ab5553-489b-4c41-89b4-5c897e3ef066&usg=AOvVaw1egMN3w119fohgegpE5FM0.

Rosa Pires, A., Pertoldi, M., Edwards, J. & Hegyi, F.B. (2014). *Smart specialisation and innovation in rural areas*, S3 Policy Brief Series n° 09/2014. Seville, Spain: European Commission, JRC-IPTS.

Schirpke, U., Timmermann, F., Tappeiner, U. & Tasser, E. (2016). Cultural ecosystem services of mountain regions: modelling the aesthetic value. *Ecological Indicators, 69*, 78–90.

Stöhr, W.B. (1985). Towards a conceptual framework for research on 'selective self-reliance in Europe'. In: Musto, S. (Ed.), *Endogenous development: a myth or a path: problems of economic self-reliance in the European periphery*. Berlin: German Development Institute, EADI-Book Series 5.

Teräs, J., Dubois, A., Sörvik J. & Pertoldi, M. (2015). *Implementing smart specialisation in sparsely populated areas*. S3 Working Paper 10/2015. Brussels: European Commission. Joint Research Centre.

Torre, A. & Wallet, F. (Eds.) (2014). Regional development and proximity relations. In: *New horizons in regional science*. Cheltenham, UK: Edward Elgar.

Wostner, P. (2017). From projects to transformations: why do only some countries and regions advance? The case of the Slovenian S4. *European Structural and Investment Funds Journal (EStIF), 5*(1), 84–96.

Zukauskaite, E., Trippl, M. & Plechero, M. (2017). Institutional thickness revisited. *Economic Geography, 93*(4), 325–345. http://dx.doi.org/10.1080/00130095.2017.1331703

Part II

Smart specialisation in practice

Territorial challenges and opportunities

5 Smart specialisation at the edge of Europe

Case study of sparsely populated regions in the Arctic

Jukka Teräs, Kristiina Jokelainen, Thomas Ejdemo and Daniel Örtqvist

Introduction

Regional development initiatives based on smart specialisation – the concept that forms the basis of the new approach to regional innovation policy in the European Union (EU) – are emerging in many sparsely populated areas, which underlines the need to dig deeper into the analysis of sparsely populated regions and their specific characteristics regarding smart specialisation. In this context, sustainable utilisation of natural resources very often plays an important role.

Traditionally, the economic literature has argued that regional economic success requires physical proximity of actors, close access to larger markets/customers, and availability to utilise different kinds of knowledge and support resources. Previous research, such as Michael Porter's studies on clusters or Richard Florida's studies on the creative class, have underpinned an understanding that metropolitan areas (and metropolitan areas only) possess the conditions required for developing into hubs for a dynamic development and highly specialised activities. The concept of geographical proximity is defined by the absolute and relative spatial or physical distances between economic actors (Boschma, 2005). In previous research, it has been claimed that spatial concentration could lead to enhanced knowledge development. Close distances make information contacts and exchange of tacit knowledge easier, and the opposite – larger distances – makes such transfer more difficult (Howells, 2002).

Does it mean then that peripheral regions are doomed to serving as providers of specific raw materials and as recreation areas for the creative classes of larger cities? Several peripheral regions today reveal a positive and dynamic development based on the smart specialisation concept, thereby challenging this kind of understanding. This, in turn, calls for additional research initiatives that address the possibilities for non-metropolitan areas to also employ a smart specialisation (S3) strategy.

This chapter analyses industrial specialisation and sustainable utilisation of natural resources in peripheral regions. The key research question of the chapter is to study the applicability of the smart specialisation concept in peripheral regions with abundant natural resources. Our aim is to develop a better understanding of the possibilities and limitations of also using the S3 concept in more peripheral regions.

The chapter is structured into three main parts. First, we provide a literature review with an introduction to the key theoretical concepts relevant to the analysis of smart specialisation in sparsely populated, peripheral regions. The empirical part presents the regional specialisation approaches in two neighbouring regions in the northernmost part of the EU: Norrbotten in northern Sweden and Lapland in northern Finland. The final discussion includes an analysis of the implications for theory and practice.

Methodology

The study presented in this chapter is based on a qualitative research methodology, which partly utilises an action research approach. The authors have each worked on programmes and projects related to smart specialisation and have studied smart specialisation and related issues in Lapland and Norrbotten. The relevant literature on S3 has been reviewed, with a focus on the implementation processes. The empirical research data consist of relevant reports and field study visits by the authors in the case study regions. The authors selected Lapland in northern Finland and Norrbotten in northern Sweden as case study regions for several reasons. First, the regions have similarities in terms of population size, geography, and natural resources. Second, the innovation performance of the case study regions, as indicated by the Regional Innovation Scoreboard by the European Commission (Regional Innovation Scoreboard, 2017), has been relatively similar. Third, and equally important, the authors have excellent access to information on regional specialisation and smart specialisation processes in the case study regions of Lapland and Norrbotten.

Smart specialisation and sparsely populated areas

The EU's ten-year jobs and growth strategy, Europe 2020, was launched in 2010 to create the conditions for smart, sustainable and inclusive growth (EC, 2010). Regional policy plays an important role in the strategy. The current approach to regional innovation policy is based on a new "understanding of the role played by innovation in economic development and in particular its relationship with geography" (McCann & Ortega-Argilés, 2013, p. 187). Smart specialisation forms the basis of the new approach to regional innovation policy in the EU. The concept was first developed to address the gap between Europe and other global competitors in R&D investment (Foray & van Ark, 2007). Despite its sectoral origins, the concept was able to accommodate the place-based approach (Barca, 2009). The smart specialisation concept has been rapidly diffusing across Europe in recent years as an increasing number of regions have adapted it and designed their smart specialisation strategies departing from their own preconditions.

Smart specialisation is an ambitious regional innovation programme that was launched in the EU for the EU programme period 2014–2020. The smart specialisation programme could be considered as the most ambitious regional innovation programme introduced in the EU (Morgan, 2016). In order to receive Structural Funds, EU Member States and their regions must have an S3 strategy (ex-ante condition; see Foray et al., 2012). A key concept of smart specialisation involves an entrepreneurial discovery process for a country or region, to discover areas of focus, or domains, for securing competitiveness in the future.

The overall structure of the S3 process is presented in the European Commission's RIS3 guide (Foray et al, 2012). The six key steps for developing a regional smart specialisation strategy are: (i) analysis of the regional context and the potential for innovation, (ii) governance by ensuring participation and ownership, (iii) elaborating an overall vision for the future of the region, (iv) identification of priorities, (v) preparation of policy mix, roadmap, and action plan, and (vi) integration of monitoring and evaluation mechanisms.

Despite the rapidly increasing literature on smart specialisation, the number of studies with a focus on smart specialisation in rural and/or sparsely populated areas remains limited. The academic literature on smart specialisation contains, however, relevant inputs related to the study of smart specialisation in sparsely populated regions. Asheim, Grillitsch, and Trippl (2017, p. 75) emphasise the importance of smart specialisation being fully and correctly understood. They state that smart specialisation is not about "specialisation" but about "diversified specialisation": countries and regions should diversify their economies primarily based on existing strengths and capabilities by moving into related or unrelated sectors. Moreover, they emphasise the importance of a broad understanding of the entrepreneurial discovery process to encompass all actors that have the capacity to discover domains, not only the traditional entrepreneurs. Ylinenpää, Teräs, and Örtqvist (2016) emphasise that a region's opportunity to diversify into new industries and new knowledge bases is affected by related variety where knowledge spillovers are to occur primarily among related sectors (e.g. Frenken et al., 2007; see also Asheim et al., 2011). The presence of relatedness in a technological or market sense in the industrial structure of a region is said to be especially supportive of innovation and regional development (e.g. Content & Frenken, 2016). Ylinenpää, Teräs, and Örtqvist (2016) state that developing a regional specialisation based on only one specific focus comes with a cost of being exposed to volatile markets, and the volatility may corner a region into a structural lock-in situation.

McCann and Ortega-Argilés (2016) note that mobilisation of different stakeholders to build complementarities between them is a complex task. Smart specialisation, however, has the potential to do this – in fact, it can be made into a very practical and workable concept, narrative even, that can engage directly with a range of different actors (see also Rodrik, 2014).

Sparsely populated areas correspond to areas that can be characterised by specific spatial and demographic features, including low population located in scattered small settlement structures, continuous land masses of open landscapes, long distances to main urban centres, and often harsh climatic conditions, often accompanied by an abundance of natural resources (Gløersen et al., 2006). In Europe, sparsely populated areas can be found in the northern and eastern parts of the Nordic countries, in the Highlands and Islands region of northern Scotland, and in the central parts of Spain (Dubois & Roto, 2012). These kinds of regions have received only a very limited interest in the research literature on dynamic regional development, where the interest instead has been on urban economics and the conditions prevailing in large metropolitan areas (see, for example, Florida, 2003). Teräs, Dubois, Sörvik, and Pertoldi (2015) studied sparsely populated European regions from the viewpoint of the implementation of smart specialisation. Their analysis of the key issues focuses on the entrepreneurial discovery process, related variety, domains, mobilisation of extra-regional resources, and a broader view of innovation (see Teräs et al., 2015, p. 9). They conclude that sparsely populated regions should not be seen as regions lagging behind by definition. The sparsely populated areas have in many cases significant industrial bases, which have been quite profitable and have also attracted migration. The challenges to the regional development of sparsely populated areas include a tendency to have too few different economic activities and being overly connected to natural resources, which has made these regions vulnerable to increased global competition and shifts in demand.

Da Rosa Pires, Pertoldi, Edwards, and Hegyi (2014) note that rural areas face the risk of neglecting their innovation potential, either because there is often an urban/industrial bias towards innovation policy or because of the historical origins of the smart specialisation approach. At the same time, analyses of the concepts associated with smart specialisation reveal that the smart specialisation approach does contain several promising elements to stimulate and support innovative activities in rural areas (Da Rosa Pires et al., 2014, p. 13). Moreover, da Rosa Pires et al. (2014 p. 9–10) provide examples of successful initiatives in rural and peripheral areas that make use of natural resources in an integrated way.

An important contribution to the studies of sparsely populated regions, with relevance to smart specialisation issues, was made by the OECD (2017), which undertook a review of so-called Northern Sparsely Populated Areas (NSPA) in Finland, Norway, and Sweden. These areas are said to resemble rural regions in Canada, Australia, and Chile more closely than other EU regions. Common traits of these regions include abundant natural resources, long distances, and high costs of land transport. The OECD notes that despite their remoteness and harsh climatic conditions, the NSPA areas enjoy relatively enhanced well-being, access to housing, clean environments, and accessibility to services. At the same time, the NSPA tend to face challenges in terms of employment and income levels below their respective national averages. In addition, an important characteristic is that the natural environment plays an important role in the NSPA. The OECD (2017) emphasises the importance of *absolute advantages* as growth opportunities for NSPA.

These tend to be connected to immobile assets such as resource endowments, and typical examples include minerals and energy, forestry, renewables, and tourism. According to the OECD, policies should aim to add value based on these assets by "supporting factors that enable productivity growth such as skills, innovation, infrastructure and the business environment". In this view, smart specialisation emerges as an appropriate policy approach to regional development in NSPA, according to the OECD.

Our empirical test bed

The empirical part of this study focuses on two Arctic regions in the northernmost part of the EU, Lapland in North Finland and Norrbotten in North Sweden (see Figure 5.1).

Table 5.1 provides an introduction to the case study regions, their industrial structures, and smart specialisation approaches.

Norrbotten (Sweden): industrial structure and S3 approach

The Norrbotten region on the Swedish side of the border is a neighbouring region to Finnish Lapland with slightly more than 250 000 inhabitants living in an area corresponding to 25% of the land area of Sweden, or 100 000 km^2. With approximately 170 000 inhabitants residing on the coastline close to the regional capital Luleå, this implies that large parts of the region are extremely sparsely populated. Some of the inland municipalities have a population density as low as 0.2 inhabitants per square kilometre.

The inland part of this region is, however, the base for the region's mining industry, its forestry, and its production of hydro power, while most industries in downstream processing, such as steel, paper and pulp, wood factories, and service industries are located on the coastline. Out of the population in Norrbotten, 3.7% earn their living from agriculture, 13.8% from industry, and 82.5% from different kinds of jobs in the service sector. The largest public employers are Region Norrbotten (public health care provider with 7 425 employees) and regional municipalities such as Luleå (6 795 employees), Piteå (4 475 employees), and Boden (3 075 employees). The largest private-sector employers are the mining company LKAB (3 825 employees), the steel mill SSAB (1 225 employees), and Samhall AB, active in different industrial branches (1 075 employees). Luleå University of Technology with its 15 000 students employs 1 800 persons as researchers, teachers, and administrative staff.

The regional authority responsible for strategic regional development in Norrbotten has shifted from the Norrbotten county administrative board to the Norrbotten county council as of 2017. This shift means a transfer of responsibility (and control over funding) from an authority that represents the national government in the region to an organisation governed by a publicly elected council. Still, the expert groups assigned to revise the strategic documents, such as the region's innovation strategy (RIS), has been

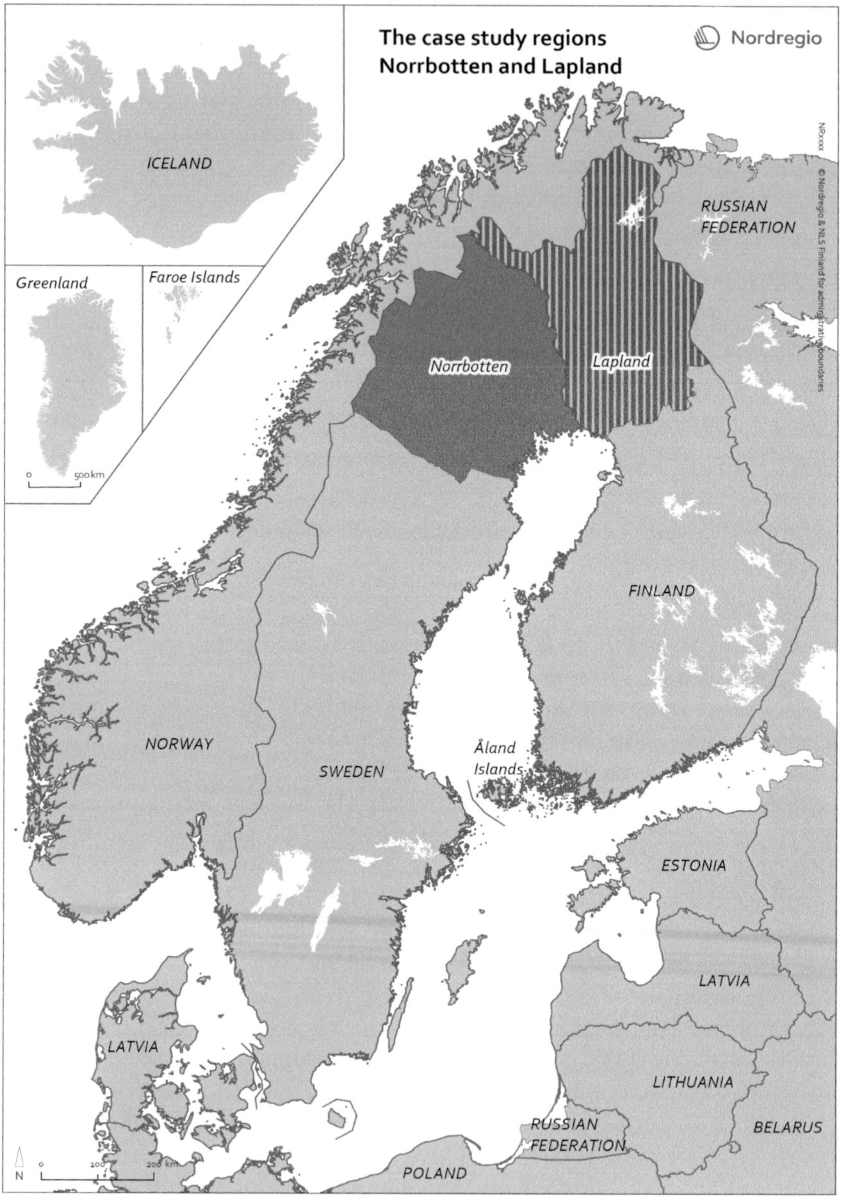

Figure 5.1 Case study regions: Lapland and Norrbotten
Source: Nordregio/Eeva Turunen

Factor	*Norrbotten*	*Lapland*
Population in 2017 (Regionfakta, 2018; Statistics Finland, 2018)	251 295	179 223
Key industrial structure	Process industry: pulp and paper, mining, steel production, energy supply, tourism	Mining and metallurgic sector Bioeconomy, pulp and paper, tourism
S3 governance	The County Council of Norrbotten is the governing body, with responsibility for regional development since 2017 • The Regional Innovation Strategy (2013–2020) identified six "focus areas" characterised as areas for smart specialisation • The revised Regional Innovation Strategy for Norrbotten 2030, to be published in 2018, emphasises smart specialisation with related variety as the central element	Regional Council of Lapland as the major governing body throughout 2012–2018 • S3 strategy process 2012–2013, followed by Arctic Smartness Development Programme and Arctic Smartness Concept to launch regional smart clusters • In 2018, update to the Lapland strategy for international collaboration and further specification of the smart specialisation strategy
S3 documentation	S3 priorities and objectives embedded in Regional Innovation Strategy (which is not an outright smart specialisation strategy document) The draft document of the revised Regional Innovation Strategy 2030 emphasises smart specialisation, with related variety as the central element of the strategy	Smart specialisation strategy document for Lapland published in 2013 Several publications on Arctic Smartness & Smart Clusters in 2015–2017
S3 priorities	(1) Technology and service development within primary, manufacturing, and process industries; (2) test-related activities (vehicles and components, aviation, space etc.) utilising sparsely populated areas and cold climate; (3) energy and cleantech; (4) digital services; (5) cultural and creative industries; (6) intersections of the above industries	(1) Sustainable refining of Arctic natural resources; (2) sustainable utilisation of Arctic natural conditions; and (3) pursuing cross-sectoral development With the support of regional cross-sectoral cluster initiative: enabling growth in the Arctic in industries such as process industries and circular economy, rural communities, tourism safety, design facilitation, and capitalisation of development environments

Source: Authors' own analysis

left mainly intact while the responsibility has shifted. Such groups consist of representatives from public-sector, academia, and regional businesses.

In the RIS document (RIS Norrbotten, 2018), it is stated that

> the region focuses on a number of focus areas, which is termed smart specialisation. These focus areas are growth areas that are unique to the region and give room for long-sightedness. Important parties, like for instance universities and research institutes, are stimulated to go for fewer research areas, which improves the possibilities of creating unique competencies. It will also make it easier to create adaptation and collaboration with concerned parts of businesses/companies and to focus the resources to the development of the focus areas. At the same time, the world is changeable, and the support systems must therefore be flexible to encourage the innovations of tomorrow.
>
> (Länsstyrelsen Norrbotten, 2013)

In Norrbotten, the smart specialisation strategy has been closely integrated into the RIS and its regional development strategy (RUS); both are regional planning documents with a 2020 horizon. These strategic documents point out six prioritised areas for further development: (1) development of technology and services for industry, (2) testing of vehicles and equipment, (3) energy and cleantech, (4) digital service sectors, (5) cultural and creative sectors, and (6) intersections between the areas mentioned above.

In 2018, an updated version of Norrbotten's Regional Innovation Strategy will be released. The draft version of the strategy document was published in May 2018, and it highlights smart specialisation with a specific section titled "Norrbotten shall invest in smart specialisation". According to the document, Norrbotten needs to better utilise its world-leading competences and prerequisites, and this will be implemented via "smart specialisation with related varieties". The section on smart specialisation highlights the recent Facebook investment in data centres in Norrbotten as examples of good practice and draws attention to related variety as a key element of Norrbotten's approach to smart specialisation (Region Norrbotten, 2018, p. 39).

Lapland (Finland): industrial structure and S3 approach

The Lapland region, the northernmost part of Finland and the EU, is the most sparsely populated region in the EU. With an area of 100 366 km^2 and a population of slightly less than 180 000, the population density in Lapland is approximately 1.8 people/km^2. Lapland covers 25.7% of the land area of Finland but holds only 3.4% of its population. Lapland's workforce is employed in the municipal sector (30%), in state and state-owned companies (10%), and in the private sector (49%). The region of Lapland currently has one of the fastest growing economies in Finland, due mainly to the refining of natural resources and a fast-growing tourism sector. The predominant natural resources to be found in Lapland include mineral resources such as chromium, gold, platinum group minerals, iron, and phosphorus. Moreover, forestry plays an important role, with forestry production occupying about 50% of the land area.

Industrial development in Lapland is supported by business development agencies, the University of Lapland, Lapland University of Applied Sciences, two vocational institutions, and research institutions, most of which are related to the sustainable utilisation of natural resources. Together, these institutions provide industries with support and a knowledge base for further development.

The preparation for the development of Lapland's smart specialisation strategy was led by the Regional Council of Lapland, with wide stakeholder consultation during 2012–2013, and resulted in the regional smart specialisation strategy document, Lapland's Arctic Specialisation Programme (Regional Council of Lapland, 2013). Three main pillars set the scene for the smart specialisation priorities described in the strategy document: (i) refining of Arctic natural resources, (ii) utilisation of Arctic natural conditions, and (iii) cross-cutting development enabling Arctic growth. The priorities were further divided into 50 specific action proposals to be implemented during the period 2014–2020. According to the vision of Lapland's Arctic specialisation for the year 2030 presented in the strategy document, Lapland will enjoy a leading position in exploiting and commercialising Arctic natural resources and conditions. Lapland will also be the centre of international Arctic transport, information, and telecommunications. From the point of view of Lapland's future, the aspects to be highlighted are the sustainable utilisation of natural resources and natural conditions and increasing the value added of the products and services in Lapland. The most important Arctic spearhead sectors in Lapland, according to the strategy document, are the mining and metal industry, tourism, and the bioeconomy (Regional Council of Lapland, 2013).

Lapland's Arctic Specialisation Programme, which was launched in 2013, described smart specialisation in Lapland as a relatively broad concept. The smart specialisation strategy process in 2012–2013 was followed by a more detailed follow-up process starting in 2014 (Teräs & Mäenpää, 2016). By highlighting specific cross-cutting specialisations, the foundation for the regional smart cluster approach called the Arctic Smartness concept was initiated. Five smart clusters were established as flagship initiatives: (i) Arctic Industry and Circular Economy, (ii) Arctic Rural Communities, (iii) Arctic Design, (iv) Arctic Safety, and (v) Arctic Development Environments. To implement the flagship initiatives into practice, a wide range of regional development projects were implemented in 2015–2018 to engage regional stakeholders, to use a wide range of external expertise to support the process, to develop synergic funding of the initiatives, and to be an active and visible actor positioned at the level of EU Smart Specialisation development.

In Lapland, smart specialisation has been seen from the very beginning as a very practical concept that brings in new insights into regional development and supports initiatives to present Lapland as an important part of Europe with access to global value chains, too. The Regional Council of Lapland, including its management, has shown significant commitment to the adoption of the smart specialisation concept in Lapland. The Regional Council of Lapland has also supported the mobilisation of smart specialisation in Lapland and has utilised international networking opportunities created by smart specialisation. Smart specialisation has been used in Lapland at three major levels. First, it has been used to direct regional structural and rural development funds towards jointly agreed specialisation topics in order to gain maximum cumulative impact. Second, smart specialisation has been used to steer regional collaboration to capitalise regional knowledge bases towards common development targets. Third, smart specialisation has acted as an important tool for Lapland to become recognised as an attractive and knowledgeable partner in the EU. The clustering work related to smart specialisation in Lapland is particularly a methodological approach to dig deeper into the entrepreneurial discovery processes that contribute to involving the different actors and to building favourable ecosystems for joint entrepreneurial development.

Cross-case analysis

Before comparing the smart specialisation approaches in Lapland and Norrbotten, it is worthwhile to note that there are several similarities to be found between Norrbotten and Lapland regarding location, industrial structure, and innovation system. First, the regions both occupy distant locations far from European and Nordic capital regions and have low population densities and harsh Arctic climatic conditions. Second, their industrial structures are dominated by large industrial actors that utilise the natural resources of the respective regions. Third, both regions invest in developing Arctic tourism as an additional economic backbone. Fourth, both regions have high levels of educational institutes, combined with developed and organised innovation systems. Both regions score relatively highly in the European Innovation Scoreboard ranking (Regional Innovation Scoreboard, 2017). There are, however, some differences between Lapland and Norrbotten regarding industrial structure and innovation system, too. In the mining industry, Norrbotten largely relies on the Swedish mining companies LKAB and Boliden, whereas Lapland has attracted several international mining companies. The latest development in the Arctic bioeconomy in Lapland includes new, large-scale investment plans with considerable Chinese involvement (Kaidi project in Kemi and Boreal Bioref in Kemijärvi).

There is a significant difference to be noted in the application of the smart specialisation concept between the regions of Lapland and Norrbotten. Lapland was one of the early adopters of the smart specialisation concept: the region had already joined the EU JRC smart specialisation platform in 2013, the regional smart specialisation strategy was launched in 2013, the implementation of the smart specialisation strategy has been intense in the years 2015–2018, including, for example, the creation of five smart clusters, and the national and international visibility – including even the regional branding – of the smart specialisation work in Lapland has been remarkable. In Norrbotten, the smart specialisation work has been seen as an embedded part of the strengthening of the key focus areas of Norrbotten, which is reported in the RIS/RUS documents. As of 2018, Norrbotten has not yet prepared/published its regional smart specialisation strategy document. Norrbotten has, however, prepared regional development analyses and future scenarios based on the smart specialisation concept (see, for example, Ejdemo et al., 2016).

Two commonalities can be distinguished in these region's S3 priorities: (a) they place some emphasis on natural resource-based industries where, in particular, forest-based resources and certain minerals occur relatively abundantly in Lapland and Norrbotten and industrial structures have been established that process and refine these commodities for the export market. Given that these regions have long-term experiences in these sectors, they are able to draw on industrial infrastructure and competences, including business and research environments that have accumulated over time. Furthermore, (b) they leverage natural conditions that are particular to these areas as strengths. These conditions include contrasts between seasons in terms of climate and daylight, most notably the cold winters, and sparsely populated areas. The cold winters and sparsity are often considered as disadvantages, but both Lapland and Norrbotten recognise that the natural conditions in these regions offer domains for potential (and existing) commercial opportunities.

Given these similarities and the relative proximity of these regions to each other, there should also be opportunities to foster increased exchanges of knowledge and ideas across the border. Indeed, these regions are similar in many respects, which suggests they may resort to competition, but their industries and, in a wider perspective, their areas of smart specialisation may be more accurately characterised as *related* in either a technological or market sense, rather than as identical. Cross-border exchanges already occur between individuals, companies, and universities in the area, but as both regions, to some extent, face challenges in critical mass, developing the connections between these regions further to open up their industrial, business, and research environments to increased collaborations could enhance the opportunities for successful entrepreneurial discoveries in these northern sparsely populated areas.

Regarding the adoption of the concepts of related variety and smart specialisation, there is an attempt in Lapland to combine cluster development with smart specialisation by 'smart clusters', that is, five interconnected clusters/cluster initiatives with synergies. The regional smart specialisation activities in Lapland upgrade and develop regional industries with the help of smart clusters. One of the key ideas behind smart clusters is the creation and promotion of combinations through unrelated knowledge bases, leading to new, related industries (Asheim et al., 2017, p. 79). For example, the smart clusters combine expertise from different industry sectors but also from industry and educational institutions in Lapland. In Norrbotten, it is widely considered that the regional industrial structure is too largely dominated by a few industries and a few actors. In fact, there is a need to not intensify the industrial specialisation process further but to find new and innovative ways for smart diversification in which Norrbotten would diversify its economy primarily based on its existing strengths and capabilities by moving into related or unrelated sectors (Asheim et al., 2017, p. 79). The draft document of the revised RIS for Norrbotten (Region Norrbotten, 2018) highlights related variety as an essential concept of the forthcoming smart specialisation efforts in Norrbotten.

Regarding governance of the regional smart specialisation development process, the Regional Council of Lapland has led the regional smart specialisation strategy and implementation work in Lapland since 2012. The entrepreneurial discovery process has recently taken place within the smart clusters, but the Regional Council of Lapland has coordinated and promoted the entrepreneurial discovery process (EDP) since the smart specialisation strategy process started in 2012. In Norrbotten, the regional authority responsible for strategic regional development shifted from the county administrative board to the county council in 2017.

Conclusions

The study of the applicability of the smart specialisation concept in peripheral Nordic regions highlights several issues of interest.

First, sparsely populated regions should not be seen categorically as lagging behind by definition. Sparsely populated regions face specific challenges, such as, for example, long distances, lack of critical mass of actors, and often harsh climatic conditions, but many sparsely populated regions perform well in comparison to many other regions with larger populations and more central locations. When applying the smart specialisation concept in sparsely populated regions, the specific characteristics of the region need to be taken into account – but with the assumption that the measures typically to be taken in developing less-favoured regions are not the only measures to be taken into account.

Second, the concept of smart specialisation seems to be quite adaptable to sparsely populated regions – at least in the Nordic Arctic regions. The analysis of Lapland presented in this chapter demonstrates especially well the ability of sparsely populated regions to adapt the smart specialisation concept to their regional development plans and implementation programmes. The combination of abundance of natural resources and lack of critical mass needs to be taken into account, however, when adapting smart specialisation to sparsely populated regions. At the same time, the analysis presented in this chapter illustrates that over the relatively short period of time during which smart specialisation has been implemented in the EU, significant variations in the adoption of the concept can be identified even between regions with significant similarities in industrial structure and innovation systems. In the case of the Nordic Arctic, the relevant regions represent, respectively, a category of early adopter (Lapland) and a category of latecomer (Norrbotten) when it comes to the pace of adoption of the smart specialisation concept. This does not mean, however, that, in Norrbotten, smart specialisation has not taken place in recent years. For example, the revised Norrbotten RIS document (Region Norrbotten, 2018) highlights Facebook data centre investment in Luleå as "a very good example of smart specialisation in Norrbotten", although the Facebook investment has not always been connected to smart specialisation. This raises a broader question: are more of these 'de facto' smart specialisation initiatives unrevealed, and undocumented, in sparsely populated areas?

Third, this analysis of Nordic Arctic regions suggests some factors that contribute to success in applying smart specialisation in sparsely populated regions. Governance and leadership of the development process of smart specialisation play significant roles. The ability to engage and mobilise regional actors behind a smart specialisation process is highlighted as a crucially important factor, as well as having key persons, one could even say smart specialisation mavericks, showing the way and inspiring actors to gather behind a joint vision with prioritisations and policy mixes. Mobilising actors and key individuals behind implementation of a joint smart specialisation strategy seems to be even more important than an orthodox adoption of the somewhat complex key terms of the smart specialisation concept such as, for example, the entrepreneurial discovery process or domain. Smart specialisation can act as a powerful tool for regional branding, too. It is also interesting to note that Nordland County in northern Norway has also adapted the smart specialisation concept, even though Norway, as a non-EU country, does not need to prepare the smart specialisation strategies in order to raise EU structural funds (see Nordland County Council, 2015). Lapland, Norrbotten, and Nordland have relatively advanced regional innovation systems compared to many other sparsely populated regions – an issue of importance when studying further the factors that contribute to success in applying smart specialisation in sparsely populated areas.

Finally, it needs to be stated that the long-term impact of smart specialisation in sparsely populated regions remains to be seen; it is far too early to judge the long-term success of the approach at this stage in the evolution of smart specialisation in EU (and some additional non-EU) regions. The early results, especially in Lapland, encourage regional actors to continue to redouble their efforts to fully utilise the smart specialisation concept. One should not, however, rely too much on smart specialisation alone in developing sparsely populated regions. Smart specialisation complements and provides new approaches to more traditional regional development. The major challenges of decreasing population and critical mass still remain in sparsely populated regions, but there is optimism that smart specialisation, if taken seriously and systematically, can provide additional tools and measures to tackle these issues, too, in the future.

References

Asheim, B.T., Boschma, R., & Cooke, P. (2011). Constructing regional advantage: platform policies based on related variety and differentiated knowledge bases. *Regional Studies*, *45*(7), 893–904.

Asheim, B.T., Grillitsch, M., & Trippl, M. (2017). Smart Specialization as an Innovation-Driven Strategy for Economic Diversification: Examples from Scandinavian Regions.

In: Radosevic et al. (2017): *Advances in the Theory and Practice of Smart Specialisation*. Cambridge, MA: Academic Press.

Barca, F. (2009). *An agenda for a reformed cohesion policy: A place based approach to meeting EU challenges and expectations*. Brussels: European Commission.

Boschma, R. (2005). Proximity and innovation: A critical assessment. *Regional Studies, 39*(1), 61–74.

Content, J., & Frenken, K. (2016). Related variety and economic development: A literature review. *European Planning Studies, 24*(12), 2097–2112.

Da Rosa Pires, A., Pertoldi, M., Edwards, J., & Hegyi, F.B. (2014). Smart specialisation and innovation in rural areas. S3 Policy Brief Series 09/2014.

Dubois, A., & Roto, J. (2012). Making the best of Europe's sparsely populated areas. On making geographic specificity a driver for territorial development in Europe. Nordregio Working Paper, 15.

EC (2010). European Commission, Europe 2020: Commission proposes new economic strategy in Europe. Press release March 3, 2010. Accessed October 2018 at: http://europa.eu/rapid/press-release_IP-10-225_en.htm?locale=en.

Ejdemo, T., Söderholm, P., Ylinenpää, H., & Örtqvist, D. (2016). Regional förnyelse av och i Norrbotten En meta-analys av länets utvecklingsförutsättningar. Luleå tekniska universitet.

Florida, R. (2003). *The rise of the creative class: And how it's transforming work, leisure, community and everyday life*. New York: Perseus Book Group.

Foray, D., Goddard J., Beldarrain J., Landabaso, M., McCann, P., Morgan, K., Nauwelaers, C., & Ortega-Argilés, R. (2012). *Guide to research and innovation strategies for smart specialisation (RIS3)*. Brussels: European Commission.

Foray, D., & van Ark, B. (2007). Smart specialisation in a truly integrated research area is the key to attracting more R&D to Europe. *Knowledge for Growth. European Issues and Policy Challenges, 1*, 26–28.

Frenken, K., Van Oort, F., & Verburg, T. (2007). Related variety, unrelated variety and regional economic growth. *Regional Studies, 41*(5), 685–697.

Gløersen, E., Dubois, A., Copus, A., & Schürmann, C. (2006). *Northern peripheral, sparsely populated regions in the European Union and in Norway*. Stockholm: Nordregio.

Howells, J.R.L. (2002). Tacit knowledge, innovation and economic geography. *Urban Studies, 39*, 871–884.

Länsstyrelsen Norrbotten. (2013). Innovationsstrategi för Norrbottens län 2013–2020. (https://www.norrbottenskommuner.se/media/1453/innovationsstrategi-foer-norrbottens-laen-2013-2020.pdf)

McCann, P., & Ortega-Argilés, R. (2013). Modern regional innovation policy. *Cambridge Journal of Regions, Economy and Society, 6*(2), 187–216.

Morgan, K. (2016). Nurturing novelty: Regional innovation policy in the age of smart specialization. *Environment and Planning C: Government and Policy, 35*(4), 1–15.

Nordland County Council. (2015). Innovative Nordland. Innovation strategy for Nordland 2014–2020. (https://www.nfk.no/_f/i83b99f70-1c31-4c7c-bf64-59e66b4bb567/innovation_strategy_web.pdf)

OECD (2017). OECD Territorial Reviews: Northern Sparsely Populated Areas.

Region Norrbotten. (2018). *Regional utvecklingsstrategi för Norrbotten 2030*. Version Remiss May 1,2018. Luleå: Region Norrbotten.

Regional Council of Lapland. (2013). Lapland's Arctic specialisation programme. (http://www.lappi.fi/lapinliitto/c/document_library/get_file?folderId=53982&name=DLFE-21455.pdf)

Regional Innovation Scoreboard. (2017). Brussels: European Commission database. (http://ec.europa.eu/growth/industry/innovation/facts-figures/regional_en)

Regionfakta. (2018). (http://www.regionfakta.com/Norrbottens-lan/IN-ENGLISH-/Population/Population/)

RIS Norrbotten (2018). (http://www.norrbotten.se/upload/IB/lg/regio/R4GG/Innovation%20Strategy.pdf)

Rodrik, D. (2014). When ideas trump interests: Preferences, worldviews, and policy innovations. *Journal of Economic Perspectives*, *28*(1), 189–208.

Statistics Finland. (2018). Population statistics. (https://www.stat.fi/tup/suoluk/suoluk_vaesto_en.html)

Teräs, J., Dubois, A., Sörvik, J., & Pertoldi, M. (2015). Implementing smart specialisation in sparsely populated areas. Joint Research Centre. *S3* Working Paper 10/2015. Brussels: European Commission..

Teräs, J., & Mäenpää, A. (2016). Smart specialisation implementation processes in the North. *European Structural and Investment Funds Journal*, *4*(2), 75–86.

Ylinenpää, H., Teräs, J., & Örtqvist, D. (2016). Innovation networks in different industrial settings: From flexible to smart specialization. *European Journal of Spatial Development*, *63*, 1–17.

6 The wisdom of the fathers?

Regional/rural development policy and structures for the Highlands and Islands of Scotland 1965–2015, through the lens of smart specialisation

Andrew Copus

Introduction

This chapter reflects upon the activities of the longest-established regional development agency of the UK, the Highlands and Islands Development Board (later renamed Highlands and Islands Enterprise), which recently celebrated its 50-year anniversary. The author argues that, although in the early years there were some celebrated mistakes, on the whole the agency's activities provide an illustration of the fact that, as others have noted (Foray et al., 2011), the broad principles of smart specialisation have been followed, in some contexts many years before the term was invented in 2008.

The Highlands and Islands of Scotland

Although fragmented in terms of present-day administrative structures, the Highlands and Islands of Scotland (Figure 6.1) has an enduring historical and cultural identity in the minds of Scottish people, and many from further afield perceive it as representing the essence of Scottish distinctiveness. This integrity is reflected in the fact that the Highlands and Islands is, according to Eurostat's classification, a single NUTS 2 region. It comprises six NUTS 3 regions, three of which are entirely made up of islands, the other three being on the Scottish mainland.

The grounds on which the Highlands and Islands could be described as 'less favoured' are not difficult to discover. They include sparsity of population and a history of out-migration, remoteness from centres of economic activity, and (until recently) an economy dependent upon resource-based activities, combined with relatively low levels of productivity.

The Highlands and Islands cover more than half (52%) of the land area of Scotland, but are home to less than 9% of its population (slightly fewer than 470,000 persons). The average population density of the region (including the main city of Inverness) is 11.6 persons per square kilometre. However, in the north-west of the mainland part of the area, this figure falls to approximately 7 per square kilometre. Net out-migration and population decline

Figure 6.1 The Highlands and Islands of Scotland
Source: HIE

have characterised the region from before detailed records began in the second half of the nineteenth century, right through to the third quarter of the twentieth century. The hardships of the rural population of 'crofters', which were the push factor for out-migration for generations of Highlanders and Islanders, have passed into folklore.

According to most measures of peripherality, the region is the most remote in the UK, and, in a European context, is surpassed in this respect only by parts of northern Norway, Sweden, and Finland. Although there have been great improvements in the transport infrastructure in recent decades, the region still has many roads that are not really suitable for modern logistics, and the coast and islands are dependent upon a network of ferries. Basic and relatively expensive air services operate out of 11 publicly owned airports. Transport and travel infrastructure have implications for both the cost of doing business and for daily life. They also present challenges for the delivery of services such as education and health care.

Prior to 1999, the gross domestic product (GDP) per capita of the Highlands and Islands was less than 75% of the EU average, rendering the region eligible for development assistance through the EU's Structural Funds (Objective 1). Historically, low productivity was associated with a predominantly rural economy dominated by small-scale farming, fishing, textiles (Harris Tweed), and forestry.

However, in recent decades there has been an increasing divergence between, on the one hand, a number of nodes of growth, notably around Inverness and the Inner Moray Firth area, together with parts of Orkney and Shetland, and on the other, the sparsely populated hinterland. This means that average regional statistics, for example, for population change, employment, or output, need to be interpreted with care. For example, although the long-term decline in the population of the region as a whole was reversed from the late 1960s, the more remote and insular parts of the region are still experiencing losses. The prosperity of Inverness and the Inner Moray Firth has cost the region as a whole its special status for EU Structural Funds, whilst (for example) parts of the Western Isles still show high levels of deprivation and poverty. Such polarisation of development can also be observed, in microcosm, in terms of demographic change in the Northern and Western Island groups, where the outer Isles have continued to 'shrink' whilst the population of the larger and more accessible islands has expanded.

This chapter focuses on the story of the two development agencies that have had responsibility for the Highlands and Islands during the last 50 years – the Highlands and Islands Development Board (HIDB), which was in place from 1966 until 1990, and Highlands and Islands Enterprise (HIE), which took over from 1991, and continues today. Before describing the activities of the HIDB and HIE, it will be helpful to place them against the backdrop of the unique history of the region, within the broader context of the evolving UK/Scottish governance framework, and in relation to the evolving overarching ethos of Scottish economic development and regional policy.

The governance context

In retrospect, it is rather striking to reflect upon just how much has changed, in terms of the way in which Scotland and the Highlands and Islands are administered, since the mid-1960s. The importance of this is that it serves to underline just how exceptional the HIDB/HIE has been, within a highly centralised and increasingly 'spatially blind' UK policy context.

Prior to 1999, the 'highest' level of administration in Scotland was a UK government department, known as the Scottish Office, located in Edinburgh and under the overall direction of the Secretary of State for Scotland, a senior member of the UK government 'cabinet' in Whitehall, London. The Scottish Office was responsible for all aspects of public administration in Scotland, except those (such as defence and foreign policy, fiscal, economic, and social welfare policy) that were managed in London. Some aspects, notably the education and legal systems, were, for historic reasons, completely separate from their counterparts in other countries of the UK. Others, such as agriculture, forestry and fishing, health care, planning, housing, utilities, and the emergency services, were administered separately, but under more or less common regulations. Regional and economic development seems to have occupied an intermediate position. In other words, some aspects were controlled by Whitehall, whilst many others, especially those that were more explicitly focused on specific localities, were seen as the responsibility of the Scottish Office. As one might expect, the two major political parties (Conservative and Labour) have, generally speaking, followed different philosophies with regard to regional intervention or support, with the latter being much more favourably disposed to Keynesian policies, and the former preferring to rely upon market mechanisms. However, it would be fair to say that, especially at the beginning of our period and, to an extent, even today, 'spatial planning' is too strong a term to describe regional policy in the UK and Scotland, even during periods when Labour were in power.

In 1999, following a 1997 referendum that showed a majority of the Scottish people were in favour of an elected Scottish Parliament, the Scottish Assembly was set up. The constitutional arrangement means that the UK (Westminster) Parliament remains the supreme level of governance but that the Scottish Assembly (later renamed the Scottish Parliament when the Scottish National Party gained power in 2011) has 'devolved' power to legislate over all matters not 'reserved' by the UK Parliament. In the context of this chapter, the key area of devolved responsibility is economic development. From 1999, the Scottish Office was renamed the 'Scottish Executive', and from 2011 it became the 'Scottish Government'.

In order to understand the role and significance of the HIDB and HIE, it is also necessary to know a little about local government arrangements in Scotland. Unlike, for example, the Nordic countries, Scotland's equivalent of municipalities (Districts) underwent early and radical reform. At the beginning of our period, in 1966, there were basically two tiers of local governance: Counties and

Districts. In 1975, a local government reform created ten large 'Regions' and 56 smaller constituent 'Districts', each with their own set of powers. The three island groups (Shetland, Orkney, and the Western Isles), though relatively small, were awarded the same powers as the 'regions' of Highland and Strathclyde, which covered most of the remainder of the HIDB area. At the lower level, there were nine Districts fully within the HIDB boundary and three that were partly within it. In 1996, the two-tier arrangement was replaced by 32 'unitary authorities' or 'Councils'. The HIDB/HIE area now comprised all of the three island areas, Highland, Argyll and Bute Councils, parts of Moray, together with some islands in the Firth of Clyde that are part of mainland Council areas, such as Dumbarton and North Lanarkshire.

This story of local government reform is important as context for the story of the HIDB and HIE for two reasons. The first is that the process has affected much more than just boundary changes; it has structured a gradual centralisation of responsibility that has rendered the current Councils little more than agents for the delivery of national (Scottish and UK) policies, with very little freedom for local initiatives to respond to local challenges. This is a process common to the other countries of the UK. In Scotland it has led to an organised campaign for greater local autonomy[1]. To some extent it explains the importance of having a separate, more local/regionally orientated development body, such as the HIDB or HIE. The second reason for explaining the rather 'messy' evolution of local government in the Highlands and Islands is to illustrate the fact that the HIDB was 'parachuted in' with little or no integration with the existing local administrative structures.

The importance of historical legacies

Although the HIDB was the first development board set up in the UK, and in some ways remains unique, it did not 'come from nowhere', and the enthusiasm and optimism that characterised its early years can best be understood against the backdrop of the socio-economic history of the region. It has always been a "place apart" (Perchard & MacKenzie, 2013), where the Clan system of societal organisation survived into the modern era, and which suffered punitive cultural repression in consequence of it being perceived as the origin of a series of challenges to English rule during the seventeenth and eighteenth centuries. In the eighteenth and nineteenth centuries, the eviction of small tenant farmers (crofters) in order to establish extensive sheep grazing enterprises (a process known as 'clearance'), and the subsequent out-migration and depopulation, have passed into folklore and popular culture. By the final quarter of the nineteenth century, the UK government was forced to act in response to the poverty of the region, and to the plight of those crofters who had chosen to remain, eking out a precarious existence on marginal land. In 1886, the first of a series of 'Crofting Acts' was passed, which gave a degree of security of tenure, the right to transfer tenancies to heirs, and so on. Over the following century, crofting developed into a distinctive (and protected) way of life, characterised by pluriactivity, combining small-scale agricultural activities with fishing or a range of other activities, including, in some areas, craft manufacturing, such as weaving, or local services. The 'crofting counties', as they were known, became synonymous with population decline and were perceived as an area 'left behind' by modern economic development, and therefore requiring public support.

In this context, it is easy to appreciate what the Secretary of State for Scotland, Willie Ross, meant when, in his 1965 House of Commons speech announcing the setting up of the HIDB, he described the region as having had a "shabby deal by history" and the highlander as "the man on Scotland's conscience". Arguably, such a region, such a deprived group, deserved some special treatment.

The HIDB and HIE as institutional structures[2]

When the HIDB was initially set up it operated from a single office in Inverness. Within a couple of years, a branch office was set up in Shetland, and this was soon followed by an office in the Western Isles, and, by 1980, the work of the Board was organised in a number of 'area teams' (Hughes, 1980).

Although the HIDB was, in a sense, a 'top-down' intervention under the auspices of the Scottish Office, from the beginning, Board staff were sensitive to the differing needs of different parts of their area, and strove to respond appropriately. However, when the Conservatives took control in Westminster in 1979, neo-liberal and New Public Management approaches were quickly reflected in the replacement of the HIDB by HIE. The word 'Enterprise' in the new title was highly significant. HIE in Inverness became an 'umbrella' body, commissioning local economic development activities from ten Local Enterprise Companies (LECs), reflecting a continuing commitment to 'local development'. These LECS were technically private companies, run by boards that incorporated local business leaders, which provided assistance to local entrepreneurs and which were monitored and evaluated by HIE according to specific and measurable performance targets. In addition to economic development, the LECs had responsibility for implementing national training policy. Outside the Highlands and Islands, a parallel body, Scottish Enterprise (SE), performed a similar function, coordinating a set of 12 LECs. The HIE LECS differed from their SE counterparts in having a remit for social development.

The next big change in the HIE structure came in 2008 when responsibility for training was transferred to a new national body, Skills Development Scotland. In 2011, a further reorganisation led to the demise of the LECs, their day to day support for enterprises being transferred to a scheme operated by the Councils, known as 'Business Gateway'. HIE is thus today a very much smaller and more centralised organisation than at any time since the early days of the HIDB. It now focuses on supporting high-growth businesses, regional growth sectors, the low carbon economy, and fragile communities[3]. Further reform is under consideration, though a 2016 proposal for the merging of HIE with SE and Skills Development Scotland was recently abandoned in favour of adding an umbrella strategic enterprise and training board[4].

Looking back on the Highlands and Islands in 1966, and the tasks facing the staff of the newly established HIDB, the contrast with the situation in 2017 is very striking. To a great extent, the vocabulary of challenge and decline has been superseded by that of opportunity and growth potential. In the next section, the author will attempt to characterise the evolution of the practical intervention strategy employed by the HIDB and the HIE across the half century.

Policy evolution and the role of experiments

Although 'actions speak louder than words', in this context, both are important: strategic policy statements help us to understand the thinking behind the activities of HIDB and HIE, even though much of it was of necessity reactive and pragmatic. It will be convenient to divide this narrative into two periods, coinciding with the lifetimes of the two agencies. Of course, there were no 'cliff edges' of changes in approach or style at the end or beginning of these periods, the evolution was gradual, and the division into discreet periods is simply for the sake of clarity and convenience.

HIDB 1966–1990

In his foreword to the first Annual Report (HIDB, 1966), Robert Grieve, the first chairman of the HIDB, characterised the ultimate goal of its activity as "adding another perfectly possible way of life to that in the great cities" and "offering that alternative to the important minority in any urbanised country who wish to take it. . .". Faced with a wide range of views on how the new board should proceed, Grieve argued that

> The board. . .must take the lead here and declare a broad set of policies which it believes can meet the needs and desires of the country in general, the Highlander in particular, and eventually lead to the solution of the Highland problem.
>
> (HIDB, 1966, p. 3)

He went on to list the potential policy solutions as follows:

1 **Agriculture** – though this was unlikely to deliver any additional employment and thus help to slow out-migration. Also, it was primarily the responsibility of the Scottish Office Department of Agriculture and Forestry.
2 **Forestry** – an expansion of planting (sensitive to landscape and ecological concerns) was "one of three great hopes for employment and a more secure Highland economy" (HIDB, 1966, p. 3). However, it was a long-term project and the responsibility of another agency, the Forestry Commission.

3 **Tourism** – "the second great prop available to us. . .tourism can make a rapid impact on the economy of the Highlands and the numbers of people that the area can support. . ." (HIDB, 1966, p. 3). The twin tasks were better marketing and extension of the season, without damaging the environment.
4 **Fishing** – still important but with locally specific needs and potentials.
5 **Manufacturing industry** – considered by Grieve to be the "third main prop". The Board "increasingly regard it as the most relevant of all with regard to the immediate need to stem a substantial proportion of the emigration of the talented sons and daughters from the Highlands and Islands. . . . It is our clear duty to see that this most important and most deficient element of the Highland economy is furnished; it should be recognised by all that we should devote a substantial proportion of our effort to it. Manufacturing industry is very poorly represented in the Highlands and Islands. Without it, the region will continue to lack any real possibility of a substantial enough rise in numbers to give credibility to Highland regeneration" (HIDB, 1966, p. 4). The strategy would comprise three elements: (i) supporting proposals for entrepreneurship or in-migration of enterprises wherever they come forward; (ii) the provision of advance factories and sites; and (iii) support for 'major growth points', where the geographic conditions seem favourable – "the Moray Firth is unquestionably the most important of these areas" (HIDB, 1966, p. 4)
6 **Crofting** – Grieve reluctantly acknowledges crofting to be a key to retaining population within the region, but only if opportunities for additional employment are available. Thus, forestry, tourism, and small-scale manufacturing development must be complementary.

After listing the above priorities, Grieve refers to the oft-repeated concern about the balance of development within the region. "No matter what success is achieved in the Eastern or Central Highlands. . . the Board will be judged by its ability to hold population in the true crofting areas" (HIDB, 1966, p. 5).

The activities of the Board over the following 24 years broadly reflect Grieve's priorities, though there were some additions, and learning processes led to shifts in approach. This learning was largely a consequence of some conspicuous failures that have tended to distract the attention of commentators from the many small successes.

Of Grieve's three sources of employment growth, the first, forestry, saw little direct activity by the Board, since support for planting was outside their remit. However, one notable and lasting success was the Norbord plant near Inverness, which, since 1985, has been making 'oriented strand board' from small quantities of roundwood timber produced in the region.

The Board was very much more active in the support of tourism. From the beginning, this involved 'place marketing', at first within the UK, but later internationally. Within the region, the Board at first supported, and later took responsibility for, a network of Tourist Information Offices, equipping them with an early computerised accommodation booking system. A wide range of attractions were supported, many, like the ski resorts of the Spey Valley, Cairngorm, and the Nevis range, aimed at extending the season.

The fishing (and aquaculture) industry possibly became more of a focus for the HIDB than Grieve anticipated. For example, a Fisheries Development Scheme resulted in the construction of more than 30 modern boats, a number of individual skippers were funded to convert to shellfish harvesting, training courses were supported in a Shetland College, a fish processing plant was established in the Western Isles, and the development of fish farming was supported in a variety of ways, including by funding research and through capital grants.

The Board's support for manufacturing industry, or rather a couple of major projects, has, as already implied, coloured the perception of its role, to an extent that seems disproportionate (Smith, 1982; Hughes, 1983). The first of these projects was a pulp and paper mill at Corpach, close to Fort William, which opened in 1964 (before the HIDB was set up). Although the HIDB could not claim to have brought this development to the Highlands, it was nevertheless associated with its closure less than 20 years later in 1981. At its peak, it employed almost 1,000 people, and its development led to house building and transport improvements in the Fort William area. The second project was a large aluminium smelter, constructed on agricultural land beside the Cromarty Firth. The choice of site reflected the deepwater access for bauxite bulk carriers and, it is generally supposed, access to cheap hydro-power from the Highlands. In fact, the plant was tied into an expensive deal (presumably for political reasons over which HIDB had no influence) with the Hunterston nuclear plant more than two hundred kilometres away on the Firth of Clyde. This was a flagship project, but its expensive energy source made it an early victim of the 'double dip recession' experienced by the UK in 1981.

Another large-scale industrial project that added to the impression that the HIDB was over-reliant upon a growth pole strategy was the experimental nuclear energy research establishment at Dounreay in Caithness. Like the Corpach mill, this was a development that predated the establishment of the HIDB, though the Board used its high-technology image as part of its place marketing to try to attract more businesses to the far north. This, unfortunately, meant that it was also associated with the decision to decommission the site in 1989.

In the 1970s, the discovery of oil in the North Sea stimulated interest in the potential for oil rig construction yards in various parts of the Highlands, including Nigg and Ardesier on the East Coast, but also Kishorn in Wester Ross and Arnish on the Isle of Lewis. For obvious reasons, these activities had a limited lifespan, and these yards soon added to the impression that industrialisation in the Highlands and Islands was a boom and bust process. Various projects for petrochemical plants were proposed but did not come to fruition. More successful and sustainable were the 'transhipping' facilities of Flotta in Orkney and Sullom Voe in Shetland.

It is important, however, to try to dispel the false impression that the HIDB's strategy for manufacturing was solely concerned with large-scale 'Fordist' projects, or that there was a blind faith in growth pole processes. There was also a lot of quiet work, through the HIDB's network of local offices, supporting both indigenous entrepreneurs and small businesses who chose to move into the less developed parts of the region. Many of these were local food and drink producers or craft enterprises.

In addition to supporting the sectors anticipated by Grieve in 1966, the HIDB soon became involved in improving the infrastructure upon which development depended. A crucial area of activity was in improving transport and communications. The HIDB concerned itself with roads, railways, ferries, and air transport. One of its most important contributions was in ensuring the continuation of ferry services to remote communities that depended on them. During the late sixties and early seventies, roll-on roll-off ('RORO') ferries were introduced, revolutionising the process of loading and unloading. The HIDB campaigned for many years for 'Road Equivalent Tariffs'. A new bridge at Ballachulish (1975) cut journey times between Glasgow and Oban. In the early eighties, the Board assisted the Islands of Fair Isle and Foula in setting up community electricity schemes. Right at the end of its life, in 1989, the HIDB was exploring the possibility of supporting the roll-out of ISDN networks across its region. The importance of these background infrastructure activities cannot be underestimated as facilitators for the development that would follow in the next 25 years; they gradually made the Highlands and Islands feel less remote.

HIE 1991–2015

The transition from HIDB to HIE was a structural discontinuity that reflected a change in the complexion of political power at the national level (the Thatcher/Major years). The more gradual 'evolution of development' approach was, in part, driven by lessons learned during the HIDB years, in part by involvement in the implementation of European rural and regional development policy, and was also very much a reflection of the academic discourse of the time.

As we have already seen, the HIDB had got its fingers burned by the conspicuous failures at Invergordon and Corpach, and had already moved away from such approaches in favour of a broader spread of smaller interventions supporting mostly indigenous entrepreneurs. By 1990, the HIDB still had a substantial property portfolio (HIDB, 1990, p. 49), but the merging of Scotland's training agency into the new HIE/LEC structure reflected the increasing recognition of human capital and innovation as a key to development. These, and other, 'soft' factors also began to come into the foreground as transport infrastructural improvements addressed some of the peripherality issues and information and communications technology began to make certain kinds of service industries feasible in the region.

Exposure to the European discourse on rural/regional development began in 1982–87 when the Outer Hebrides was selected for an experimental 'Integrated Development Programme' (IDP), which brought together a range of agricultural improvements, with support for the nascent industry of fish farming and investments in infrastructure (Houston, 1987). Later in the year that the IDP was completed, the Highlands and Islands was awarded Objective 5b status for the 1987–93 Structural Fund programming period. Between 1994 and 2006, the region moved into Objective 1. However, the accession of Eastern European countries in 2004 pushed the EU GDP per capita average down and, combined with improvements in the Highlands and Islands, led to the region becoming a 'Statistical Effect' region for the 2007–2014 period, and thereafter a 'Transitional' region. From the early 1990s onwards, the Highlands and Islands has participated in a succession of LEADER/CLLD programmes (Black & Conway, 1995). Although the governance structure of these successive programmes evolved, HIDB/HIE remained a key player, and was very much part of a learning process about integrated development and place-based approaches. The Objective 5b Rural Enterprise Programme was quite a big step forward in this respect.

The evolution of the approach followed by HIE and the LECS also reflected the changing academic discourse, with its increasing emphasis on enterprise, innovation, the role of small and medium-sized enterprises (SMEs), local development contexts, information and learning, human capital, and so on. This was the period when reliance upon Fordist manufacturing and 'cumulative causation' of the 1950s and '60s was giving way to 'postmodern' ideas and approaches, such as those presented by Piore and Sabel's (1984) 'Second Industrial Divide', Porter's (1990, 1995) work on innovation and clusters, Storper (1993), Morgan (1997), and Asheim's (1996, 1999) 'Learning Regions', and the 'Industrial Districts' of the third Italy (Belussi, 1996). The concept of institutional thickness' (Amin & Thrift, 1995) began a period of preoccupation with governance. Broadly speaking, this shift could be summed up as a move away from individual investments in 'hard capital' and towards a more holistic approach in which the importance of 'softer' elements was recognised.

Thus, the structural discontinuity between HIDB and HIE was associated with an incremental rather than revolutionary change in terms of ethos and intervention logic, and it was not until the Scottish Assembly/Executive took over from the Scottish Office that a major policy restatement was issued, in the form of "A Smart Successful Scotland" (Scottish Executive, 2001a, 2004b) and "A Smart Successful Highlands and Islands" (HIE, 2005).

The Highlands and Islands document states:

> Our aim is to enable people living in the Highlands and Islands to realise their full potential on a long-term sustainable basis. The aim is founded on the belief that the people who live here have the prospect of enjoying one of the most fulfilling existences in the developed world.
>
> (HIE, 2005, p. 14)

This aim was to be achieved through four priorities for action: (i) strengthening communities, (ii) developing skills, (iii) growing businesses, and (iv) making global connections. These activities were to be achieved within the context of an ethos of sustainability:

> Enabling people to realise their full potential is about utilising our resources wisely in a way that assists current residents to improve their lives, without constraining the ability of future Highlands and Islands residents to make their own improvements from an enriched, rather than depleted, resource-base.
>
> (HIE, 2005, p. 15)

Although each of the four priorities is then elaborated with reference to the specific needs of the Highlands and Islands region, it is significant that Smart Sustainable Highlands and Islands was designed to be coherent within a hierarchy of policy documents issued by the Scottish Executive. At the 'top' of this hierarchy was the overarching Framework for Economic Development in Scotland (Scottish Executive, 2001b, 2004a). This provided the context for "A Smart Sustainable Scotland" (2001a, 2004b), which sets out the policy framework for the Enterprise Network (HIE and Scottish Enterprise), and the principles established here were developed in more detail in the HIE's own document.

In 2007, the SNP administration introduced a National Performance Framework[5], a complex structure of objectives and performance indicators relating to all aspects of Scottish Government activity. Within this framework, economic development is carried out within guidelines set out in a document entitled "Scotland's Economic Strategy" (Scottish Government, 2015). The Framework Agreement and Operating Strategy documents under which HIE currently operates are very clear that

> HIE's primary purpose, (. . .) is to focus its activities on the achievement of the SG's purpose of creating a more successful country with opportunities for all of Scotland to flourish through increasing sustainable economic growth. Ministers expect HIE to do this by aligning its vision, purpose and priorities with the SG's published Programme for Government (PfG), Scotland's Economic Strategy (SES) and National Performance Framework (NPF).

There is thus a very real sense in which the HIE is now expected to conform to a set of principles that were applied throughout Scotland. This contrasts strongly with the 'exceptionalist' ethos (Perchard & MacKenzie, 2013) that led to the establishment of the HIDB 30 years before, when the region was seen as "a place apart" and having special needs. The feeling that the Highlands and Islands and HIE have been 'mainstreamed' is reinforced by a number of diagrams in "A Smart Sustainable Scotland" (Scottish Executive, 2001, 2004), which give a clear message that policy and strategy originates in the Scottish Government (then Executive), but that the two Enterprise Agencies are required to adapt it to regional contexts.

Since responsibility for day to day support for SMEs and entrepreneurs was transferred to Business Gateway and the Councils, and 'routine' training responsibilities shifted to Skills Development Scotland, HIE's role has become more strategic. It now focuses on supporting economic activities that have a particular growth potential within the region, and developing the preconditions for such growth. Key opportunities include renewable energy, tourism, local/quality food and drink, knowledge-based services, and creative industries. This is essentially a subset of the Key Sectors identified in Scotlands Economic Strategy (Scottish Government, 2015).

Although the HIE still supports transport infrastructure projects, improving broadband access has been a key focus in recent years. Triple Helix concepts are also extremely influential, with a substantial proportion of HIE's budget being used to support the University of the Highlands and Islands and associated research institutes.

What does the HIDB/HIE story tell us about smart specialisation in practice?

> Clearly Scotland has been pursuing a smart specialisation approach, without using the term, in its Key Sector focus.
>
> (Scottish Parliament European and External Relations Committee, 2012)

The term smart specialisation was not invented or popularised for at least a couple of decades after the HIDB began its work. Even today it is not explicitly referred to in any of the HIE's policy documents. However, the question we have set ourselves is: to what extent did the HIDB and HIE, during their half century of activity, learn, by experience, ways of working to support economic activity in the Highlands and Islands that were, in essence, aligned with smart specialisation principles?

Prior to the introduction of 'Smart Specialisation' to the European regional policy discourse in 2008, the accepted 'dogma' of regional/growth policy was that the public sector should support innovation by enhancing the preconditions, such as regional research and development capacity, or education and skills, but that they should beware of any temptation to promote any kind of sectoral specialisation. For example, Foray et al. (2011) state that

> departing from such neutrality is always dangerous since it implies guessing the future developments of markets and technologies and this opens the door to all those little monsters that economists like to eradicate: wrong choices, picking winners, market distortions. According to the dogma, it is much better to leave any issue concerning sectoral strategies, specialisation, or direction to the "magical chaos of the blind watchmaker". Any notion of specialisation policy was a taboo in policy discussion, particularly in the main policy institutions.
>
> (Foray et al., 2011, p. 3)

Smart specialisation provided a way around this restriction at a time when recession was sharpening the appetite for new solutions. This was achieved by taking the choice of regional specialisation out of the hands of policy practitioners and placing this responsibility in the context of a 'neo-endogenous' selection process called 'entrepreneurial discovery' (Foray et al., 2011; Rodríguez-Pose & Wilkie, 2017). This process builds upon the tacit knowledge (about regional assets, opportunities, constraints etc.) of individual entrepreneurs, and upon their ability to spot opportunities, and to initiate innovative activities. A range of other actors, such as research and development facilities, and a range of supporting institutions, including development agencies, are mobilised to support the nascent specialisation, so that it can begin to develop the (external) economies of scale and scope that are necessary for longer-term competitiveness in a globalised context. Entrepreneurial discovery, although initiated by individuals, is not a purely bottom-up process. Top-down and public-sector and policy inputs alternate in a "bi-directional iterative dynamic" (Foray et al., 2011, p. 10). It is an essentially inclusive process, in which institutional context (both in terms of organisations and 'rules of the game') and governance are crucial (Rodríguez-Pose & Wilkie, 2017).

Thus, at the heart of smart specialisation is the idea that every region or locality has a unique set of constraints to which it should adapt, and opportunities that it should exploit, and that these point to specific development models and paths. Successful configurations are not necessarily transferable. Not every region can be a Silicon Valley. Regional development processes need to be carefully adapted to build upon local strengths, whether they are natural resources, human or social capital, cultural traditions, or institutional capacities. Charles, Gross & Bachtler (2012) suggest that smart specialisation has much in common with the older term regional innovation strategy, but that it is distinctive in the following elements:

- a strong emphasis on building upon regional strengths; in other words, it is a strongly 'place-based' in approach
- a balancing emphasis on interregional connectedness and integration into globalised circuits of economic activity.

We have seen that in many ways the Highlands and Islands of Scotland of today are very different from those in which the HIDB was established in 1965. Over the 50 years, both the day to day management/implementation of the agency and the overall development strategy have evolved almost beyond recognition.

Although the Highlands and Islands is a relatively large region to be the subject of a single smart specialisation process/strategy, it is nonetheless true to say that giving the Highlands and Islands a dedicated regional development agency was a clear signal of recognition that a differentiated approach, reflecting regional specificities, was required. Furthermore, the early move to set up local offices throughout the region shows a recognition of the need to build the kind of relationships with local business communities that are a very important part of an entrepreneurial discovery process.

In terms of strategy, during the first 25 years, the HIDB followed a mixed approach. History has not been kind in highlighting its mistakes, and failing to acknowledge its achievements. Undoubtedly, the prescription of Fordist manufacturing industry as a remedy for out-migration from remote rural areas can be criticised. It was, perhaps, 'dumb diversification' rather than smart specialisation. However, looking beyond this conspicuous error, the HIDB also promoted a range of initiatives that, with the benefit of hindsight, have been shown to be 'smart' – especially support for fish farming, tourism, food and drink processing, and crafts. In retrospect, the choice of these specialisms was the consequence of fairly intensive interaction between embedded local HIDB staff and the entrepreneurial community. Furthermore, these were set against a backdrop of infrastructure, human capital, and community development investments that have played an important facilitating role. As such, it would not be stretching the terminology to describe the activities of the HIDB during the 1970s and 1980s, and in the early years of the HIE, as a process of entrepreneurial discovery.

Although the HIE era began with an approach that looked more like neo-endogenous development, with each LEC having a degree of apparent autonomy within the monitoring and guidance framework administered by HIE, it has ended with a more centralised model. Perhaps the recent strategic focus on 'growth industries' can be considered compatible with the smart specialisation concept to the extent that such activities capitalise on the specific territorial assets of the region.

Thus, in retrospect, the history of the development agencies of the Highlands and Islands provides evidence of elements of smart specialisation approaches throughout the past 50 years. However, these have emerged as common sense' responses to regional change and development issues, rather than from an explicit paradigm or ideology. Furthermore, they have expressed themselves through different governance and strategic structures, proving that more centralised policy arrangements are not necessarily inimitable to the regional/local flexibility commonly associated with smart specialisation.

Notes

1 Commission on Strengthening Local Democracy in Scotland http://www.localdemocracy.info/news/final-report/ [accessed 3rd October 2018]
2 For an interesting anecdotal history of the HIDB/HIE, including early promotional films, see http://timeline.hie.co.uk/ [accessed 3rd October 2018]
3 http://www.hie.co.uk/about-hie/our-priorities/default.html [accessed 3rd October 2018]
4 http://www.bbc.co.uk/news/uk-scotland-highlands-islands-39442747 [accessed 3rd October 2018]
5 http://nationalperformance.gov.scot [accessed 3rd October 2018]

References

Amin, A., & Thrift, N. (1995). Globalisation, institutional thickness and the local economy. In: P. Healey, S. Cameron, S. Davoudi, S. Graham & A. Madanipour (Eds.). *Managing Cities, The New Urban Context*. Chichester, UK: Wiley.

Asheim, B. (1996). Industrial districts as learning regions: a condition for prosperity, *European Planning Studies*, *4*(4), 379–400.

Asheim, B. (1999). Innovation, social capital and regional clusters: on the importance of co-operation, interactive learning and localised knowledge in learning economies, paper presented at the Regional Studies Association International Conference, Bilbao, Sept 18–21.

Belussi, F. (1996). Local systems, industrial districts and institutional networks: towards a new evolutionary paradigm of industrial economics? *European Planning Studies*, *4*(1), 5–22.

Black, S., & Conway, E. (1995). Community-led rural development policies in the Highlands and Islands: the European Community's leader programme, *Local Economy*, *10*(3), 229–245.

Charles, D., Gross, F., & Bachtler, J. (2012). Smart specialisation and cohesion policy – a strategy for all regions? *IQ Thematic Paper*, *30*(2), 1–51. Retrieved 3rd October 2017 from http://www.clusterpolisees3.eu/ClusterpoliSEEPortal/resources/cms/documents/2012.06.20_Smart_Specialization_and_Cohesion_Policy_-_A_Strategy_for_All_Regions.pdf.

Foray, D., David, P., & Hall, H. (2011). Smart specialization: from academic idea to political instrument, the surprising career of a concept and the difficulties involved in its implementation. MTEI-Working Paper 2011-001. Lausanne, Switzerland: Management of Technology & Entrepreneurship Institute, École polytechnique fédérale de Lausanne. Retrieved 3rd October 2018 from: https://infoscience.epfl.ch/record/170252/.

Highlands and Islands Development Board (HIDB). (1966). *First Annual Report of the HIDB*. Inverness, Scotland: Highlands and Islands Development Board.

Highlands and Islands Development Board (HIDB) (1990). *Twenty-Fifth Annual Report of the HIDB*. Inverness, Scotland: Highlands and Islands Development Board.

Highlands and Islands Enterprise (HIE). (2005). *A Smart Successful Highlands and Islands, An Enterprise Strategy for the Highlands and Islands of Scotland*. Inverness, Scotland: Highlands and Islands Enterprise. Retrieved 3rd October 2018 from http://timeline.hie.co.uk/media/1371/hie-story-a-smart-successful-hi-2005.pdf.

Houston, G. (1987). Assessing the I.D.P. for the western isles, *Scottish Geographical Magazine*, *103*(3), 163–165. DOI: 10.1080/00369228718736714

Hughes, J.T. (1980). *An outline of the powers and work of the Highlands and Islands Development Board*. Inverness, Scotland: HIDB.

Hughes, J.T. (1983). HIDB development policy: a response, *Scottish Geographical Magazine*, *99*(2), 121–124. DOI: 10.1080/00369228308736558

Morgan, K. (1997). The learning region: institutions, innovation and regional renewal, *Regional Studies*, *31*(5), 491–503.

Perchard, A., & MacKenzie, N. (2013). Too much on the Highlands? Recasting the economic history of the Highlands and Islands. *Northern Scotland*, *4*(1), 3–22.

Piore, M., & Sabel, C. (1984). *The second industrial divide: Possibilities for prosperity*. New York: Basic Books.
Porter, M.E. (1990). *The competitive advantage of nations*. London and Basingstoke: Macmillan.
Porter, M.E. (1995). The determinants and dynamics of national advantage. In: J. Drew (Ed.) *Readings in international enterprise*. London/New York: Routledge.
Rodríguez-Pose, A., & Wilkie, C. (2017). Institutions and the entrepreneurial discovery process for smart specialization. In: D. Kyriakou, M. Palazuelos Martínez, I. Periáñez-Forte, & A. Rainoldi (Eds.) *Governing Smart Specialisation* (pp. 34–48), London: Routledge.
Scottish Executive (2001a). *A Smart, Successful Scotland: Ambitions for the Enterprise Networks*. Edinburgh: Scottish Executive. Retrieved 3rd October 2018 from http://www.gov.scot/Resource/Doc/158455/0042945.pdf.
Scottish Executive (2001b). *The Way Forward: FRAMEWORK for Economic Development in Scotland*. Edinburgh: Scottish Executive. Retrieved 3rd October 2018 from http://www.gov.scot/Resource/Doc/158281/0042858.pdf.
Scottish Executive (2004a). *The Framework for Economic Development in Scotland*. Edinburgh: Scottish Executive. Retrieved 3rd October 2018 from http://www.gov.scot/Resource/Doc/25725/0025718.pdf.
Scottish Executive (2004b). *A Smart, Successful Scotland: Strategic direction to the Enterprise Networks and an enterprise strategy for Scotland*, Edinburgh. Retrieved 3rd October 2018 from http://www.gov.scot/Resource/Doc/26800/0027981.pdf.
Scottish Government (2015). *Scotland's Economic Strategy*. Edinburgh: Scottish Government. Retrieved 3rd October 2018 from http://www.gov.scot/Publications/2015/03/5984.
Scottish Parliament European and External Relations Committee. (2012). *Horizon 2020: Written Evidence from Scotland Europa, Scottish Enterprise, Highlands and Islands Enterprise and The Scottish Funding Council*. Retrieved 3rd October 2018 from http://www.parliament.scot/S4_EuropeanandExternalRelationsCommittee/Inquiries/Submission_from_Scotland_Europa_Scottish_Enterprise_Highlands_and_Islands.pdf.
Smith, J.S. (1982). The Invergordon Aluminium smelter – growth policy gone wrong? A note, *Scottish Geographical Magazine*, *98*(2), 115–118. DOI: 10.1080/00369228208736524
Storper, M. (1993). Regional "worlds" of production: learning and innovation in the technology districts of France, Italy and the USA, *Regional Studies*, *27*(5), 433–455.

7 The role of biorefineries in the revitalisation of (old) industrial rural regions

Alexandre Dubois and Iryna Kristensen

Introduction

Many European rural regions have identified the bioeconomy as a future pillar of their regional development strategies, enabling them not only to contribute to the achievement of overarching Sustainable Development Goals at national and European levels, but also to unlock new opportunities for regional growth. This focus has led regions to identify the bioeconomy as a potential domain of the Smart Specialisation Strategies (S3). Regional bioeconomy initiatives are envisaged to combine sustainable exploitation of biomass, whether coming from agriculture or forestry, and promotion of new market outlets for bio-based products. By means of this, an internal process of retooling and optimising traditional resource-based activities is combined with an external process of integrating regional actors into new industrial value chains. As an economic process, achieving a transition of the regional bioeconomy refers less to upscaling of the existing commodity export *filière*, where internationalised actors often dominate the flows in and out of the regional economy, than to a change of scope that considers biomass production as the starting point for engaging in multiple industrial processes. In a nutshell, the transition aims less at retooling the existing production capacity and reinforcing the position of commodity providers in a linear global value chain, than to widen the market opportunities by integrating multiple value chains with future growth potential and to shorten the number of intermediaries between territorial economic agents and global markets.

Territorial biorefineries are concrete endeavours to operationalise the bioeconomy on a regional scale. This chapter aims to examine how the establishment of biorefineries contributes to the regeneration of regional economic development trajectories in old-industrial rural regions based on innovative developments and applications of bio-based products and processes. We first delve deeper into the concept of the territorial biorefinery and its relation to territorial development, the bioeconomy and smart specialisation. The cross-analysis of the two illustrative cases presented in this study highlights the similarities and differences in the governance arrangements that have enabled the integration of such industrial development into the region's socio-economic fabric. This chapter will look especially at how the advancement/transformation of traditional industries can contribute to a revitalisation of resource-based economies.

Territorial development

A central notion addressed in this chapter is the notion of territoriality. Territoriality deals with how 'places' are socially constructed, created and reproduced through the interaction of social relations across time and space (Soja, 1989; Paasi, 2009). Territoriality is thus an inclusive process leading to the identification and characterisation of actors with a certain geography. Hence, a territory is less constructed by delineating the inner and outer boundaries of a socio-economic space than by the emergence of the recombination of institutional, social and economic elements along with features of the natural or physical environment (Filippi, Frey & Torre, 2011). Thus, a 'territory' is not simply a physical space that engulfs social and economic activities (Filippi et al., 2011), but a geographical entity that is constructed by and shapes interdependencies among actors and pertains to collective action, contractual relations and organisational trust for its governance (Torre, 2006). Moreover, the boundaries of a territory may be "moving" (Torre & Wallet, 2014, p. 653) as the interactions between the actors evolve over time due to both internal changes and adaptation to external processes of change.

Within this framework, the scenery for economic interactions is not formed as a mosaic of self-contained and adjoined socio-economic systems, be they states or regions, but rather as a system of interdependencies leading to intertwined spatialities (Dubois & Carson, 2016). Territorial development thus emerges as a collective capacity to sustain and reinvent interdependencies between space (inwards and outwards), time (past, present and future) and capital (human and natural). These perspectives on territorial development are strongly aligned with recent theoretical developments about neo-endogenous development. Neo-endogenous development invokes the necessity for territorial actors to mobilise available local resources and the need to incorporate extra-local factors, requiring high levels of shared identity and coordination capabilities (Bosworth & Atterton, 2012; Torre & Wallet, 2014). The neo-endogenous development approach emphasises the importance of both external knowledge acquisition and localised learning through networking (Virkkala, 2007).

The place of the bioeconomy in smart specialisation

Marsden and Farioli defined bioeconomy as "both the science and practice of utilising living things (natures) to produce a much wider range of goods and services" (Marsden & Farioli, 2015, p. 335). The latter entails a "redeployment of farm-based resources into non-food or fibre products" (Sæther, 2015, p. 112) that generates new revenue streams in rural communities (McCormick & Kautto, 2013). De Besi and McCormick (2015) characterised bioeconomy as

> an economy in which the basic components of materials, chemicals and energy are derived from renewable biological resources [. . .] bioeconomy involves a transition away from the use of fossil-based resources and towards the production of renewable biomass and the conversion of this biomass into food, feed, energy, biofuels, and bio-based products.
>
> (De Besi & McCormick, 2015)

At the European level, Scarlat et al. (2015) acknowledged that the successful transition towards bioeconomy will "rely on the advancement in technology of a range of processes, on the achievement of a breakthrough in terms of technical performances and cost effectiveness and will depend on the availability of sustainable biomass". The combination of organisational and technological innovations and sustainable biomass production will likely require a systemic territorial approach that integrates developments taking place in both urban and rural regions across the continent.

The implementation of an ambitious European and national agenda for the bioeconomy has given rural regions a renewed interest in their primary production capabilities and promoted a retooling of their resource-based economies. In this light, bio-based activities have become an evident pillar of these regions' S3. A recent pan-European study of the implementation of the bioeconomy showed that 207 out of 210 EU regions included "bioeconomy related aspects" in their 2014–2020 Research and Innovation priorities and plans, essentially linked to the agrifood sector but also "bio-based fuel and energy" (Spatial Foresight, SWECO, ÖIR, t33, Nordregio, B. Group & Infyde, 2017). However, the level of readiness to harness the potential of the bioeconomy varies greatly between European regions, as many regions in Europe (35.7%) have a low level of bioeconomy maturity due to a lack of human capital and efficient production processes (Spatial Foresight et al., 2017). The pan-European study thus emphasises the pertinence of using a "value chain perspective" encompassing the multiple stages of industrial development, including supply, research, processing and marketing (Spatial Foresight et al., 2017).

This means that the transition towards regional bio-based economies is considered by regional authorities as a 'low-hanging fruit', i.e. a potential that may be harnessed rather swiftly because biomass production is significant, in one form or another, in most EU regions. What we need to point out, though, is that the effectiveness of this transition rests not only on the availability of biomass production capabilities, but also on other factors such as knowledge inflows, market potential, logistics and local governance. Moreover, the presence of industrial capabilities appears critical to the harnessing of this potential. The transition to bio-based regional economies based on an industrial and territorial ecology approach entails a "profound transformation of the organisation of the territory" in relation to material flows through the territory and the exchange of information and the sharing of knowledge between public and private actors (Ceapraz et al., 2016, p. 54).

Territorial biorefineries: enacting the regional bio-based economy

A biorefinery may be approached as "a new business model involving the complete valorisation of biomass in energy, food, feed, biomaterials and bio-based chemicals" (Sauvée & Viaggi, 2016). More specifically, Ceapraz et al. (2016) defined the concept of 'territorial biorefinery' as "a new means of biomass development based on 'doubly green' chemistry and the principles of territorial and industrial ecology applied to this industry". Biorefineries may serve as a catalyst for the revitalisation of old-industrial and rural areas since they provide incentives for sustaining agricultural activities and thereby counterbalance the decline of other traditional economic activities in these regions. Biomass has increasingly been considered as an important natural asset for European territories. Its sustainable production and efficient use constitute the main pillars of the biorefinery concept (Hoeltinger et al., 2011). Biorefineries typically integrate agricultural (crop production, logging), research (lab and live experimentations) and industrial (processing and manufacturing of new materials or products) activities in the same geographical location. Although biorefineries are often physically located on former industrial sites at the interface between urban and rural landscapes (urban fringe), their relational geographies are complex: social and ecological outcomes may be felt locally, whereas economic benefits and anticipated markets are much wider in a sectoral (i.e. feeding into different industrial value chains) and geographical (i.e. internationalised) sense. Investigating such clusters necessitates taking a multi-actor and multi-scalar perspective (Gobert, 2016), hence the use of the term *territorial* to characterise these socio-technical systems. As socio-technical systems, territorial biorefineries have been examined using different frameworks, including an 'organisational systems and networks perspective' (Sergent & Cazals, 2015) or an institutionalist approach (Beaurain & Brullot, 2011).

Sergent and Cazals (2015) further outlined that biorefining essentially consists of transferring the traditional industrial model developed in fossil fuel-based chemistry and energy production to biomass processing. Such systems need to be strongly anchored in the technological and cognitive development trajectory of the local innovation milieu (Sergent & Cazals, 2015), and the scope of change induced is dependent on context-specific features (Näyhä & Pesonen, 2014). Sergent and Cazals (2015) further questioned how the focus on 'green' chemistry is compatible with the current economic paradigm based on low prices and economies of scale. The success of territorial biorefineries thus also depends on the development of new business models based on economies of scope. The concept of a territorial biorefinery integrates actors according to the logic of proximity (in the sense of an enhanced collective coordination of individual actions) and complementarities between actors (Ceapraz et al., 2016).

By feeding into multiple value chains instead of consolidating and optimising their position in a single *filière*, based on a linear commodity-process-product-market sequence, territorial biorefineries seek to generate economies in related technologies and related diversification (Boschma et al., 2017) at the scale of both an industrial cluster and a territory. In that regard, territorial biorefineries can be deemed a solid basis for developing new domains. Indeed, smart specialisation scholars have defined a domain as a mid-grained economic unit that stretches across several sectors or activities that offer greater possibilities to promote learning and generate knowledge spillovers (McCann & Ortega-Argilés, 2013). However, this may represent a challenge for old-industrial regions as those are typically "overspecialized in mature technologies and industries experiencing declining", thus possibly faced with an unwillingness to change and "lock-in" (Coenen et al., 2013). Other scholars have argued that "development measures for old-industrial areas often have to be strategically oriented on breaking path dependency and facilitating the renewal of regional economy" (Tödtling & Trippl, 2005). Hence, harnessing the potential for developing territorial biorefineries in old-industrial rural regions will necessitate a difficult trade-off between relying on and breaking the past development trajectory.

If the argument supporting the establishment of territorial biorefineries is rather well framed, less attention has been paid to *how* these socio-technical clusters actually appear and develop. The literature has emphasised the potential conflicts between social and industrial logics taking place at different spatial scales. These clusters have often been portrayed as being "part of the community" (Selfa et al., 2015). However, in practice, the social acceptability of these industrial projects often arrives "end of pipe", as Gobert (2016) phrased it, i.e. only at later stages of the implementation processes, with little possibility for the community to influence project development. Moreover, there is little systemic understanding of the extent to which communities of practices and interests that are dominant in upstream (e.g. agricultural cooperatives) and downstream (e.g. industrial clusters) flows feed into each other. Developing systemic thinking with regard to upstream and downstream flows (Brullot & Gobert, 2014), especially in relation to territoriality, becomes a prerequisite. Various researchers have also questioned the idea of territorial anchoring of infrastructure that leads to resilient local development (Raufflet, 2014).

Method

This chapter examines empirically the development process of two biorefineries, Processum in Örnsköldsvik (Västernorrland, Sweden) and Bazancourt-Pomacle (Champagne-Ardenne[1], France). The material deployed to support this examination consists essentially of secondary sources, such as academic publications, research accounts and documentation or other material from the biorefineries' homepages. In the case of Processum, direct contacts were made with some biorefinery actors in order to access documentation that was not available publicly. In the case of Bazancourt-Pomacle, the empirical analysis focused on synthesising the rich corpus of scientific publications dedicated to this specific biorefinery cluster.

Based on these accounts, we then propose a cross-analysis highlighting the main differences and similarities between the processes developing these biorefineries and how they addressed issues related to multi-actor, multi-sectoral and multilevel coordination. Our research question deals with the extent to which biorefinery development can be a platform for 'smart' regional development, in terms of using the existing knowledge and competences of the past industrial heritage to feed future-oriented specialisations.

We characterise our two case study regions of Västernorrland (Sweden) and Champagne-Ardenne (France) as *old-industrial rural regions* in light of the historical legacy of economic activities in these regions converting biomass production into products feeding global value chains – paper pulp and the wine industry, respectively. In that respect, these regions' territorial assets consist of extensive biomass availability and industrial infrastructure and competences. In general, old-industrial regions are associated with a certain decline in the regional economy (Boschma & Lambooy, 1999). Such regions epitomise the transition from an era of industrialisation towards the knowledge economy. The case of biorefineries supports the notion that biomass production, industrial capabilities and knowledge-intensive activities can not only be compatible with each another but may also cross-fertilise each other.

The two regions selected nonetheless offer interesting contrasts for undertaking such a comparative study. In a typology of Territorial Innovation Systems, the region Champagne-Ardenne belonged to the category of 'smart and creative diversification areas' (a low degree of local applied knowledge, some internal innovation capacity, high degree of local competences), whilst the mid-Sweden region (including the counties of Jämtland and Västernorrland) belonged to the category of 'smart technological application area' (a high product innovation rate, a limited degree of local applied science and a high creativity that allows external basic and applied science knowledge to be translated into innovation) (Camagni & Capello, 2013).

With respect to employment structure and dynamics, the two regions seem to be diametrically opposed. The mid-Sweden region has an employment rate above the 75% level set by the Europe 2020 agenda, and the level has generally increased since 2009. In contrast, the Champagne-Ardenne region has a rate that is level with this threshold and has declined during the period 2009–2016 (Nordregio, 2018). With respect to R&D intensity, the Champagne-Ardenne and Västernorrland regions appear to have similar levels, between 0.5 and 1% as a share of Gross Regional Product, which is well below the EU28 average of 2% (Nordregio, 2017).

Case study 1: Processum

The "new regional industry initiatives" (Tesar & Bodin, 2012) – the result of "entrepreneurial experimentation" in the aftermath of the wood industry crisis as a major occurrence – is a perfect example of the regional economic regeneration processes in Västernorrland County, with the growing biorefinery cluster in Örnsköldsvik as a central component. Such initiatives are rooted in bottom-up entrepreneurial approaches; yet the county is part of a group of Swedish regions that have not yet formalised their 'smart' activities into a comprehensive S3 strategy.

Örnsköldsvik is a municipality in Västernorrland County, located along the Gulf of Bothnia in northern Sweden, with a population of 56 139 inhabitants (SCB, 2017). Historically, the economic welfare of the northern towns was determined by the proximity to and abundance of forested areas. The main industries of Örnsköldsvik are thus pulp and paper, forestry and engineering (Tesar & Bodin, 2012). Industrial production in Örnsköldsvik makes a significant contribution to Sweden's total net exports (about 3%), considering that the population of Örnsköldsvik constitutes less than 0.5% of the total population (North Sweden Cleantech, 2018).

During the 1990s, the pulp and paper industry suffered from a global recession, creating a risk of substantial slowdown in regional economic activity and job losses: around 5,000 jobs were lost in the Örnsköldsvik area (Tesar & Bodin, 2012). The situation was further aggravated by increased imports of raw forest products – leading to substantial downsizing of several large companies – as well as raising concerns about the environmental damage caused by certain industrial operations (Arbuthnott et al., 2010; Teräs et al., 2014). This resulted, for instance, in the closure of bleach plants (Arbuthnott et al., 2010).

In the face of these challenges, regional entrepreneurs and politicians came together to search for new solutions and markets to avert over-reliance on a single value chain and thus reduce the risks of economic downturns (Tesar & Bodin, 2012; Teräs et al., 2014). The urge to undertake innovative actions stimulated dynamic networks and intersectoral dialogue on possible alternatives for industrial renewal "that could be expanded into new business and industrial processes within their struggling region" (Arbuthnott et al., 2010). The diverse solutions were territorially anchored, implying that new business ideas emerged from the region's natural resource abundance (i.e. forestry and the wood industry) as well as existing industrial capabilities and competence basis. The outcome of this 'experiment' was a new regional biorefinery initiative marking industrial transformation towards higher-value outputs (Arbuthnott et al., 2010; Tesar & Bodin, 2012; Hansen & Coenen, 2013). The idea was quickly supported by both the municipality of Örnsköldsvik and the county government of Västernorrland, and in 2003 Processum Technology Park AB[2] was established to coordinate and facilitate the development of high-value products and energy solutions with wood as the raw material. The biorefinery is founded upon an existing infrastructure on the site of the original pulp mill[3], located close to the High Coast of Sweden. Biorefinery inputs – the feedstock (timber) – are both imported (from abroad) and (mainly) domestically produced.

Gradually, the cluster expanded in the area, and in 2005 the Biorefinery of the Future[4] initiative, aimed at creating a regional innovation environment for forestry-based biorefinery development, was undertaken (Hansen & Coenen, 2013). Since 2008, the annual turnover of Processum has increased from SEK 10 to 38 million, the number of employees has grown from 3 to 30, and around 200 new jobs have been created on the Domsjö site in Örnsköldsvik. In 2013, the Processum Interest Association sold 60% of its shares to SP Technical Research Institute[5] and became a subsidiary of the SP group. This, together with a comprehensive research infrastructure (biorefinery pilot and demo resources), has resulted in business opportunities for the providers of R&D and engineering services, as well as, for example, mechanical and electrical services. This has also opened the door for national, European and international research collaborations that generate important synergies with different resources and stakeholders. For instance, the Horizon 2020 project SYLFEED aims to convert production of single-cell protein from residual streams from the forestry industry, unlocking and further developing synergies between biotechnology, forestry and the fishing industry.

The biorefinery in Örnsköldsvik has had a long-ranging effect on local development and dynamic synergy creation, based on biorefinery outputs such as heat. SEKAB utilises sulphite ethanol from Domsjö Biorefinery waste products to produce fuel and green chemicals, which deliver a low-carbon footprint. Wastewater from the Domsjö facility and the chemical plants run by Akzo Nobel and SEKAB is processed by the biological treatment plant for purification and biogas production. Biogas is further reused by the Domsjö facility in the drying processes of lignosulphonate. Examples of technical concepts that are already on, or really close to, the market: Purimeth for purification of stripper gases (produces useful methanol and reduces the NOx emissions from a sulphate mill), CelluApp (the Sekab E-tech process for production of, for example, second generation bioethanol), the torrefaction technique developed by Bioendev, verified in an industrial demo unit, Single Cell Protein from forest industry residual streams for use in fish feed, Green liquor sludge for different applications in the mining industry (for example, as an oxygen barrier when covering mine waste), lignin as an additive for concrete or lately as a binder in pellets for animal feed.

Research activities are linked to the major industries and are conducted in cooperation with Umeå University and Mid Sweden University, contributing to diversified industrial development. Applied research is conducted in Processum, which is an important node in the national bioeconomy. Companies providing engineering services (More, Eurocon and PulpEye) and R&D (More and RISE Processum) are located at the site in close proximity to business partners and customers. In 2008, Domsjö Fiber was founded as a cooperation between the municipally owned energy company Övik Energi AB and, at the time, the privately owned biorefinery Domsjö Fabriker AB – a joint raw material procurement company. A couple of new companies (e.g. PulpEye, Mopsys) and subsidiaries (e.g. Eurocon Site Base) were also started at the site.

Ten years of cluster cooperation within the framework 'The Biorefinery of the Future' has resulted in 61 new products, services or processes; 58 prototypes; more than 100 approved patents; 10 new companies and about 30 business expansion investments or establishments. There are 20 paying member companies; however, the functional network is much larger, including national and international partners from industry, academia as well as research institutes. The number of companies involved annually in R&D projects has doubled over the past five years, amounting now to more than 100.

Case study 2: Bazancourt-Pomacle

The territorial biorefinery project is instrumental to the operationalisation of Champagne-Ardenne's Smart Specialisation Strategy, complimentarily to sustainable production practices in the wine industry (Peltier, 2014). This pillar is in itself multidimensional as it seeks to coordinate interventions and promote synergies across the material sciences and chemistry, energy, resource management agrifood sectors (Peltier, 2014). The Bazancourt-Pomacle biorefinery in Champagne-Ardenne in France is an interesting example of a successful territorial economic transition based on industrial symbiosis as a result of its 'technological road map' (Debref, 2012). Industrial symbiosis refers to the synergies that take place between actors located on the biorefinery site (Schieb et al., 2016). The development of the territorial biorefinery is thought to sustain the traditional know-how from the region's economic legacy in terms of industrial and agricultural development, to develop innovations related to new technical and technological applications, to maintain a certain level of exchanges in the local economy and to position the regional economy along multiple global value chains, thus diminishing its vulnerability to market volatility from one specific sector. The biorefinery has its own ecosystem of start-ups emerging from R&I projects within the cluster. Approximately EUR 0.5 billion was estimated to have been raised in the past few years through the start-up ecosystem, in addition to the R&I projects conducted to the value of around EUR 1.5 billion (Philp & Winickoff, 2017). The strong imbrication of public and private partnerships means that for every one euro committed from public money, another two euro has been leveraged from the private sector (Philp & Winickoff, 2017).

The biorefinery is located 15 km north of Reims, in the middle of a vast agricultural area that counts among the most productive in Europe. The biorefinery is one of the most integrated existing biorefineries in Europe, containing several facilities: wheat processing (Chamtor), an industrial demonstration plant (BioDemo), a sugar beet refinery (Cristal Union), ethanol production (Cristanol and Procéthol 2G), a mutualised research centre (ARD) and a cosmetology centre (Soliance) (Chauvet, 2013). Concentrating multiple activities in relation to the production of bio-based products on a single site facilitates synergies between different activities related to biorefining, especially between two types of ecosystems, one industrial and one R&D, namely, the innovation platform BRI (Chauvet, 2013). The biorefinery thus contributes to the increased relatedness of bio-based activities, not only by intertwining material flows among facilities, but also by creating a shared knowledge base platform that introduces novelty and spillovers from one value chain to the next. These enmeshed flows aim at improving the economic efficiency of the cluster by reducing the need to source in material flows from elsewhere and limiting its environmental impacts (Thénot & Honorine, 2017).

Some figures will enable us to get a better sense of the scale of this industrial facility. The biorefinery employs 1200 persons directly and contributes to about 600 indirect local jobs (e.g. 24/7 employment shifts during the sugar beet harvest); it produces over 3 million tons of diversified biomass (2 million tonnes of sugar beet and 1 million tonnes of wheat) over an area of 160 ha; it represents a cumulated investment of EUR 1 billion (2012 adjusted) with EUR 20 million invested annually; it has an output of 20 products or by-products (food, feed, fuel) for a sales value of around EUR 650 million (Schieb et al., 2016).

The Bazancourt-Pomacle biorefinery is part of the IAR (Industries et Agro-Ressources) cluster, a joint investment between the Picardie and Champagne-Ardenne regions, whose goal is to structure the agro-industrial value chain on the site around non-food applications of biomass, sourced from algae, forestry and agriculture, and the development of green chemistry (Chauvet, 2013). Green chemistry extracts various vegetal components for the production of biofuels, biomolecules used in cosmetics and pharmaceutics and biomaterial destined to enter the industrial process of multiple sectors such as construction, packaging, automobile and aeronautics.

One important feature of this model is that it rests on strong functional linkages between agricultural developments, technical and organisational innovations and industrial applications. Access to large quantities of biomass is a critical factor, and thus biorefineries are often located in rural areas, close to where biomass is produced, creating a strong link between industrial actors and associated agricultural producers to the creation of new added value (Jarry & Thomas, 2012). According to Schieb et al. (2016), geographical proximity and clustering are instrumental to the unfolding of economies of scale and economies of diversification that are determinants of the biorefinery's competitiveness. In the case of the Bazancourt-Pomacle biorefinery, Jarry and Thomas (2012) counted around 200 members in the cluster, including biomass producers, agro-industrial actors and chemists, as well as end users such as actors from the construction, health and cosmetics sectors.

If agro-industrial relations are foundational to the territorialised biorefinery model, a particular feature of Bazancourt-Pomacle is its integration of an open innovation ecosystem, which was strongly supported by the regional farmers' union (Thénot & Honorine, 2017). Thénot and Honorine (2017) further noted the key role of the highly entrepreneurial territorial farming system as a driver for the establishment of the biorefinery. From the 1990s onwards, the site expanded by successively adding new facilities, such as a starch-glucose production unit (Chamtor) and an R&D pole (ARD). This development was made possible by the large investments made by the two large local agricultural cooperatives (Vivescia and Cristal Union) combined with support from local authorities (Thénot & Honorine, 2017). Only in the mid-2000s have the regional authorities of Picardie and Champagne-Ardenne invested in the site to develop the IAR cluster as part of the competitiveness poles developed across France (Thénot & Honorine, 2017).

Such strong functional and institutional linkages contribute to the anchoring of the biorefinery project into the territorial socio-economic fabric. According to Jarry and Thomas (2012), the strength of the IAR cluster's unique environmental, industrial and institutional ecosystem is its ability to ensure an important local supply of biomass, to host state-of-the-art industrial facilities and diversified R&D innovation systems and to benefit from voluntarism in regional policy interventions.

There are two ongoing developments that are notable and may consolidate this territorial anchoring. First of all, as more academic partners are associated with the biorefinery, a new building physically hosting these partners is being built. Two well-renowned universities based in Paris (CentraleSupélec and AgroParisTech) have joined the project, which will consolidate the positioning of the cluster in national and international research and innovation networks. It will also further attach the development of scientific knowledge necessary for the future development of the biorefinery to the site. Second, an experimental farm has recently been created on a nearby site formerly occupied by an army aerial base (Thénot & Honorine, 2017). This platform is thought to be used as a test site for developing more efficient future farming practices and to enable local agriculture to thrive by regenerating local know-how and practices (Thénot & Honorine, 2017).

Cross-case analysis

A further cross-examination of both case studies provides important insights and perspectives on the processes of multi-actor engagement mechanisms, the level of imbrication between multiple sectoral value chains, the importance of territorial governance and the extent to which communities have been involved in the implementation process. Table 7.1 synthesises the key features of the biorefinery projects under scrutiny in this chapter.

A critical factor for the successful establishment of biorefineries is their relatedness to locally present biomass production and industrial facilities. Whether biomass comes from forestry (Processum) or agriculture (Bazancourt-Pomacle), having a large enough domestic supply of biomass ensures a certain level of stability in the volume and price of inputs necessary for biorefinery activities and significantly reduces the vulnerability of downstream product-and-process development activities to large fluctuations in the global commodity markets. In practice, it also means that representatives of territorial commodity producers (e.g. farmers' unions in the French case) are directly involved in the biorefinery partnership project. The development of a biorefinery largely relies on the mobilisation of pre-existing industrial competences, networks and infrastructure, which emphasises how biorefineries need to be understood as an extension and transformation of the industrial legacy and development trajectory of a territory and not a radical departure from it. This means that the biorefinery contributes to the regeneration of collaborative networks and interdependencies at the territorial level and promotes entrepreneurial cooperation and knowledge mobilisation among the economic agents involved.

Table 7.1 Cross-case synthesis summary table

Elements for comparison	*Processum, Sweden*	*Bazancourt-Pomacle, France*
Geographical location of biorefinery	Close to the High Coast of Sweden, on the site of the original pulp mill, where all necessary infrastructure is already in place. ~500 km north of Stockholm	In a rural region with large agricultural biomass production and industrial heritage. Accessible location at 140 km east of Paris
Locally sourced inputs	Timber	Sugar beet and cereals (e.g. wheat)
Biorefinery outputs	Green chemicals, biofuel and construction materials, road surfacing materials and organic cotton	Green chemicals, food, animal feed, energy, ethanol, materials, cosmetic ingredients
Movers/innovators in (industrial) transformation processes	Regional entrepreneurs	Farmers' unions, agricultural cooperatives, regional authorities, sugar production company
Modes and mechanisms of interaction	Strong university–industry–government cooperation	Collaborative research between actors on site. Cooperative business model: creation of new facilities through joint ventures
Industrial linkages and synergistic networking	Synergy creation along and between value chains. Locally available biorefinery pilot and demo resources aid bridging the gap between branches and value chains	Synergies of material flows promotes *de facto* multi-actor governance practices between cluster actors. In-sourcing of external scientific knowledge base through localisation of research campus and experimental facilities

Source: Authors' own analysis

The interdependencies between biorefinery actors can be characterised as a combination of functional, institutional and cognitive mechanisms. The overlapping of input and output material flows between biorefinery actors creates an incentive for them to collaborate and align their development strategies on the basis of valorising shared interests and addressing joint challenges. Hence, functional interdependencies and cognitive proximity among actors reinforce the bonds between actors and consolidate the institutionalisation of the biorefinery as a collaborative territorial development.

The clustering of actors on the site of the biorefinery appears to facilitate cross-sectoral collaboration initiatives that may generate an impact on science, industry and society. Our case studies show that the cohabitation of R&D and industrial facilities unlock new opportunities for bridging the gap between fundamental research performed at university laboratories and product-and-process development leading to new market outlets. The presence of demonstration, experimental and testing facilities on the biorefinery sites has been instrumental in internalising knowledge flows and shortening the pathway from research to market. The biorefinery complex functions as a cluster in related variety, by inducing specialised diversification processes across related sectors, which may be associated with a geographical manifestation and concrete operationalisation of the concept of 'domains' in smart specialisation thinking (Foray et al., 2011; Asheim & Grillitsch, 2015).

For these types of clusters to thrive in rural settings, i.e. with an absence of economies of agglomeration, emphasis needs to be put on embedding knowledge production and application in the rural bio-based economy. Enhancing knowledge flows amongst biorefinery actors creates communication channels able to unlock localisation economies. Indeed, looking at the development trajectories of our two cases, it become apparent that there is a push towards the implantation of process-oriented knowledge capabilities (demo and experimental facilities, local offices of metropolitan universities) beyond the development of new products. The aim is to create a self-sustaining cyclical process from research to market. However, this requires deeply collaborative relationships between actors at different stages of the biorefinery process, i.e. biomass producers, industrial actors and experimental research laboratories. In order to continually attract these types of competences, partnership ventures are set up, which, for instance in the French case, translated into the installation of local offices and laboratories of two Parisian universities on the biorefinery site through a joint partnership venture. Hence, a key challenge for the sustainable development of biorefinery projects is to find a suitable governance model to attract and embed knowledge production and application, as this requires different modes of coordination than the industrial processes of biorefineries (Schieb et al., 2016).

Finally, our two case studies show that biorefineries are powerful territorial development tools to attract financial capital and investments to old-industrial rural areas. As a rule of thumb, non-public extra-regional investments are difficult to attract to such settings due to weak and uncertain returns on investment.

An interesting feature is that biorefineries are first and foremost a means to make the most of the financial capital already present in the region by combining public, private and research investments. Indeed, many of the early investors are the traditional commodity exploiters and industrial actors of the territory. Biorefinery projects enable biomass producers to project themselves in the future and invest in what could lead to stability and expansion of the market outlets for their commodities at hand. Biorefineries promote the convergence of the interests of local industries (e.g. less sensitive to global or sectoral downturns), regional/local public authorities (e.g. increase in well-paid and qualified local employment opportunities) and academia (e.g. securing long-term funding to support fundamental and applied research). Hence, as a territorial development instrument, biorefineries operationalise a systemic approach to local development that includes investments in both hard and soft infrastructure (North & Smallbone, 2006). The convergence of local investments and the attraction of long-term external funding through partnerships and joint ventures unlock a *multiplier effect* for the local economy as financial capital invested in the biorefinery complex feeds multiple industrial processes simultaneously.

Concluding remarks

In this chapter, we raised the question of understanding if and how biorefineries as collective projects may have leverage to become a platform for enacting 'smart' territorial development, in terms of using the existing knowledge and competences of the past industrial heritage to feed future-oriented specialisations. The cross-case analysis showed that biorefineries have indeed offered new prospects for old-industrial rural regions to revitalise their regional economies through the skilful combination of biomass production, industrial capabilities and knowledge-intensive activities. The two cases illustrated the evolution of the biorefinery cluster towards an increasing integration of scientific knowledge production capabilities on the site of the cluster, whereas earlier stages focused essentially on industrial applications of knowledge developed elsewhere. In that respect, biorefineries are constantly and gradually developing entities that require flexible governance arrangements to cater for present challenges whilst preparing future prospects through experimentation and research.

These case studies showcase the potential for such initiatives to territorialise and operationalise the visions of territorial actors at the intersection of regional bioeconomies and innovation strategies. Biorefineries thus showcase how territoriality and bio-based economies may be combined in an enabling of sustainable place-based development (Barca et al., 2012). Research into territorial biorefineries is still scarce. The complex nature of biorefineries allows them to benefit especially from interdisciplinary research that brings together insights from economic geography, territorial development and innovation policy, rural studies, biotechnology and industrial system management, to mention just a few.

Although territorial biorefineries appeared under those pages as a particularly efficient tool that may be mobilised by policymakers to promote territorial development and economic revitalisation in old-industrial and rural regions, this model rests on two main pillars. First, a truly abundant source of biomass production must be available in the immediate vicinity of the cluster. This ensures that the expansion of the biorefinery model, progressively integrating numerous actors, will not depend on the importing of biomass products that would make the whole model vulnerable to fluctuations in the global commodity market. Second, the intervention of powerful territorial actors (e.g. the farmers' unions in the French case) is required to inject the necessary investments as well as drive the process in its early stages, and for the reconfiguration and redesign of the collegial structure governing cluster development. The latter is especially important for addressing potential tensions among actors. This is due to the fact that the complexity of biorefineries as relational constructs means that it might be difficult to achieve in practice, given what is at stake and who the stakeholders are.

Acknowledgement

The authors would like to thank Jan Nyman for providing information on Örnsköldsvik and Processum.

Notes

1 Following the regional reform of 2014, the Champagne-Ardenne region was merged with Alsace and Lorraine to form the Grand-Est region.
2 Cluster organisation.
3 The pulp mill in Domsjö was established by Mo and Domsjö AB in 1903.
4 A regional VINNVÄXT initiative and a hub for forest biorefinery development. In 2008, with support from member companies, the municipality, the county government and universities, the Biorefinery of the Future initiative wins a VINNVÄXT award.
5 In 2016, SP Technical Research Institute of Sweden, Innventia and Swedish ICT merged to become RISE Swedish Research Institute. As a consequence, SP Processum changed its name to Processum and is a subsidiary of the RISE group.

References

Arbuthnott, A., Eriksson, J., & Wincent, J. (2010). When a new industry meets traditional and declining ones: an integrative approach towards dialectics and social movement theory in a model of regional industry emergence processes, *Scandinavian Journal of Management*, *26*(3), 290–308.

Asheim, B., & Grillitsch, M. (2015). Smart specialisation: sources for new path development in a peripheral manufacturing region. CIRCLE-Center for Innovation, Research and Competences in the Learning Economy. Lund: Lund University.

Barca, F., McCann, P., & Rodríguez-Pose, A. (2012). The case for regional development intervention: place-based versus place-neutral approaches, *Journal of Regional Science*, *52*(1), 134–152.

Beaurain, C., & Brullot, S. (2011). L'écologie industrielle comme processus de développement territorial: une lecture par la proximité, *Revue d'Économie Régionale & Urbaine*, (2), 313–340.

Boschma, R., Coenen, L., Frenken, K., & Truffer, B. (2017). Towards a theory of regional diversification: combining insights from evolutionary economic geography and transition studies, *Regional Studies*, *51*(1), 31–45.

Boschma, R., & Lambooy, J. (1999). The prospects of an adjustment policy based on collective learning in old industrial regions, *GeoJournal*, *49*(4), 391–399.

Bosworth, G., & Atterton, J. (2012). Entrepreneurial in-migration and neoendogenous rural development, *Rural Sociology*, 77(2), 254–279.

Brullot, S., & Gobert, J. (2014). L'écologie industrielle et territoriale: une expression possible de l'intelligence territoriale? International seminar towards sustainable territorial intelligence: the scales of the resilience. Second Great-West Meeting of Territorial Intelligence.

Camagni, R., & Capello, R. (2013). Regional innovation patterns and the EU regional policy reform: toward smart innovation policies, *Growth and Change*, *44*(2), 355–389.

Ceapraz, I.L., Kotbi, G., & Sauvee, L. (2016). The territorial biorefinery as a new business model, *Bio-based and Applied Economics*, *5*(1), 47–62.

Chauvet, J.-M. (2013). BRI: an innovation platform in the heart of an integrated biorefinery. From biomass to bioproducts. ARD Agroindustrie Recherches & Développements.

Coenen, L., Moodysson, J., & Martin, H. (2013). Renewal of mature industry in an old industrial region: regional innovation policy and the co-evolution of institutions and technology. CIRCLE Paper 7.

De Besi, M., & McCormick, K. (2015). Towards a bioeconomy in Europe: national, regional and industrial strategies, *Sustainability*, 7(8), 10461–10478.

Debref, R. (2012). The paradoxes of environmental innovations: the case of green chemistry, *Journal of Innovation Economics & Management*, (1), 83–102.

Dubois, A., & Carson, D. (2016). Placing northern development: the case of North Sweden, *Local Economy*, *31*(7), 795–811.

Filippi, M., Frey, O., & Torre, A. (2011). The modalities of territorial embeddedness of French cooperative groups. In: Torre, A., & Traversac, J. B. (Eds.) *Territorial Governance, Local Development, Rural Areas, and Agrofood Systems* (pp. 43–63). Heidelberg: Springer.

Foray, D., David, P., & Hall, H. (2011). Smart specialization: from academic idea to political instrument, the surprising career of a concept and the difficulties involved in its implementation. MTEI-Working Paper 2011-001. Lausanne, Switzerland: Management of Technology & Entrepreneurship Institute, École polytechnique fédérale de Lausanne.

Gobert, J. (2016). D'une acceptabilité à une réflexion multiscalaire sur les systèmes socio-techniques: exemple des bioraffineries, *La revue électronique en sciences de l'environnement*, *16*(1).

Hansen, T., & Coenen, L. (2013). Value chain analysis of biofuels: Örnsköldsvik in Sweden. TOP–NEST, Project number: RD 2011-42, Nordic Energy Research.

Hoeltinger, S., Schmidt, J., & Schmid, E. (2011). The green biorefinery concept: optimal plant locations and sizes for Austria, *Journal of the Austrian Society of Agricultural Economics*, *21*(1), 147–156.

Jarry, B., & Thomas, D. (2012). Les alternatives végétales aux ressources fossiles – concept et enjeu territorial, *Les Entretiens IAR*, 15–16 novembre 2011, Chantilly. Laon.

Marsden, T., & Farioli, F. (2015). Natural powers: from the bio-economy to the eco-economy and sustainable place-making, *Sustainability Science*, *10*(2), 331–344.

McCann, P., & Ortega-Argilés, R. (2013). Transforming European regional policy: a results-driven agenda and smart specialization, *Oxford Review of Economic Policy*, *29*(2), 405–431.

McCormick, K., & Kautto, N. (2013). The bioeconomy in Europe: an overview, *Sustainability*, *5*(6), 2589–2608.

Näyhä, A., & Pesonen, H-L. (2014). Strategic change in the forest industry towards the biorefining business, *Technological Forecasting and Social Change*, *81*, 259–271.

Nordregio (2017). Research &Development intensity in 2014. Stockholm: Nordregio. Retrieved October 2018 from http://www.nordregio.org/maps/research-development-intensity-in-2014/.

Nordregio (2018). State of the Nordic Region 2018. Stockholm: Nordregio. Retrieved October 2018 from http://www.norden.org/en/state-nordic-region

North, D., & Smallbone, D. (2006). Developing entrepreneurship and enterprise in Europe's peripheral rural areas: some issues facing policy-makers, *European Planning Studies*, *14*(1), 41–60.

North Sweden Cleantech (2018). Örnsköldsvik. Retrieved October 2018 from http://northswedencleantech.se/sv/om-oss/var-region/ornskoldsvik/.

Paasi, A. (2009). The resurgence of the 'Region' and 'Regional Identity': theoretical perspectives and empirical observations on regional dynamics in Europe, *Review of International Studies*, *35*(Supplement S1), 121–146.

Peltier, M. (2014). Synthesis of the research & innovation strategies for smart specialisation of French regions, KNOWING European Programmes 2014–2020, 2015.

Philp, J., & Winickoff, D.E. (2017). Clusters in industrial biotechnology and bioeconomy: the roles of the public sector, *Trends in Biotechnology*, *35*(8), 682–686.

Raufflet, E. (2014). De l'acceptabilité sociale au développement local résilient, *La revue électronique en sciences de l'environnement*, *14*(2).

Sæther, B. (2015). Microfirms in peripheral areas: how can evolutionary economic geography contribute in studies of diversification? A case study from Norway. *Norsk Geografisk Tidsskrift-- Norwegian Journal of Geography*, *69*(2), 112–120.

Sauvée, L., & Viaggi, D. (2016). Biorefineries in the bio-based economy: opportunities and challenges for economic research, *Bio-based and Applied Economics*, *5*(1), 1–4.

Scarlat, N., Dallemand, J.-F., Monforti-Ferrario, F., & Nita, V. (2015). The role of biomass and bioenergy in a future bioeconomy: policies and facts. *Environmental Development*, *15*, 3–34.

SCB (2017). Folkmängd i riket, län och kommuner 31 december 2017 och befolkningsförändringar 1 oktober–31 december 2017. Totalt. Retrieved October 2018 from http://www.scb.se/hitta-statistik/statistik-efter-amne/befolkning/befolkningens-sammansattning/befolkningsstatistik/pong/tabell-och-diagram/kvartals--och-halvarsstatistik--kommun-lan-och-riket/kvartal-4-2017/.

Schieb, P.A., Lescieux-Katir, H., Thénot, M., & Clément-Larosière, B. (2016). *Biorefinery 2030*, Heidelberg: Springer.

Selfa, T., Iaroi, A., & Burnham, M. (2015). Promoting ethanol in rural Kansas: local framings and cultural politics. *Journal of Rural Studies*, *39*, 63–73.

Sergent, A., & Cazals, C. (2015). L'industrie papetière face au développement de la bioraffinerie lignocellulosique. Dynamiques institutionnelles et perspectives territoriales. *Économie rurale*, (5), 13–30.

Soja, E.W. (1989). *Postmodern geographies: The reassertion of space in critical social theory*. London/New York: Verso.

Spatial Foresight, SWECO, ÖIR, t33, Nordregio, B. Group, & Infyde (2017). Bioeconomy development in EU regions. Mapping of EU Member States'/regions' Research and Innovation plans & Strategies for Smart Specialisation (RIS3) on Bioeconomy for 2014–2020. Luxembourg: European Commission.

Teräs, J., Lindberg, G., Johnsen, I.H.G, Perjo, L., & Giacometti, A. (2014). Bioeconomy in the Nordic region: regional case studies. Nordregio Working Paper 2014:4.

Tesar, G., & Bodin, J. (2012). *Marketing Management in Geographically Remote Industrial Clusters: Implications for Business-to-Consumer Marketing*. Singapore: World Scientific Publishing Company.

Thénot, M., & Honorine, K. (2017). La bioéconomie industrielle à l'échelle d'une région: la bioraffinerie de Bazancourt-Pomacle, tremplin d'une stratégie territoriale. *Annales des Mines-Réalités industrielles, FFE.*

Tödtling, F., & Trippl, M. (2005). One size fits all?: towards a differentiated regional innovation policy approach. *Research Policy, 34*(8), 1203–1219.

Torre, A. (2006). Collective action, governance structure and organizational trust in localized systems of production. The case of the AOC organization of small producers. *Entrepreneurship & Regional Development, 18*(1), 55–72.

Torre, A., & Wallet, F. (2014). Towards new paths for regional and territorial development in rural areas. *European Planning Studies, 23*(4), 650–677.

Virkkala, S. (2007). Innovation and networking in peripheral areas – a case study of emergence and change in rural manufacturing. *European Planning Studies, 15*(4), 511–529.

8 Models of institutional governance for smart specialisation

A comparative study of Asturias and the Basque Country

Jaime del Castillo and Jonatan Paton

Introduction

Territorial development has become increasingly more important in economic policy insofar as many current macro trends have been explained from a micro economic standpoint (Paton, 2014). Consequently, territories now play a decisive role as scenarios in which competitive advantages are built that generate economic prosperity over time (Del Castillo et al., 2017).

The debate regarding territorial development is focused on the contextual factors that make some territories more prosperous than others, how they vary over time and, finally, the actions that can influence them.

The case of old industrialised regions (OIRs) is a good example for putting all these issues into practice: following their initial emergence, due to a different supply of resources that increased the efficiency and concentration of manufacturing in them, the passing of time and, above all, the change in productivity models put at risk the suitability of these locations with the development of new competitive factors. The decline suffered by most of the OIRs placed them in a situation characterised by most of the elements found in less-favoured regions (LFRs) nowadays, such as geographic marginality and poorer communication infrastructures, over-specialisation in obsolete and non-competitive sectors, traditional mindsets averse to change, rigid labour markets and low levels of social capital (Vázquez, 1994; García Blanco, 1998).

However, within this context, some OIRs were able to not only identify these new conditioning factors, but to adapt their economic structure to the new context, whereas others, on the contrary, were unsuccessful and remained in a situation of decline.

The purpose of this study is first to analyse the decisive factors in situations where territories with an industrial past, following changes in international competitiveness models, have been affected by a deep crisis and are forced to reconfigure their economic base.

Second, it aims to identify and characterise success and failure models in economic transformation policies, analysing the similarities between OIR experiences and theories of current smart specialisation (S3) models promoted in Europe and the potential transfer to LFR reality. To that end, the analysis will be focused on two OIRs in Spain – Asturias and the Basque Country since the time of their decline in the 1970s and 1980s.

Lastly, based on these cases, to identify and highlight lessons that will respond to the current demand for both these less-favoured territories to successfully develop economic transformation processes in line with S3 approaches.

Theoretical framework

Although the phenomenon of declining industrial regions is present in certain areas of emerging and developing countries[1], it reached its peak in various European countries in the 1980s[2]. Therefore, the analysis of the underlying factors in situations of decline will be based on a review of literature that goes back mainly to the 1980s and 1990s. Nevertheless, their structural nature is clear over time, propitiated by factors related to technical change that are exogenous to the territories (Rees, 1979; Markusen, 1985; Steiner, 1985; Del Castillo, 1989a, 1989b; Del Castillo et al., 2017) and that contribute to "generate new social, political and institutional problems on a territorial level" (Musto, 1989).

Boschma and Lambooy (1999) mention three structural characteristics, namely, regional size, division of work level in the economic structure and the relative level of specialisation with respect to other neighbouring territories. Previously, Jacobs (1984) argued that economies specialised in few activities are more exposed to international crises. Together with these, other authors also consider the institutional component (Wadley, 1986; Nelson, 1995). However, this component may act as a limiting factor due to social and cultural resistance (Del Castillo, 1989a); this is the 'lock-in' effect that the historical accumulation of knowledge and social principles sometimes generates (Storper, 1992). The historical heritage may be, according to some authors (Martin, 2009; Valdaliso, 2013), both a limiting and an opportunity factor by conditioning the sectors that may arise from specialisation and diversification, or, in S3 terms, territorial diversification capacities as a mechanism for reversing a declining trend.

In any case, Paton et al. (2017) consider these factors as "an interrelated system in which acting on one or more factors separately and without coordination will lead to a less than optimal development".

Thus, since the literature points out that economic decline is caused by a combination of exogenous and endogenous factors, territorial policy is justified to reverse a process of decline, as well as to develop traditional LFRs (Cunningham, 1982; Del Castillo, 1989c).

Del Castillo (1989b) stresses the importance of having a good territorial strategy in place with all the above-mentioned factors as well as the participation, involvement and commitment of both public and private agents. Valdaliso (2013) reaffirms that this territorial strategy must be founded on a series of assets, players and capacities available and highly dependent on the territory.

Hassink (1998) mentions three key elements: (i) the energising of public institutions, (ii) the capacity of the territory to define, agree on and set up a common project and (iii) the density of its social relations.

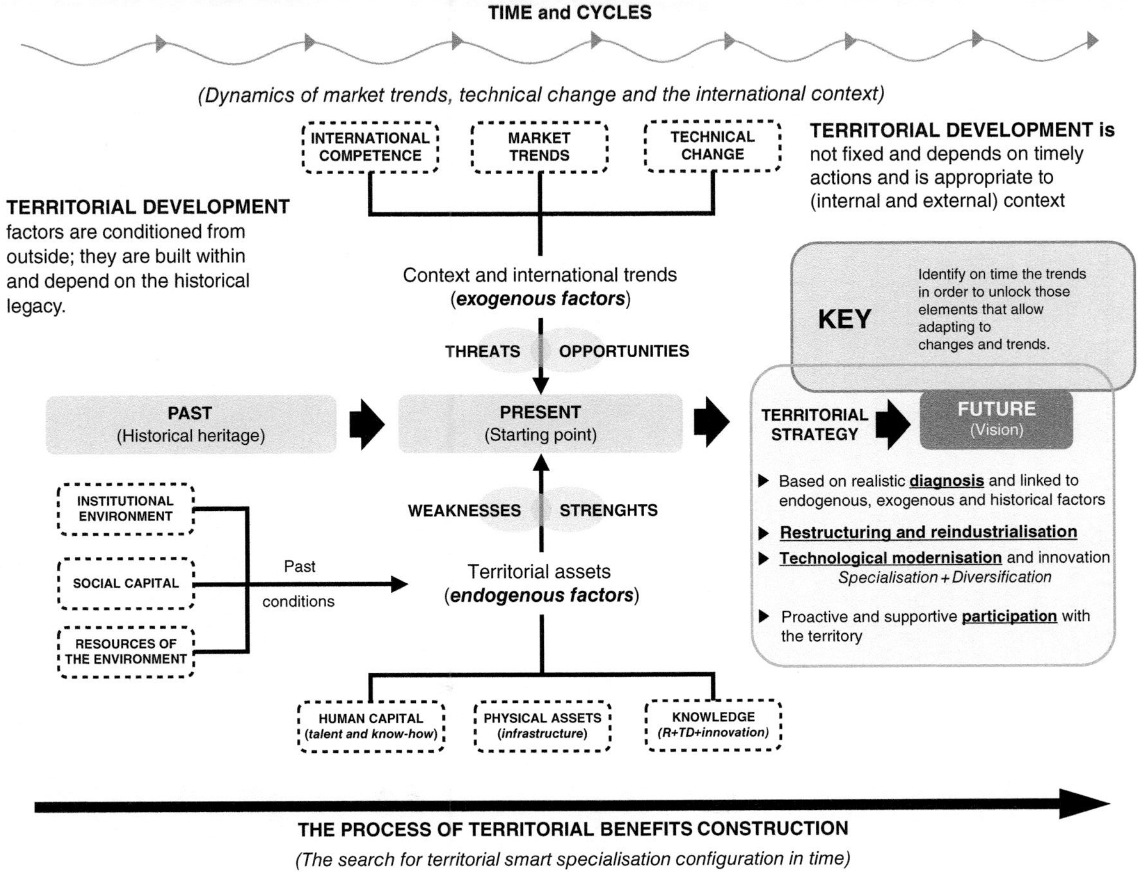

Figure 8.1 Factors in territorial decline

Source: own elaboration

The policies observed in the analyses of regions in decline indicated that it was necessary to determine the type of economy to be developed (Irigoien, 1982): the products, technologies, investments and market sectors to be covered, the organisational and economic integration of the territory and the position it is willing to play within the new international context. As can be seen, a relatively direct similarity exists with current S3 models (JRC, 2012; Barroeta et al., 2013; Brennan and Rakhmatullin, 2015; Sörvik at al., 2016): which territorial specialisation and/or diversification strategy to use within the international context, considering that any action plan must be defined and implemented on a participatory basis. In fact, many authors have emphasised that S3 is not a new concept, but a rediscovery of territorial development applied to regions in decline (Asheim, 2013; Barroeta et al., 2013). Thus, some authors consider S3 more as part of a process that is ongoing (Orkestra, 2014; Del Castillo et al., 2015) and that formally integrates the historical know-how of territorial development (Del Castillo et al., 2017).

As can be seen, the literature of the 1980s and 1990s makes clear allusions to many S3 elements: the need to respond quickly to changes of context (Del Castillo, 1989b), the need to focus on a limited number of specialised diversification priorities (Cunningham, 1982) based on the economic and social characteristics of the territory (Wadley, 1986), having a good participatory and mobilising strategy (Irigoien, 1982; Del Castillo, 1989b), the need for an initially micro enterprise approach to foster the process (Irigoien, 1982; Hassink, 1998) and the pertinence and optimality of concentrating support on the most promising areas, with the vision of generating a subsequent drag-along effect (Cunningham, 1982).

The analysis in the next section will allow us to reference the similarities addressed within the cases of Asturias and the Basque Country, two examples of OIRs in Spain that went through processes of S3.

Comparative evolution of the Basque Country and Asturias

The identification of the factors linked to territorial decline in Asturias and the Basque Country has been made from the main variables described in the theoretical framework (Figure 8.1).

The GDP per capita figures show that the differences between the Basque Country, Asturias and the Spanish average, have increased considerably since the decade of the 1980s: in 1986, the Basque Country and Asturias accounted for 131.1% and 92.6% relative to the Spanish average; in 2014, the figure for the Basque Country increased to 149.0%, while that of Asturias decreased to 87.7%. Furthermore, according to data from the Instituto Nacional de Estadística (INE, Spanish National Statistics Institute), the population decline was more pronounced in Asturias than in the Basque Country during the almost 40 years since the 1980s, which therefore indicates a much smaller growth in GDP.

Other indicators from INE (labour productivity, exports and R&D) reinforce these differences in economic growth:

- In relation to productivity, the figures obtained show a better evolution in the Basque Country up to the year 2000. During the period 2000–2010, both regions seem to have evolved in a similar way, but after 2010 the economic crash appears to have hit Asturias harder again.
- As for exports, the foreign trade data published by the Spanish Ministry MINECO (Datacomex database) shows a significant change in their composition: although Asturias maintained an important concentration of semi-elaborated products, the Basque Country has progressively diversified to niches related to finished product and value-added segments (e.g. capital goods, automotive and aeronautical industries).
- Lastly, regarding R&D effort in terms of GDP, the Basque Country grew from 0.81% at the end of the 1980s to more than 2% in 2015, while Asturias, with 0.4% in 1987, recorded a much more modest increase to 0.8% in 2015.

According to Pontikakis et al. (2009), the unequal composition of the economic structure may help us to understand the causes of the differences between territories, and here between Asturias and the Basque Country.

Taking into account the employment specialisation coefficient of both regions, at the beginning of the 1990s, Asturias had a relative specialisation in energy (7.12) and the primary agricultural and livestock sectors (1.36). In the case of the Basque Country, specialisation in 1990 was confined to manufacturing, with a very significant value (1.65).

Nonetheless, in 2014, the specialisation structure varied considerably in the case of Asturias, as the result of restructuration processes: the energy sector lost 76.4% of its level of specialisation (falling to 1.68), as did the primary sector, which fell by 32.3% (to 0.92%), unlike industry, which increased by 50% (standing at 1.13 in 2014). In the case of the Basque Country, the restructuration process did not generate any significant changes in the coefficient of specialisation of employment, which actually increased from 1.65 to 1.71 (see Graph 8.1).

The importance of the manufacturing sector in both regions also requires a detailed analysis of the composition of this activity. In the case of Asturias, there is a group of industrial sectors that represent a very important part of all industrial production, and, in addition, they concentrate the major part of exports from Spain. Nonetheless, between 2000 and 2010, their importance in the total production of Asturias has declined (top left-hand quadrant): metallurgy, mechanical equipment, chemicals, motor vehicles and other transport materials.

Another group of industrial sectors that also accounts for a considerable percentage of the total production of Asturias have continued to grow in importance since the decade of the 2000s, as well as having a certain potential for exports: other metal products, other food, paper, rubber and plastics.

In the case of the Basque Country, a large number of industrial sectors represent an important part of total industrial production (a higher level of diversification than in Asturias), and also have very high export percentages, such as metallurgy, motor vehicles, other metal products, electronics and electrical equipment, rubber and plastics, other transport materials and chemicals (see Graphs 8.2 and 8.3).

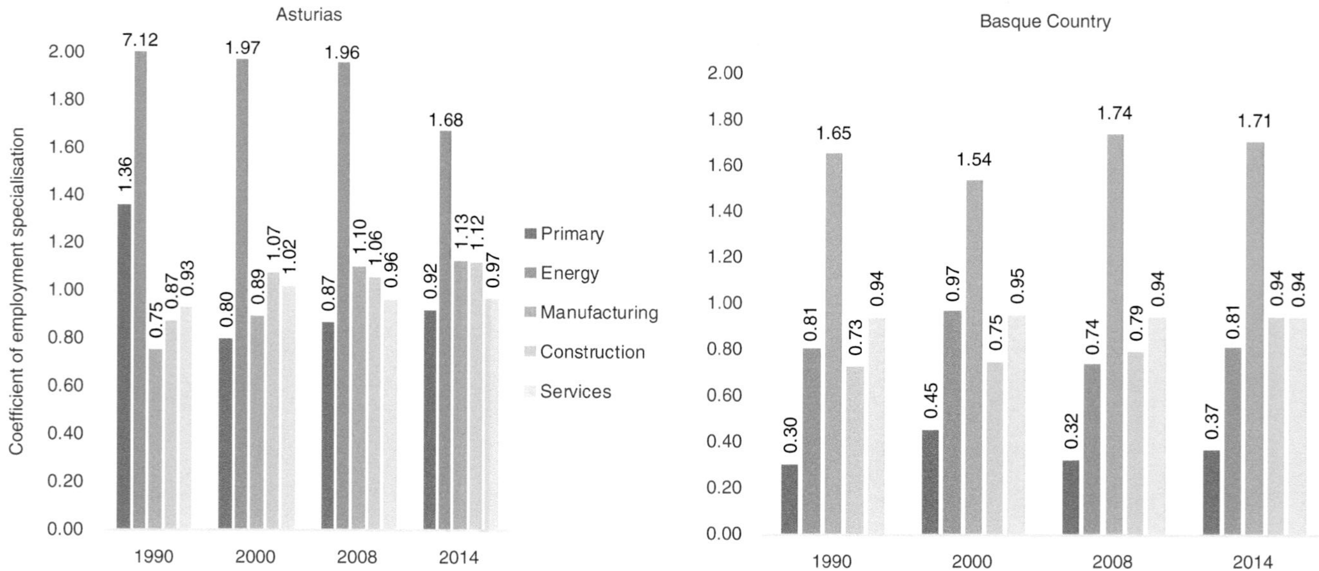

Graph 8.1 Evolution of employment specialisation coefficient by sector

Source: own elaboration from National Statistics Institute (INE) on employment figures

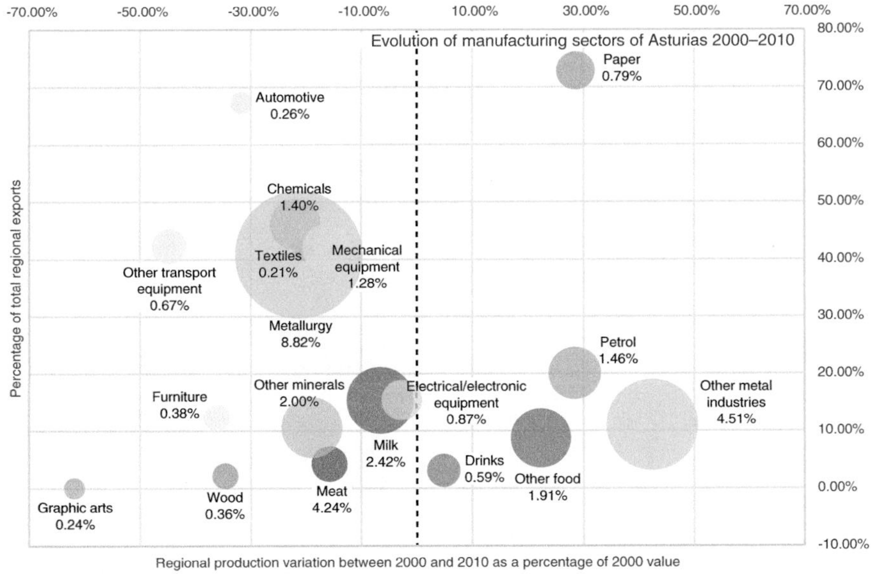

Graph 8.2 Evolution of manufacturing sectors in Asturias 2000–2010

Note: Size of each ball represents percentage of total regional production

Source: own elaboration from regional accounts – SADEI

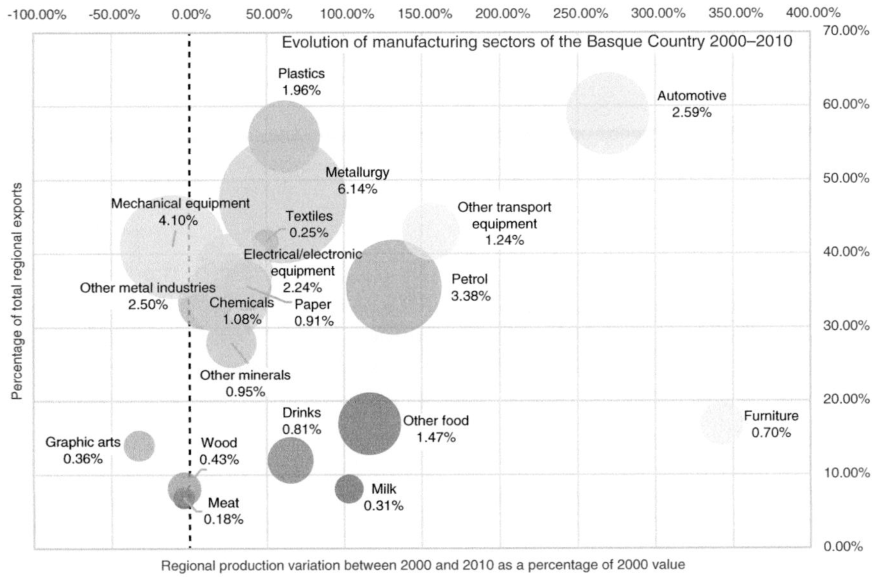

Graph 8.3 Evolution of manufacturing sectors in the Basque Country 2000–2010

Note: Size of each ball represents percentage of total regional production

Source: own elaboration from regional accounts – EUSTAT

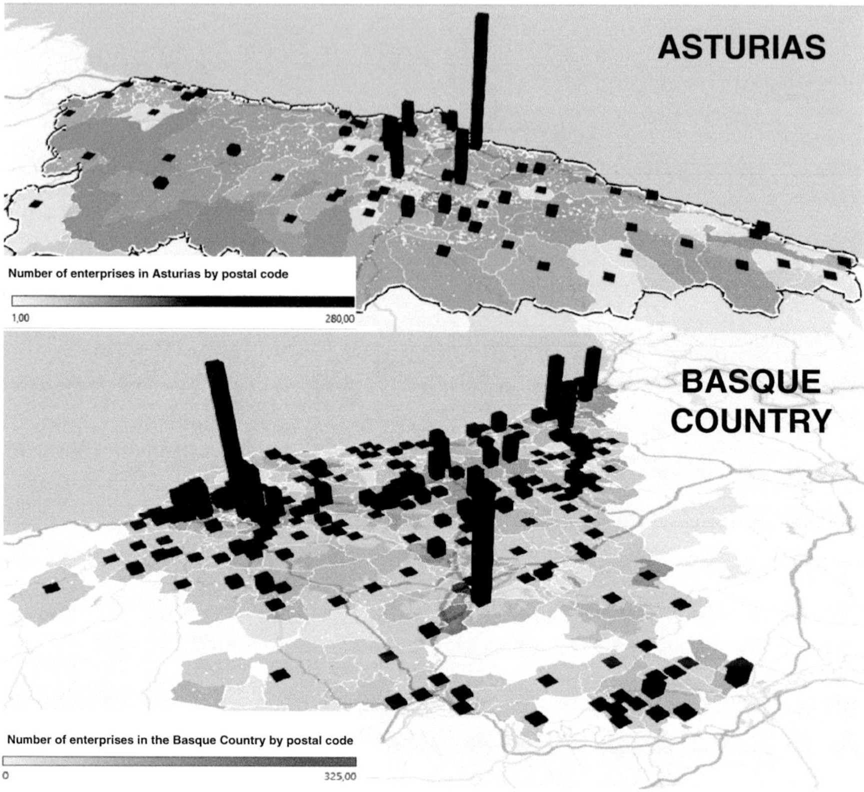

Figure 8.2 Location of economic activity in Asturias and the Basque Country: number of enterprises by postal code (2016)

Source: own elaboration

As for location phenomena, the SABI database describes the location of industrial companies in both regions in 2016. As shown on the maps, the business concentration level in the Basque Country is considerably higher because the absolute number of companies and their employment levels are almost triple those of Asturias, and these companies are dispersed across a geographic area that is half the size, among other reasons (see Figure 8.2).

Lastly, another factor from the theoretical framework that can demonstrate the different behaviour of Asturias and the Basque Country is the level of interrelationships across industrial sectors over time. The following graphs reflect the commercial relations of industry with other sectors in both regions between 2000 and 2010.

In Asturias, in 2000, 95% of intermediate purchases by industry were concentrated in 13 subsectors (more than half from manufacturing). Between

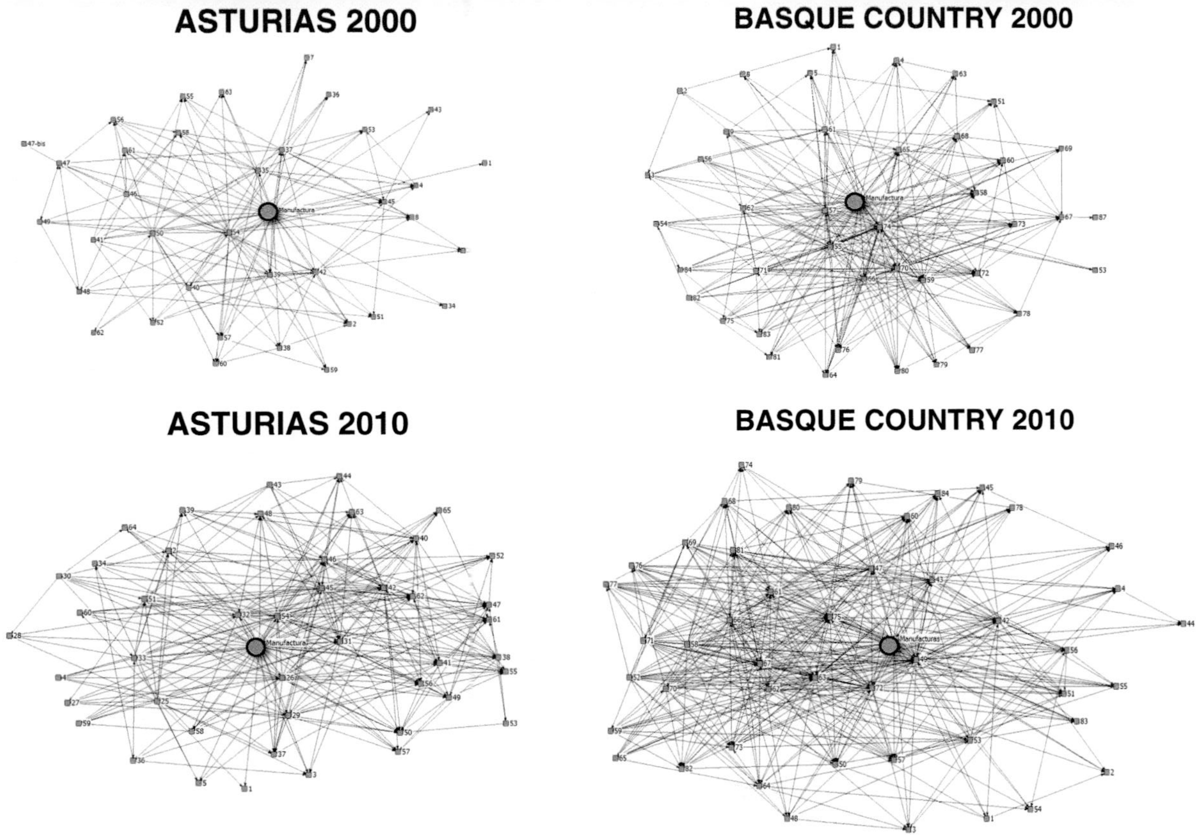

Figure 8.3 Input–output relationship among economic sectors in Asturias and the Basque Country: 2000 and 2010 comparison

Source: own elaboration

2000 and 2010, they appear to undergo a slight increase, as reflected in a denser network of relations and, in short, the increased complexity of the value chain.

In the Basque Country, in 2000, 95% of intermediate purchases by industry were concentrated in 15 subsectors (and, like Asturias, more than 60% from manufacturing). In 2010, input purchases grew considerably, but, unlike what was observed in Asturias, this change led to a significant diversification to new sectors with which no relations had previously been established. For example, in the case of advanced services to industry, whereas in Asturias there was a reduction to a minimum percentage, in the Basque Country they increased considerably (see Figure 8.3).

These seem to indicate that, in line with the theoretical postulates, the density of industrial networks during the decade under study can explain the differences between Asturias and the Basque Country: as Paton (2014) says, this higher complexity in the Basque Country value chains and greater associated diversity in the Basque Country could explain the positive externalities linked to diversification processes, i.e. innovation and opportunities arising from hybridisation between diverse but related sectors.

Along with these economic factors, other aspects related to institutional setting will be analysed in the next section.

Basque Country case: analysis of regional development policies

The Basque Country clearly presents the three policy phases considered in the theoretical framework review and, in particular: 1980–1985 is characterised by restructuring policies; 1985–1990 is characterised by reindustrialisation policies; and the 1990s and subsequent years are characterised by measures and actions focused on new competitive models based on innovation and technology.

Basque reindustrialisation phase: 1980–1991

The 1970s and the first few years of the 1980s were characterised by a series of imbalances that had developed in the Basque economy related to land availability, the technology gap, an excessive concentration of investment in a few mature sectors in a process of decline and a low level of tertiarisation (Plaza and Velasco, 2001). These imbalances were accentuated by the economic crash, which led to the unemployment levels of the region reaching 25%. Within this context, the Basque Government decided to implement an active policy that was contrary to the 'laissez-faire' neoliberal economic ideology prevailing at that time (Azua, 2006).

The first group of policies (1980–1985) included restructuring measures aimed at complementing funds channelled by the Central Government to Basque industry (Gobierno Vasco, 1983). However, despite the restructuring priority, the regional government simultaneously implemented another type of action focused on the integration of new technologies into businesses (IMI[3], CN-100[4] or ECTA[5] programmes) and on promoting internationalisation (representative offices abroad and export consortiums). Regional technological policy had two focal points (Jaureguizar, 1996): support in the consolidation of Technological Centres and the creation and strengthening of business R&D units (at that time, the R&D system was basic, with no Public Research Entities, a young university system and a business sector with no knowledge of R&D). In this setting, the Sociedad para la Promoción y Reconversión Industrial (SPRI, Regional Economic Development Agency) played an increasingly important role in managing the policies defined by the regional government.

Competitiveness phase: 1991–2001

During the 1990s, the importance of competitiveness in the Basque Government strategy constituted an important step forward in the configuration of a territorial strategy and in connecting different agents of the innovation system. This new strategy stressed the need to position technology, knowledge and innovation as the bases of territorial development, and this was a differentiating element with respect to other Spanish regions (Paton, 2014).

One of the most distinguishing characteristics was the step from a 'top-down' to a 'bottom-up' approach (Moso and Olazarán, 2001). Various cluster associations were set up with the intention of providing tools to identify and transmit business needs to knowledge suppliers (mainly Technological Centres).

The new cluster policy gave rise to the creation of committees to facilitate the identification of sectoral technologies and innovations (Moso and Olazarán, 2001), which were also included in the regional technological policy actions, namely, the Industrial Technology Plan (PTI) 1993–1996 and the Science and Technology Plan (PCT) 1997–2000 (Gómez Uranga and Álvarez, 1996).

The government also set up several initiatives focused on business management and the promotion of quality, and in 1993 the Euskalit Quality Promotion Agency was founded.

Knowledge and innovation phase: 2001–2010

At the end of the 1990s, the emphasis on innovation and knowledge was finally consolidated. However, this emphasis led to the creation of a multitude of support plans and programmes, generating duplicity and difficulties in coordination (Paton, 2014; Del Castillo et al., 2017).

In parallel, the regional government decided to promote sectoral diversification to new emerging markets: Biobask 2010 (biotechnology), Nanobasque 2015 (nanotechnology) and Tourgune (tourism) strategies were defined. Additionally, three agencies were set up to roll out policy actions in these sectors.

In 2007, Innobasque (the Basque Innovation Agency) was set up with the aim of disseminating innovation throughout Basque society. At this time, Ikerbasque was also created to promote excellence in basic research by attracting international researchers in priority areas of the region.

Towards smart specialisation: 2010–. . .

At the end of 2009, in a context of international crisis, the Basque Government was targeting its resources at a mix of actions for reconfiguring the sectors in crisis and promoting competitiveness through traditional technology and innovation support measures (Del Castillo et al., 2017).

Simultaneously, the European Commission established a condition for obtaining funds related to R&D within the Cohesion Policy, consisting of a smart specialisation strategy (S3). At that time, the Basque Government was already immersed in the process of defining a new Science, Technology and Innovation Plan (PCTI), which served as a basis for preparing that specialisation strategy. This strategy defined three priorities: advanced manufacturing, energy and biosciences.

The historical review of the policies set up in the Basque case highlights the many similarities between current S3 understanding and the Basque experience since the 1980s. This has led different authors (Navarro et al. 2011; Orkestra, 2014; Paton, 2014; Del Castillo et al., 2017) to affirm that what is termed the "Great Basque Transformation" was in actual fact an S3 process that has been operating for more than 30 years and originated in the reconfiguration processes undertaken to face situations of industrial decline.

Asturias case: analysis of regional development policies

The case of Asturias is a true reflection of a region that, based on a singular supply of natural mineral resources (coal), founded its development model on a mining and iron metal-based industrialisation process.

Over time, the liberalisation process suffered by the Spanish economy at the end of the 1950s and the beginning of the 1960s (which ended with Spain joining the Common Market in the 1980s) and the energy crisis of the 1970s caused the economy of Asturias to undergo a profound recession (García Blanco, 1998). This context, together with conditioning factors related to its economic, social and institutional structure, made it difficult for Asturias to overcome this situation, and the region was converted into the prototype of an 'old industrial area' (Pichierri, 1989).

Prada (2011) concludes that the strong regional dependence on mining and the iron and steel industry aggravated the situation during the crisis of the 1970s and 1980s, which generated a social sentiment of "bewilderment and pessimism".

Reconversion and restructuring policies phase: 1980–1990

The first symptoms of decline in the mining industry of Asturias in the 1960s and the polarisation of the economy based on the iron and steel industries gave rise to various early reconversion policies during the Francoist regime. However, the end of the dictatorship and the later decentralisation process in Spain, along with the lack of a stable government, delayed the implementation of a policy capable of offsetting the decline of the region's economy.

In 1983, two very important measures were implemented in Asturias: Employment Promotion Funds (FPE) and Urgent Reindustrialisation Zones (ZUR). The first of these was an employment policy measure (benefits, requalification and creation of jobs). The second was a combination of territorial and sectorial policies to certain Spanish regions (including Asturias) for encouraging the reindustrialisation of areas in decline.

ZUR policies were a new type of instrument adapted to the territory (Velasco and Del Castillo, 1988) and focused on palliating the loss of jobs generated by the reconversion, increasing the efficiency of investment towards new technologies and products (this is diversification and modernisation).

In any case, as indicated by Ruíz-Valdepeñas (1992), none of the ZUR in Asturias met the initial objectives, which led to an important loss of direct jobs during the 1980s (Fernandez García, 1988).

After ZUR in 1988, the Regional Incentives Law (LIR) was implemented, which established first an even clearer differentiation between territories with Economic Promotion Zones (ZPE) with a greater focus on income and unemployment problems, and, second, Industrial Zones in Decline (ZID) in which the industrial adjustment process was maintained.

Review of the model in the 1990s: reindustrialisation and modernisation: 1991–2011

All of the above led to a review of the industrial policy in the 1990s (Vázquez, 1994): the selection and stimulation of a growing number of activities and simultaneous support for modernisation and restructuring of the two major industrial areas of Asturias. In any case, the different restructuring, reindustrialisation and modernisation measures were characterised by a relative slowness in comparison with other economies in a similar situation (i.e. the Basque Country).

Despite the complexity and heterogeneity of the factors leading to the situation of decline after the 1970s and 1980s, various studies appear to point to four factors (Vázquez, 1994):

1. insufficient supply of communication infrastructures, which led to a certain marginality as compared to the major Spanish and European communication routes
2. imbalances in the labour market, aggravated by the difficulty in retaining qualified workers and their integration into the labour market
3. imbalances in the business fabric: low levels of private capital, cost strategies, bureaucratic organisational structures, excessively strong dependence on public support and low technological and educational levels
4. relatively lower levels of scientific and technological capital in the territory, with the key really lying in combining quantity with applicability, and the need to prioritise a limited number of niches.

In addition to these four elements, García Blanco (1998) adds the strong influence of trade union organisations and the reactive attitude of workers in traditional industries, which conditioned social and institutional interaction and posed difficulties in adjusting and adapting to the new conditions.

Another aspect that is not as clear in traditional analyses but is reflected in the analysis of the input–output relations of Asturias's economy is the low industry–services integration. Vázquez (1994) says: "The private and institutional supply of services to companies in Asturias is low and provided by services outside the region. The demand is also low, particularly for technological and management services."

The combination of these six factors created a strong barrier that made it difficult to overcome the crisis, and also contributes to decline. The difficulty in efficiently reallocating resources and making the most of the endogenous advantages blocked the emergence of new activities that could transform the regional economy.

The industrial policy of Asturias during this period is the result of the achievements of the ZUR, ZID and ZPE policies until the beginning of the 1990s and was relatively intense in terms of industrial reactivation through the generation of industrial zones and territory-based incentives. Through its development agency, Instituto de Desarrollo Económico del Principado de Asturias (IDEPA), the regional government designed and set up different plans between 1990 and 2008 aimed at creating a new supply of land to favour business development and attract investment. Also, IDEPA defined and implemented three Regional Research Plans in the periods 1989–1993, 1994–1999 and 2001–2004. Following this, a new plan was defined with a wider focus (PCTI 2006–2009), which was last updated between 2013 and 2017. The Smart Specialisation Strategy (S3) was also defined during this period.

Other measures implemented by the regional government during the 2000s were based on financial support for investment, entrepreneurship, innovation and internationalisation. Along with these, efforts were made to improve the infrastructures and services for supporting industry (i.e. communications, industrial land and energy infrastructures) as well as to provide an advanced supply of services to industry through the creation of a network of technological centres, business partnerships (clusters) and vouchers for industrial companies.

Towards smart specialisation: 2012–. . .

The S3 strategy of Asturias was set up between 2012 and 2014 following a participatory reflection on regional competitiveness. In this strategy, 16 priorities were selected, grouped into six areas of specialisation. Two of the areas are targeted at markets (Steel Pole and Healthcare Pole), while the other four areas of specialisation represent opportunities for diversification through interrelations based on broad technological domains (IDEPA, 2014).

The S3 entailed an interesting rethinking process in Asturias focused on new ways of public support in the region: first, by trying to reduce the gap between research and enterprise and seek diversification based on the traditional strengths of the territory, and second, by developing new policy instruments. This latter aspect is also clearly observed in the reformulation of IDEPA's internal and support instruments (IDEPA, 2016).

Lessons for other OIRs and LFRs

Over the last few decades, territories have had to face radical structural changes, mainly as a consequence of the extension of the knowledge economy, globalisation, the liberalisation of markets and the appearance of emerging countries that redefine the division of labour in global value chains. These processes have accelerated as a result of the dizzying pace of technological change. Such change has been accompanied by, and has been the cause of, relocations of productive activities to countries with better conditions (in terms of costs and more and more often in terms of talent and knowledge).

The industrial decline processes experienced by the regions of Asturias and the Basque Country during the 1970s and 1980s, and the way in which both regions responded through their policies to these situations, provide us with lessons on how to face the challenge of surfing the 'waves' of innovation and the obsolescence of previous territorial competitiveness models.

As the case studies of Asturias and the Basque Country demonstrate, the situation of decline was very much linked to the prevalence of an established mental mindset that inhibited the system's capacity to develop self-generated growth by exerting a depressive effect on the business potential of the regions. Furthermore, this prevalence did not give rise to a sectorial diversification process, but rather to a specialisation process, thus consolidating the levels of dependency of these territories on activities that accumulated assets and employment in segments that were gradually becoming obsolete in relation to new international trends.

Thus, a regional specialisation process was generated that was, in turn, limited by the progressive disassociation of these regions from elements of economic dynamism and by the flourishing of external diseconomies: a scarcity of quality land, excess specialisation, the inflexibility of the labour market, social conflict and resistance to change.

As a brief outline, certain lessons can be summarised from the regional cases analysed:

- Territorial-based policies are able to improve local factors through basic tangible capacities (communication infrastructures and private services of a high quality), business and cooperation capacities (social capital, transparency and information, organisational transparency), knowledge capacities (infrastructures for the generation and transfer of knowledge, promotion of talent and qualification) and diversification and specialisation capacities (new opportunities for enterprise, ensuring an adequate setting for attracting and retaining economic activity and talent).

- Many of the results observed are linked to the externalities generated from the coherent and systemic approach followed between the mentioned policy dimensions.
- The intensification of capital levels obviously requires an effort obtained internally, but without forgetting the possibilities of adapting external resources (investment, technology, know-how, etc.).
- Industrial transformation requires increased integration of technology into production, and also a greater presence in global value chains.
- The effects of investment and mobilisation will lose their intensity and efficacy if they are not accompanied by a series of changes in the productivity structure towards value-added activities, actions to rectify the imperfections of the internal market (inflexibility and aversion to change), institutional development and cooperation between economic and social agents (social and labour conflict, resistance to change).
- Here, the improvement in human capital and the change in the mental mindset should not be limited to workers only, but must include the entire organisation and, in particular, company management.

The cases analysed show the opportunities behind enhancing the existing possibilities in related activities in terms of production and technology: a mix that means not seeking specialisation or diversification as isolated elements but searching for specialised diversification.

The cases of Asturias and the Basque Country show the differences in terms of how the territorial development policy has been defined and implemented:

- improving local conditions and factor endowment, promoting business modernisation through indirect, systemic actions that require the existence of an adequate and well-structured institutional basis of promotion, coordinated by a shared strategy
- an integral and systematic territorial strategy over time with an appropriate design and an efficient execution, active, positive engagement of economic and social agents, a large dose of institutional cooperation and social concertation, a strong motivation and a radical change in certain mindsets that existed prior to the crisis (see Figure 8.4).

In conclusion, beyond the underlying physical and tangible elements of the industrial model in both regions, the findings of the study lead one to believe that it was more a question of intangible elements linked to the role played by the regional agents, the business fabric and society itself that in each case advanced towards a non-formalised model based on the need to adapt to the new international conditions arising from a crisis. In other words, in each region the different performance levels have been the result of a complex combination of inner capacities and socio-cultural mindsets regarding change and, specifically, the way regional policies have been able to guide these elements in a coherent and systematic direction towards territorial development.

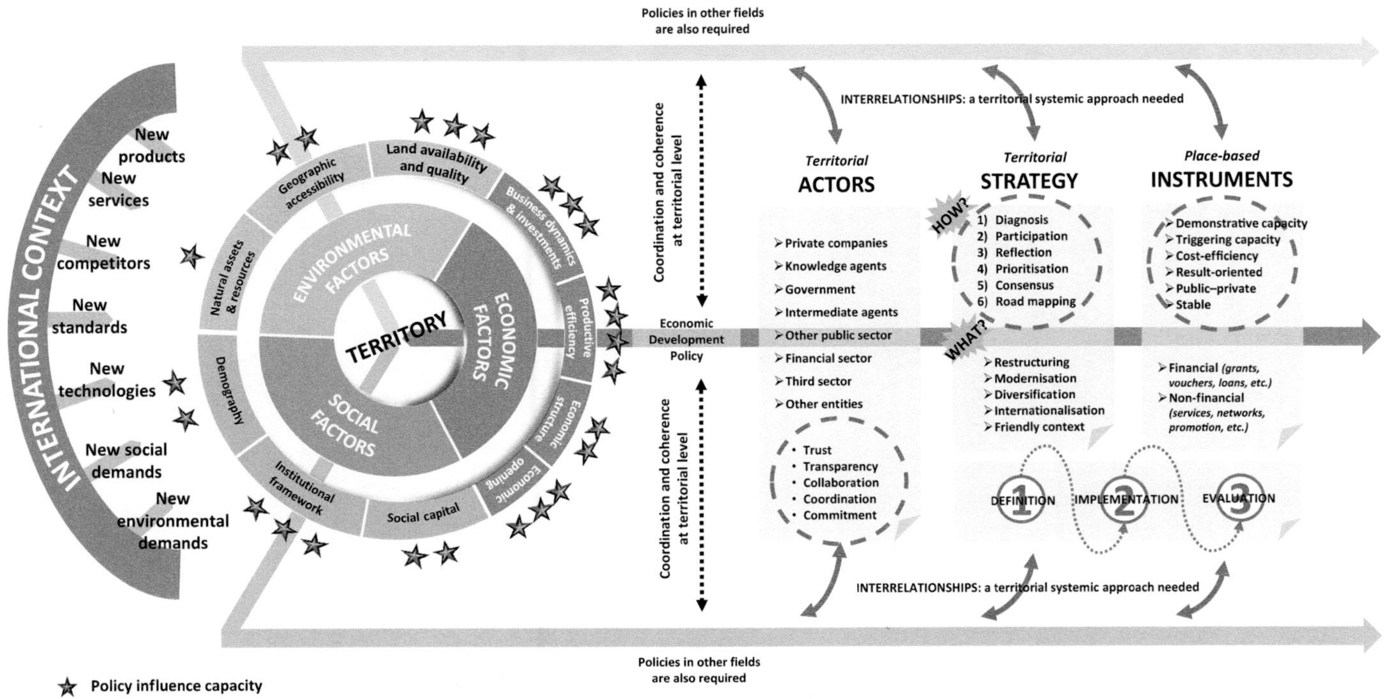

Figure 8.4 Success factors from the old industrial regions cases: a smart specialisation process for less-favoured regions

Source: own elaboration

Notes

1 For example, this work is based on the results of a preliminary study carried out for the Government of Chile within the framework of its Strategic Programme for Smart Specialisation in Advanced Manufacturing. However, concerns about the possibilities of economic transformation models based on natural resource advantages are a constant in many developing countries. Other references can be found in Barroeta et al. (2017).

2 One example of this is seen in the Symposium organised by the Chamber of Commerce of Bilbao, the University of the Basque Country and the Association of Regional Science of the Basque Country in June 1981, attended by representatives from the European regions of Saarland (Germany), Lorraine (France), Wales and Scotland (UK) and Wallonia (Belgium).

3 Programme for the Incorporation of Microelectronics into Industry: this consisted of training centres targeted at citizens to allow them to become familiar with new technologies and the use of computers.

4 100 CNC Programme: its objective was to modernise the production sector and generate a demand for digitalisation for machine tools by financing the purchase of numeric control machines in Basque companies.

5 Advanced Technical Design Equipment Programme: similar to CNC-100 but for financing the purchase of complex, automated production equipment.

References

Asheim, B. (2013). Smart specialization – old wine in new bottles or new wine in old bottles? Presentation at the ERSA Conference, 28 August, Palermo.

Azua, J. (2006). Política Industrial y Competitividad: El caso del País Vasco. Boletín Informativo Techint 321.

Barroeta, B., Gómez, J., Paton, J., Palazuelos, M. and Cabrera, M. (2017). Innovation and Regional Specialisation in Latin America. Seville: JRC Technical Reports..

Barroeta, B., Paton, J. and Del Castillo, J. (2013). Etapas para elaborar una RIS3. INFYDE Working Paper No. 7.

Boschma, R. and Lambooy, J. (1999). Why old industrial regions decline? An exploration of potencial adjustments strategies. European RSA Conference. Dublin.

Brennan, L. and Rakhmatullin, R. (2015). Global Value Chains and Smart Specialisation Strategy. Seville: JRC Technical Reports.

Cunningham, E. (1982). Participation in the seminar: Regiones industrializadas en declive, Bilbao.

Del Castillo, J. (1989a). Social rigidities as a factor of decline in old industrial regions: the case of the Basque Country. In: J. Del Castillo, M. García Crespo and A.S. Musto (Eds.) *Spatial Aspects of the Technological Change*. Spain: UPV/EHU.

Del Castillo, J. (1989b). Elementos para una política regional en áreas industriales tradicionales. In: J. Del Castillo (Ed.) *Regional Development Policies in Areas in Decline*. European Association of Development Research and Training Institutes EADI.

Del Castillo, J. (1989c). The regional aspects of the technological policy. In: J. Del Castillo, M. García Crespo and A.S. Musto (Eds.) *Spatial Aspects of the Technological Change*. Spain: UPV/EHU.

Del Castillo, J., Paton, J., and Barroeta, B. (2015) Smart specialisation for economic change: the case of Spain. *Symphonya. Emerging Issues in Management*, pp. 30–34.

Del Castillo, J., Paton, J. and Barroeta, B. (2017). The Great Basque Competitive Transformation towards sustainable innovations. In: L. Kebir, O. Crevoisier, P. Costa and V. Peyrache-Gadeau (Eds.) *Sustainable Innovations and Regional Development*. Cheltenham, UK: Edgar Elgar Publishing.

Fernandez García, A. (1988). La reconversión industrial en España: impacto regional y trasformaciones espaciales. *ERIA*, *17*, 191–200.

García Blanco, J.M. (1998). Declive económico y políticas regionales: el caso de Asturias. *Revista Española de Investigaciones Sociológicas*, *83*, 87–119.

Gobierno Vasco (1983). Organización de la Política Industrial y Energética. Vitoria.

Gómez Uranga, M. and Álvarez, B.A. (1996). Análisis de las estructuras de interfaz en el sistema de innovación del a C.A.V. *Ekonomiaz*, *35*, 213–243.

Hassink, R. (1998). What does the learning region mean for economic geography? Paper presented at the RSA International Conference, Frankfurt, Germany.

IDEPA (2014). Estrategia RIS3 de Asturias 2014–2020. Oviedo

IDEPA (2016). Plan Estratégico del Instituto de Desarrollo Económico del Principado de Asturias 2017–2019. Oviedo

Irigoien (1982). La economía de Euskadi. Presentation at the seminar: Regiones industrializadas en declive. Bilbao

Jacobs, J. (1984). *Cities and the Wealth of Nations*. London: Penguin Books.

Jaureguizar, J. (1996). Política Científica y tecnológica en la CAPV. In: XII Congreso de Estudios Vascos: Ciencia, Tecnología y cambio social en Euskal Herria. Euskao Ikaskuntza. Donostia, pp. 163–180.

JRC (2012). Guide on Research and Innovation Strategy for Smart Specialisation: RIS3 Guide. Sevilla.

Markusen, A. (1985). *Profit Cycles, Oligopoly and Regional Development*. London: McMillan.

Martin, R. (2009). Rethinking regional path dependence: beyond lock-in to evolution. *Papers in Evolutionary Economic Geography*. Utrecht University.

Moso, R. and Olazarán, M. (2001). Actores, ideas e instituciones: políticas tecnológicas regionales y creación del sistema I+D en la Comunidad Autónoma del País Vasco. In: M. Olazarán and M. Gómez Uranga (Eds.) *Sistemas Regionales de Innovación*. Spain: UPV/EHU.

Musto, A.S. (1989). Challenges to European economics and politics. In: J. Del Castillo (Ed). *Regional Development Policies in Areas in Decline*. Germany: European Association of Development Research and Training Institutes EADI.

Navarro, M., Aranguren, M.J. and Magro, E. (2011). Smart Specialisation Strategies: The Case of the Basque Country. *Orkestra* Working Paper Series in Territorial Competitiveness. Donostia.

Nelson, R.R. (1995). Recent evolutionary theorizing about economic change. *Journal of Economic Literature*, *33*(1), 48–90.

Orkestra (2014). Informe de Competitividad del País Vasco. Donostia.

Paton, J. (2014). Los clusters. Piezas clave de la economía del conocimiento. PhD thesis. Spain: UPV/EHU.

Paton, J., Del Castillo, J. and Barroeta, B. (2017). Sustainable Equilibrium Index: a measure to analyse the systemic dependences in territorial development. *Journal of Economics and Public Finance*, *3*(2), 239–257.

Pichierri, A. (1989). *Strategie contro il declino in aree di antica industrializzazione*. Torino: Rosenberg & Sellier.

Plaza, B. and Velasco, R. (2001). Política Industrial de las Comunidades Autónomas: Análisis de la descentralización de la Política Industrial Española 1980–2000. Círculo de Empresarios Vascos. Bilbao.

Pontikakis, D., Kyriakou, D. and Van Bavel, R. (Eds.) (2009). The Question of R&D Specialisation: Perspectives and Policy Implications. JRC Technical Reports. Seville: European Communities.

Prada, J. (2011). Desarrollo, patrimonio y políticas de revitalización en ciudades intermedias de especialización minero-industrial: el caso de Langreo (Asturias). CES del Principado de Asturias. Oviedo.

Rees, J. (1979). Technological change and regional shifts in American manufacturing. *Professional Geographer, 31*(1), 45–54.

Ruíz-Valdepeñas, H.P. (1992). Reconversión y reestructuración industrial en Asturias. *ERIA, 28*, 151–163.

Sörvik, J., Midtkandl, I., Marocchi, Ch. and Uyarra, E. (2016). How outward-looking is smart specialisation? Seville: JRC Technical Reports.

Steiner, M. (1985). Old industrial areas: a theoretical approach. *Urban Studies, 22*(5), 387–397.

Storper, M. (1992). The limits to globalization: technology districts and industrial growth. *Economic Geography, 68*(1), 60–93.

Valdaliso, J.M. (2013). Las estrategias de desarrollo económico del País Vasco: una perspectiva histórica. *Ekonomiaz, 83*, 146–174.

Vázquez, J.A. (1994). Estrategias para la reindustrialización de Asturias. *Revista Asturiana de Economía, 1*, 111–120.

Velasco, R. and Del Castillo, J. (1988). Posibles soluciones para las regiones industriales en declive. *Papeles de Economía Española, 35*, 208–218.

Wadley, D. (1986). Restructuration régionale. Paris: OECD.

9 Digital Innovation Hubs as enablers of Smart Specialisation in Sparsely Populated Areas

Jens Sörvik

Introduction

The concept of Digital Innovation Hubs (DIHs) as policy initiatives is quite recent and was formally launched in the European Commission (EC) Communication on "Digitising European Industry" (European Commission, 2016a). In this communication, a DIH is defined as helping "companies in the region become more competitive by improving their business/production processes as well as products (and services) by means of digital technology". DIHs are described as actors that also support the development of the surrounding innovation ecosystem (European Commission, 2017). The design of the DIH should be based on regional needs and existing capabilities, connecting it to S3: "every DIH will have its own specialisation, in line with the smart specialisation priorities of a region. Through the networking of DIHs, competences not available within the regional DIH may be found in another DIH" (European Commission, 2017).

This chapter explores the role DIHs can play in S3 processes in Sparsely Populated Areas (SPAs). S3 is a place-based approach addressing a region's unique development potentials through targeted efforts to support the emergence of new domains to foster regional growth through structural change (European Commission, 2012; Foray, 2015; Gianelle et al., 2016). S3 consists of horizontal measures addressing the regional innovation ecosystem, regardless of economic domains, and a limited number of priority domains, where regions make targeted efforts (McCann and Ortega-Argilés, 2014). To identify vertical domains of discovery is central to the smart specialisation concept, according to Foray (2015): "an entrepreneurial discovery is a new area of structural change that opens up, into which a whole segment of an industry can move to explore it and generate numerous innovations". This entrepreneurial discovery process (EDP) aims at identifying areas of discovery and mobilising market or entrepreneurial knowledge, R&D-based knowledge and users to know where the greater potential for regional growth is. Figure 9.1 presents a stylised strategy inspired by some of the vertical priority domains of Norrbotten and Västerbotten and some of their horizontal activities.

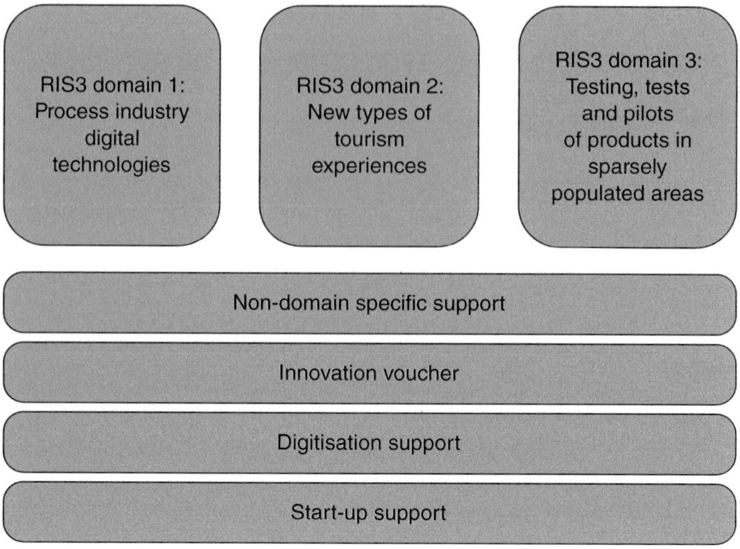

Figure 9.1 Schematic illustration of horizontal and vertical activities in an S3
Source: own elaboration

A DIH can play a role in both dimensions, horizontally, by providing digitalisation support to all sectors, and vertically, they can lead or take part in processes that mobilise stakeholders. These could include setting up arenas to identify regional challenges and opportunities, as well as orchestrating processes for developing road maps, designing targeted policy mixes and aligning stakeholder activities. A DIH can also support the S3 design process, by providing information for decision-making, both by the DIH staff's own knowledge and by mobilising stakeholders and committing them to the process. They can also secure stakeholder commitment to the S3 process after the first rounds of design have been carried out in a continuous design process (Sörvik and Midtkandal, 2017).

The specific characteristics and features of SPAs, often with abundant natural resources, large companies in primary and secondary industries and organisationally thinner regional innovation systems (RISs) (Isaksen and Trippl, 2017) with limited human capital, a lack of agglomeration economies and fewer intermediary organisations covering large distances, pose challenges for the S3 concept. At the same time, S3 has been identified as a viable approach in SPAs and that information and communications technology (ICT) is a specific enabling opportunity for SPAs. Teräs et al. (2015) pointed out that SPAs need to put an emphasis on a strategy development process incorporating even more profound regional analysis with stakeholder engagement in inclusive processes, as well as on strengthening their competitiveness with extra-regional knowledge and networking pipelines, and this even more so than other types of regions, considering the lack of critical mass. Isaksen and Trippl (2017) also emphasise the role of extra-regional knowledge and targeted public interventions for development path renewal in SPAs. Nuur and Laestadius (2010) have pinpointed the importance of support for small-firm networking and ICT. The latter can help peripheral actors overcome their locational disadvantage in terms of knowledge formation and exchanges and can provide access to markets and resources.

DIH is a relatively newly launched concept, which shares traits with clusters and cluster initiatives. The concept of clusters was popularised by Michael Porter (1990, 1998) and addresses the role of externalities from collocation of economic actors active in a related economic field. Related to this are cluster initiatives that are efforts aimed at strengthening the competitiveness of the cluster (Sölvell et al., 2003). Similarly, DIHs are ecosystems of actors involved in digitalisation, and it is a term used for policy initiatives to support digitalisation in existing industries. Many cluster organisations have worked cross-sectorially, organising multi-stakeholder projects, and have participated in regional development processes, which supports the idea of cluster organisations or DIHs taking a role in S3 processes in both their design and their implementation (European Commission, 2013, 2016b). As DIHs build upon a network of competences to support digitalisation, it is an interesting model for SPAs that need to cover large distances and cannot build up fully fledged competence centres in all locations of a territory.

This chapter explores the different roles of DIHs in S3 processes in SPAs and outlines issues and challenges based on the experiences of cluster initiatives and regional strategies in northern Swedish SPAs. A comparative case study methodology was chosen, as it broadens the range of possible data, supporting the identification of what may be regional-specific and what can be common traits, and providing a richer and deeper understanding of the data (Yin, 2003). The data for this chapter come from a literature review (academic articles and evaluation reports) and from interviews with cluster managers, regional officials, company representatives, as well as academics involved in the initiatives to get a multi-stakeholder perspective triangulating different actors' views.

Smart Specialisation in Sweden

S3 development in Sweden has not been a process that strictly follows the steps outlined in the EC's S3 guide (European Commission, 2012), and regions have supported innovation preceding the EC's requirements. In the negotiations with the EC for the 2014–2020 European Structural and Investment Funds (ESIF) programmes, Sweden declared it has a multilevel S3 framework comprising several different strategies for research and innovation, including Regional Development Strategies, Regional Innovation Strategies, the National Innovation Strategy and the Research and Innovation bill. Then, later, a few Swedish regions have developed dedicated S3 following the model proposed by the EC.

In Norrbotten, Västerbotten and Gävleborg, this is not the case. The strategies of these regions, rather, are the outcome of a long experience of working with regional innovation support. They have a systemic perspective, with different forms of horizontal support, but they also entail focused activities, such as cluster initiatives. In comparison to a description of the S3 conceptual process, the activities in these regions are not as coherent, but comprise several more parallel processes incorporating a high degree of different regional actors and projects. Yet, there are many relevant experiences from these activities that can be interpreted and understood for an S3 context. These regions are also currently engaging in processes to develop new RISs, and in these they are following the S3 concept to a greater extent.

In this chapter, the focus is on two cluster initiatives that have functioned like DIHs in their regions, in that they have worked, with projects to upgrade existing and mature industries. They have also carried out processes to mobilise actors and set up multi-stakeholder projects in their specific areas to develop new technology and market domains. The initiatives are: Fiber Optic Valley (FOV) in the Gävleborg region, focusing on broadband and sensor technologies, and ProcessIT, focusing on ICT for process industries in the Västerbotten and Norrbotten regions.

These cluster initiatives are in northern Swedish regions, which are characterised by a division into sparsely populated inland regions and agglomerations of population, as well as industries and research capabilities in coastal cities. The primary and process industries are very important (forestry, paper, mining, metals), both the large multinational companies and their suppliers.

FOV and ProcessIT are both well anchored in their respective RISs, and early on were acknowledged at the national level by being winners of the Swedish Innovation Agency VINNOVA's RIS programme Vinnväxt.[1] Process IT and FOV are also participants in the Strategic Innovation Programmes,[2] another VINNOVA programme, with the purpose of stimulating long-term relations between actors in multi-stakeholder constellations for the development of Swedish national-level areas of strength.

Fiber Optic Valley (FOV)

FOV supports commercialisation of ideas, SMEs to grow and find new markets and larger companies in matchmaking activities. The company set up innovation projects involving industry, universities and the public sector in the areas of broadband and sensor technology, also providing facilities for testing these, and supports the identification of funding. It also supports more general innovation and digitalisation efforts in the region.

FOV works in close collaboration with the research centre STC (Sensible Things that Communicate) at the Mid Sweden University, the research institute Acreo Swedish ICT (now RISE Acreo) and around 70 industrial actors, including multinational enterprises (MNEs) like Ericsson, growing companies like Hexatronics and start-ups like People in the Park, but also public actors like the municipalities and the Regional Development Agency.

FOV is working as an innovation ecosystem strengthening hub; it supports innovators, both in coastal areas and also carrying out targeted efforts to more rural areas. It has at times taken on the role of supporting structural change. As an example, Ericsson closed a large plant for fibres in Hudiksvall and FOV took on the role of supporting the change process and supported the establishment of start-ups and the training of personnel, as well as attracting a new industrial actor to the region, i.e. Hexatronics.

FOV originated out of an observation that the region had a high concentration of actors with strategic competences in broadband technologies, which started a discussion on how this could be further enhanced to benefit the region and its companies. The idea was supported by the municipality of Hudiksvall that had identified this as a possible growth area and supported a project in 1999 to set up a city-wide broadband network, which became a cornerstone of FOV's test facilities. In 2001, Acreo set up their Fibre Lab for contract research, and in 2002 they set up a national test bed for fibre optic solutions. In the neighbouring town of Sundsvall, the Mid Sweden University began to focus on fibre technology during this period.

As of 2017, FOV has become incorporated in the Swedish Research Institute group, RISE. FOV will be part of a unit providing SME support in, among other areas, digitalisation, not only in the region of Gävleborg but also on a national level. Connected to this there is an association, where industry and the public sector are members, that guides FOV's work. This was created as a way of anchoring FOV in the region.

Region Gävleborg is in the process of updating their regional innovation strategy, and in this they follow the S3 approach more closely than previously. Region Gävleborg more clearly points out priority domains (smart sustainable cities, materials technology and sustainable production, sustainable and inclusive working life and digital services and processes), in which they will work in more depth with stakeholders across different sectors. These domains were identified in a process involving representatives from regional higher education institutions, cluster organisations, innovation support organisations like incubators and science parks, the regional development agency and companies that met at several workshops to identify the domains. Region Gävleborg also used external consultants to carry out a quantitatively oriented analysis to identify key areas of strength to support the decision-making process. The region is now in the process of further narrowing down the domains, to give them more focus, and creating specific action plans for each domain.

Digitalisation is a horizontal activity that supports all areas. In this work, FOV is an important partner together with the other regional cluster organisations on ICT. The region is also increasing the number of collaborative projects and the setting up of open arenas, where clusters are considered vital because of their experience in working cross-sectorially (even though Region Gävleborg would like to increase the inclusion of civil society in these processes).

Region Gävleborg is emphasising the need to be able to provide a distributed support network, so that companies will not be required to go to central cities for support. To guarantee support also to inland areas through this type of distributed support network and on a long-term basis, Region Gävleborg and the municipality of Hudiksvall have set up a long-term contract for the service of regional innovation support from FOV, where the staff of FOV will travel to companies to provide support.

Within the region, FOV functions primarily as an innovation intermediary, and on a national level, FOV works more with a strict focus on sensors, fibres and optics. At the same time, in their new costume of RISE, they will work nationally with digitalisation support. They also participate in EU-level projects, such as the Interreg project (Erudite),[3] which focuses on the digitalisation of sparsely populated regions.

FOV had a major crisis in 2012, which led to the removal of many in-house competences and a focus on enabling others to initiate projects and assisting them in identifying funding sources – in our terms, becoming more horizontal. The respondents point to the fact that FOV's most successful role has indeed been as an innovation intermediary. The staff are knowledgeable about other key innovation actors and possible funding sources; one respondent calls the staff a "reseller of public money". The staff are also skilled and well positioned to organise cross-sectorial and collaborative projects.

The company has been running broadly targeted (entire region) projects, with support for the provision of small-sized digitalisation projects. One important project was a 'needs' inventory that yielded a good map of regional SME and industry needs, also identifying the number of SMEs with innovation potential (1000 out of 10 000 registered SMEs) and creating stronger relationships with these companies. This activity is indicated by the respondents as possibly the most vital for a cluster organisation. Another successful activity has been the digitalisation project, Kickstart, where SMEs are provided with three days of training in order to digitalise their operations. This is now being scaled up to the national level.[4]

In the beginning of its existence, FOV with its focus on broadband technologies supported regional processes of rolling out broadband, and access to a proper infrastructure is something all respondents point to as key for the competitiveness of SPAs, and it is also one of the target areas for the region's development work. FOV was involved in many projects exploring how to increase broadband coverage in sparsely populated regions. These activities were carried out to develop the region, by creating better opportunities for actors in remote areas, but also to create business opportunities for the regional technology providers.

There are two interesting FOV members located in the inner part of the region as a result of the existence of good broadband. Sense Air is a globally competitive innovation-based sensor company with a large staff of engineers and researchers. The founders wanted to live in their current location, and proper ICT infrastructure allowed them to do that. Similarly, there is People in the Park, a company that develops ICT solutions for film and TV production and carries out post-production of video online, which requires access to high bandwidth. The entrepreneur behind this company had worked outside of the region but wanted to return to live in one of the more sparsely populated parts. FOV made it easier for him to re-establish himself there. They helped with projects to get the proper infrastructure and to develop new types of software. FOV helped him both financially and to navigate different systems to succeed with his ideas and to connect him with right people to develop them further.

FOV has not worked in the manner of the S3 conceptual model of a priority area working group, developing a roadmap and policy mix. It is more of a flag-holder to stimulate developments around ICT, broadband and sensor technologies in the region and to support emerging activities. It has been one factor in facilitating the establishment of fibre optic and sensor activities in the region. It has done this through working at many levels, lending support to existing industries, start-ups and the emergence of new ideas (e.g. boosting innovation competition). FOV has also supported the development of an education services company (IFTAC) that trains and certifies broadband technicians to support broadband implementation processes. It has also worked closely with the STC research centre, which has grown from a staff of two, with the emergence of the area of forest and sensor-based ICT, to a staff of over 60. One respondent expressed it as support rather than ownership of the process of the development of broadband and sensor technologies in the region. FOV's work in conjunction with industrial development, the work of RISE Acreo and the Mid Sweden University has stimulated growth and the emergence of new industry with a more holistic profile transforming the industrial ecosystem.

At the same time, FOV seems to have become less focused domain-wise over time and is moving to a more generalised digitalisation support role, with less of their earlier focus on fibre and sensor technologies.

ProcessIT Innovations

ProcessIT Innovations is a collaborative innovation centre located at the University of Umeå and Luleå Technical University that aims to stimulate the growth of new companies and upgrade existing companies from process and manufacturing industries, by supporting the development of innovative products and services by means of digitalisation technologies through the provision of relevant research competence and support to collaborative projects.

ProcessIT originated from a process whereby a network called Internet Bay from Luleå mapped out long-term industry needs for 20 regional process and manufacturing companies. The process brought a realisation that, to solve some of the long-term and complex issues, there was a need for a more stable organisation, which led to the founding of ProcessIT in 2002.

ProcessIT members include process and engineering industries and ICT companies in the region, the universities of Umeå and Luleå, the four coastal municipalities (Luleå, Piteå, Umeå and Skellefteå) and the county administrative boards of Västerbotten and Norrbotten.

ProcessIT does not have any formal responsibility within either of the two regional innovation strategy processes, but leading staff members from the organisation have been participating in the processes of designing the regional development strategies, both in Västerbotten and in Norrbotten. The organisation also carries out several vital projects within the strategy and works closely with the regional administration. They are regarded as a long-term and important strategic partner, for which they receive institutional support.

In Norrbotten, the regional development agency is currently developing a new innovation strategy, where the focus will be to support diversification. The agency is considering having a part called the Institutional Regional Innovation System that works long term in established sectors with critical mass. There will then be one part that is more flexible in meeting new and emerging needs, such as sudden opportunities arising from foreign direct investments, like the establishment of Facebook in the region or a need to work with some types of digitalisation, which they call an entrepreneurial RIS. These are shorter-term activities that may cease after some time.

Region Norrbotten perceives that ProcessIT will play a significant role in both strengthening existing industries and in supporting emerging industries. The regional respondent indicates that ProcessIT's knowledge about the needs of the processing industry, SMEs and existing knowledge within academia is vital, as is its knowledge about global trends and bringing long-term perspectives. ProcessIT is an important partner and has participated in both designing the strategy and implementing it. However, Region Norrbotten does not see it as the leading partner in managing an S3 domain.

In Västerbotten, there are many actors and organisations that are active in supporting digitalisation. ProcessIT is one of the most well-established actors and is a trusted speaking partner for the region in strategy development and implementation. They are recognised for their knowledge of industry needs and knowledge-based opportunities. In Västerbotten, regional authorities align their regional innovation strategy with their digital agenda; they want to combine R&I with ICT and support digital entrepreneurship. ProcessIT is a partner in both regional processes, e.g. through the SPIN project that aims to speed up digitalisation processes in the region.

In Västerbotten, they are about to begin with something called digitalisation pilots that act as DIHs in connecting actors seeking help with digitalisation and competence centres and innovation support services that can help them. For this, they are considering actors that would be perceived as strictly neutral, not representing a vested interest and able to cover their geographic area. This will be divided into three geographical zones, with a pilot in each that would also collaborate.

In Västerbotten, there are various efforts ongoing to support digitalisation, with a focus also on SPAs, in which ProcessIT is participating. For example, the Inland Technology Park (Inlandets Teknikpark) that supports local industry by training staff and students in new ICT-based manufacturing skills. They have also been active in the Change Agents (Förändringsagenterna) programme, where manufacturing companies have been coached to acquire new digital solutions.

ProcessIT uses the Internet as a metaphor for distributed knowledge, describing themselves as in a network of hubs and nodes that have different knowledge and capabilities and provide a differentiated range of support. Where hubs are more loaded with deeper knowledge, this can be accessed by partners from other nodes, with fewer layers of services, as well as from hubs. The different hubs and nodes differ not only in their layers of services but also in the types of capabilities they possess. Knowledge in the different parts can be accessed and used from any entry point. ProcessIT sees itself as a hub that participates in regional, national and EU processes.

The Inland node project, in which ProcessIT is involved, reflects this idea. It is a support network founded by three municipalities, the regional administration and ProcessIT. It draws upon the specialisation of innovation support competences in the different localities (Åsele, Vilhelmina and Dorotea) and in ProcessIT. The network provides differentiated services, depending on the location, but pools and links resources to provide adequate support through the network. Connected to this also is the Technology Park of the Inland,[5] which ProcessIT supports by linking in needed skills, especially digital production management. The Technology Park supports the digitalisation of manufacturing industry in the inland area of Västerbotten and is collocated with the Malgomaj gymnasium (secondary school), which educates and develops skills related to manufacturing industry.

ProcessIT's work in developing the area around process industrial ICT can be seen as meeting the strategic issues expressed by industry, with new projects emerging over time, and supporting start-ups and developing new academic knowledge in the field. It has not been the type of priority domain development as described in the S3 concept; the approach is more that of supporting several projects within a defined niche, which evolves over time, rather than a specific plan driving towards that end.

ProcessIT provides differentiated support in different geographies and to different actors. For high-tech and larger companies, they are engaged in more complex longer-term processes on the national and global scales. For many SMEs, especially those in the inland region, it provides more routine-based knowledge and support more connected to current businesses. However, through its role and the possibility of supporting both actors and geographies, it can also support regional linkages and contacts between suppliers and global arrowhead companies. One of the respondents pointed to the fact that the larger companies are interested in a strong base of local suppliers to provide innovative solutions, and these local suppliers can follow the standards and requirements of the global markets. Furthermore, ProcessIT is also interested in establishing a good base for recruiting staff. This is needed for staying competitive in the global markets, but also to stay competitive in the internal value chains of multinational companies, where there is constant competition between different plant locations.

Central to ProcessIT's processes are investigations into the different needs of industry, where R&I needs and funding possibilities are identified and joint projects are designed. ProcessIT also scans the horizon for long-term trends in related industries and brings those to discussions with industry representatives. The industry is interested in the coming technological developments (3–8 years away) and the future changes that will require them to adapt their business models. With this in mind, networking with potential partners, such as suppliers and researchers, is most important, both to identify possibilities and to carry out joint development projects to shape the future. ProcessIT provides companies with a clearer channel into academia and facilitates collaboration; they have found it to be important that the industrial partners lead the processes and ProcessIT supports them.

ProcessIT carries out collaborative projects, involving manufacturing, the process and mining industries, suppliers and academia, that have an impact on value chains and upgrade the participants through numerous types of inventions, which would not have happened without these broad stakeholder constellations. An example is the Digital Mine Project, for which Boliden, Ericsson, Telia, Volvo CE, ABB, Wolfit, RISE SICS and Luleå Technical University are testing 5G-related technologies (sensors, vehicles, ventilation, networks, etc.) in a mine, which has led to important inputs to the respective technology domains and has created a safer mining environment.

ProcessIT has also played an important role in setting up the UMIT Research Lab, a strategic research area into real-time physics and simulation at Umeå University. This is a growing area attracting resources and researchers, which has already generated several start-ups, such as Algoryx and Elastisys, that have entered the 33-listan[6], a ranking of Sweden's most innovative companies.

ProcessIT is also part of several national- and EU-level initiatives that take a more comprehensive approach. For example, together with the cluster Automation region, it has gathered together Swedish suppliers and manufacturing and process industries into the strategic innovation programme (SIP) PiiA.[7] PiiA connects regional initiatives with national actors to develop new technology, new business models and new skills. ProcessIT is also active in the SIP for the Mining and Metal Industry.[8] On a European level, it is active in ARTEMIS,[9] an industry association for Embedded Intelligent Systems that promotes the R&I interests of its members and is driving the development of a European strategy for embedded intelligent systems.

Discussion

S3 development in SPAs differs from that in non-SPAs; there are fewer agglomerations, longer distances and a high degree of specialisation in a few areas. SPAs need to support and maintain the competitiveness of these spearheads, as well as supporting new niches and innovation activities in remote areas, with an increased need to connect to extra-regional resources.

What can be observed in the cases described above is that DIHs can play several roles: in upgrading established industries, in stimulating projects in new industrial areas and in acting as coordinators for mobilising industry. The regional respondents point to the fact, however, that a 'hubs and nodes' model may be the necessary next step for SPAs. Each location cannot develop competences in all areas, but needs to develop networks that can serve as entry points of support, which can then connect beneficiaries with relevant specialised competences to form projects or support industries. There will be a differentiation between nodes in layers of services and competences. This would form a network of innovation support actors having different focuses, competences and capabilities, depending on their geographical location and their main local needs, but that can, through active networking and knowledge of other nodes and hubs, draw upon other skill sets when there is a need to. For it to function correctly, there is a need for actors in the network, which is in constant contact with industry, academia and other parts of the innovation system, to be aware of needs and possibilities and to cater for and solve their specific needs. These needs differ between SMEs and multinationals; in simple terms, SMEs need more direct general innovation support and multinationals need more medium-term horizon projects. At the same time, it should be of interest to both SMEs and multinationals that DIHs can connect them in various projects. The intermediaries in the case regions seem to work in the regional setting more as project initiators or opportunities brokers and, especially in the inland region, more as a connector/facilitator between regional actors, with less of a thematic focus. The thematic ICT focus becomes more important when connecting some of the more advanced regional actors in national and international projects, and this especially in the case of FOV.

The clusters have had important roles in the regional strategy work, both as speaking partners for the design of strategies and in implementing activities. The clusters are signposted as important partners for their domains and are knowledgeable about academic and industry needs and competences as well as global trends. However, they have not taken on the role of leading a priority domain (the regions have not yet designed their regional strategies according to the S3 model), and some respondents raised doubts about whether the clusters could take this on.

The respondents expressed a fear that cluster organisations are pre-existing, i.e. already associated with some founding stakeholders and with certain activities that have been made possible through various funding and financing sources. Therefore, it can be a challenge to steer the actors to something new and/or to include new actors that would lead to long-term regional change. They perceive cluster organisations as being neutral agents between the actors within their domain but defending it on the outside, which could prevent them from taking on work for structural change. Thus, if a DIH is to lead a priority domain, the S3 process leaders need to give it a new or additional mandate, additional capabilities, competences, resources and incentives to be independent.

The cluster organisations studied so far do not have a broad set-up of possible policy interventions to initiate, as this lies with other actors. Therefore, the two cluster organisations examined have not yet themselves had the opportunity to set up a roadmap with a policy mix for an S3 priority area. Currently, they are not in a position on a regional level to initiate and lead an agenda of broader and more profound structural changes. If a cluster organisation or hub were to lead the development of a priority area, they would need to broaden the participation base of their working groups to involve more types of stakeholders, such as users and policy actors, beyond R&I funding. This is also something that a few respondents requested: a broader quadruple helix set-up.

At the same time, it seems as if the clusters have functioned as focal points for their domains and have supported different projects and initiatives in these areas, conducive to the emergence of more capabilities and acting upon opportunities within the defined domain. At a regional level, there have been fewer strategic long-term agendas to facilitate planned structural changes. However, when it comes to the idea of developing new economic domains more strategically, they have been part of the national-level processes developing it, especially ProcessIT with the SIPs. The process leader of PiiA argues that, to succeed both regionally and nationally, there is a need for these networks; regional efforts can only succeed if they are also connected to efforts at national and international levels, and national efforts can only succeed by connecting regional efforts. This is even more important for the SPAs, to support their regional actors to connect to national and international networks to access highly skilled and competitive partnerships.

However, one should be careful about how much can be planned; one respondent said that "plans are best written afterwards", perceiving that there is a danger that strategies become desktop fantasies and emphasising the need to depart from existing capabilities to enhance regional capabilities.

Conclusions

The findings in this chapter come from two Swedish cases, but they are relevant for other contexts. SPAs differ in both distribution and innovation capacity, with strong spearheads of specialisation but fewer other sectors. There is also a geographical spread, with deeper knowledge and more technology leaders in the urban centres of the coastal regions but fewer knowledge-intensive activities in the inland regions. There are fewer local possibilities for positive serendipitous outcomes and important global contacts. Therefore, it becomes even more important to find ways of networking and of connecting to extra-regional resources and actors in order to seek ways for diversification.

There is a need for intermediaries that can connect actors regionally and SMEs to larger companies across sectorial boundaries and outside of the region. Multinational companies need local suppliers to be able to compete in global value chains, and suppliers need their customers. At the same time, there is a strong interest in connecting to other types of knowledge and to technology leaders outside of the region. The intermediary should be able to provide relevant support to these different categories. In SPAs where there is a general lack of critical mass, it will not be possibly to cater locally to all needs. DIHs should therefore seek to model themselves on a distributed innovation support network with localised specialisations in a type of 'hubs and nodes' model.

The focus of the two clusters seems to be a sliding scale of two parameters: one is geographic scope and the other is domain focus. The cluster organisations in this study appear to work more horizontally with digitalisation and innovation support within their defining region but then engage in national projects where they are more vertically domain-focused. This is an approach that both upholds important relations in the region and establishes important extra-regional networks. One could see it as gaining critical mass and addressing common needs among regional stakeholders, while maintaining relations with all regional interests in one organisation (the cluster).

Both clusters in the study have taken part in the development of regional innovation strategies, but they are not leading any renewal areas as such. The Needs Inventory Processes seem to be important for initiating projects as well as for building relations and knowledge about the industry.

It is unclear whether the clusters have driven intended structural change in their regions. There has been a growth of R&D centres in these domains and start-ups, and companies have gained access to new technologies supporting their development and their innovation work. However, new discovery areas have not been opened up, into which many actors have moved, as Dominique Foray envisioned with the EDP term.

Cluster organisations could take on the role of leading a vertical priority area of an S3. However, already-existing organisations come with histories. Thus, for this to work, the S3 process leaders need to give the cluster organisation a new or additional mandate, additional capabilities, competences, resources and incentives to be independent. They would also need to broaden the scope of actors to engage with quadruple helix actors or broader policy domain owners.

Notes

1 https://www.vinnova.se/en/publikationer/vinnvaxt/
2 https://www.vinnova.se/en/m/strategic-innovation-programmes/
3 https://www.interregeurope.eu/erudite/
4 https://fiberopticvalley.com/aktuellt/succen-fortsatter/
5 http://inlandetsteknikpark.nu/
6 https://www.nyteknik.se/startup/33-listan/
7 http://sip-piia.se/en/
8 https://www.sipstrim.se/
9 https://artemis-ia.eu/

References

European Commission (2012). *Guide to Research and Innovation Strategies for Smart Specialisation (RIS3)*, Brussels: CEC.

European Commission (2013). *The Role of Clusters in Smart Specialisation Strategies*, Brussels: CEC.

European Commission (2016a). *Communication on "Digitising European Industry – Reaping the Full Benefits of the Digital Single Market*, Brussels: CEC.

European Commission (2016b). *The Role of Clusters in Smart Specialisation: The Smart Guide to Cluster Policy*, Brussels: CEC.

European Commission (2017). *Digital Innovation Hubs: Mainstreaming Digital Innovation Across All Sectors, Roundtable on Digitising European Industry, Working Group 1*, Brussels: CEC.

Foray, D. (2015). *Smart Specialisation: Opportunities and Challenges for Regional Innovation Policy*, London: Routledge.

Gianelle, C., Kyriakou, D., Cohen, C., and Przeor, M. (Ed.) (2016). *Implementing Smart Specialisation Strategies*. Luxembourg: DG JRC IPTS.

Isaksen, A., and Trippl, M. (2017). Exogenously led and policy-supported new path development in peripheral regions: analytical and synthetic routes. *Economic Geography*, *93*(5), 436–457. https://doi.org/10.1080/00130095.2016.1154443

McCann, P. and Ortega-Argilés, R. (2014). The role of the smart specialisation agenda in a reformed EU Cohesion Policy, *Scienze Regionali*, *13*(1), 15–32.

Nuur, C. and Laestadius, S. (2010). Development in peripheral regions: case studies in Sweden. *European Urban and Regional Studies*, *17*(3), 293–307.

Porter, M. (1990). *The Competitive Advantage of Nations*. New York: Free Press.

Porter, M. (1998). Clusters and competition: new agendas for companies, governments, and institutions. In: M. Porter (Ed.) *On Competition* (pp. 197–287). Boston: Harvard Business School Press.

Sölvell, Ö., Lindqvist, G., and Ketels, C. (2003). *The Cluster Initiative Greenbook*. Stockholm: Ivory Tower AB.

Sörvik, J., and Midtkandal, I. (2017). Continuous priority setting – in the Norwegian VRI programme. In: D. Kyriakou, M. Palazuelos Martínez, I. Periáñez-Forte and A. Rainoldi (Eds) *Governing Smart Specialisation*, London: Routledge.

Teräs, J., Dubois, A., Sörvik, J., and Pertoldi, M. (2015). *Implementing Smart Specialisation in Sparsely Populated Areas*. S3 Working Paper, European Commission, Joint Research Centre.

Yin, R. (2003). *Case Study Research: Design and Methods*. London: Sage Publications.

Interviews (information used for empirical analysis)

Åkerberg, Carina, RIS3 Manager, Region of Gävleborg

Ärlestig, Martin, EVP Plant Manager, Umeå, Komatsu

Andersson, Per-Erik, Strategist, Regional Development, Region of Norrbotten

Johansson, Anders O.E., Deputy Programme Manager, Process Industrial IT and Automation (PiiA)

Karlsson, Håkan, Editor and Post-production Producer, People In The Park Production AB

Larsson, Anders, Former CEO and Chairman of the Board, Fiber Optic Valley
Levén, Per, CSO, ProcessIT
Lindberg, Per, Dean, Malgomaj School and Project Leader, Inlandets Teknikpark
Lithner, Marcus, IT Manager, Norrmejerier
Lundström, Jonas, Head of Unit, Business Development, Region of Västerbotten
Nygård Skalman, Karin, Former CEO and Chairman of the Board, Fiber Optic Valley
Rudehäll, Magnus, Digital Strategist, Region of Västerbotten

Part III

Operationalising smart diversification

10 Diversification patterns at the regional level and their relationship to regional knowledge capabilities

Differences between advanced and less favoured regions

Andreas Reinstaller and Fabian Unterlass

Introduction

The key ingredients of S3, as defined by the European Commission, to promote economic development across regions in Europe are: the identification and analysis of the economic specialisation of regions, the identification of potential avenues to diversify established economic activities in a region into new domains with high market potential, and the development and implementation of policies that support structural adjustments towards these new fields of economic activity (Foray et al., 2011). In the context of this process, it is important to recognise that the development of the productive structures of a region is a highly cumulative, path-dependent process and any structural change is necessarily rooted in the current knowledge base and industrial specialisation of a region. If now less favoured regions (LFRs) lack diversity with respect to economic and technological activities, S3 may not be conducive to structural change and the generation of greater wealth, as well as better development opportunities as envisaged by the European Commission.

To properly understand and successfully implement S3, it is important therefore to better understand the persistence of industrial specialisations across regions, and how they can be influenced to successfully promote structural change (Boschma & Gianelle, 2014; Foray & Goenaga, 2013). Finally, it is necessary to understand whether there are differences in how these mechanisms operate across regions with different levels of economic development, and especially the LFRs. This chapter examines these questions empirically. It analyses the relationships between different channels of knowledge generation and transmission and the development of industrial specialisations at the regional level across the 28 EU countries (as of 2018). It relies on a regional industry structure matrix to break down sectoral and country-specific indicators to the regional level for these 28 countries and distinguishes between different levels of economic development.

Conceptual background

Company-level learning, path dependence and regional specialisation

Path dependence in industrial specialisations emerges because of 'local search' and 'localised technical change', which are phenomena that have been given technological and economic explanations (cf. Dosi et al., 1990). The technical explanations for local search gravitate around the nature of learning processes at the company level. The knowledge acquisition of companies is focused on the production techniques they currently use, on the markets in which they operate, and on existing information channels with other firms, customers, suppliers and external sources of knowledge generation such as research institutions. They accumulate and transform this knowledge over time through learning (e.g. learning by doing), which gradually gets embodied in individuals, company routines or technological blueprints (e.g. Dosi, 1988; Nelson & Winter, 1982). These are then perpetuated and further developed, over time giving rise to highly specific knowledge bases that enable firms to exploit existing economic opportunities related to their own idiosyncratic technological or organisational capabilities.

The economic explanations for local search focus on the importance of sunk costs and irreversibility in the choice of production techniques. Antonelli (1998), for instance, argues that

> all existing capital stocks, both tangible, such as fixed assets, and intangible, such as reputation, experience and competence, have elevated levels of durability. . . Hence it is costly to change both the amount of capital stock as well as the proportions in which it is used with other complementary inputs due to changing market conditions.
>
> (Antonelli, 1998)

Specific combinations of tangible and intangible assets linked to one another through complementarities therefore become quasi-fixed factors of production.

However, the literature has also recognised that to explore new opportunities, companies need to constantly tap into external knowledge sources (March, 1991). Hence, firms must strike a balance between on, the one hand, deepening their knowledge related to specific products or services and, on the other hand, broadening their knowledge base to be able to diversify into new products. Effective knowledge transfer between firms and external sources of knowledge (such as other firms, research institutes etc.) requires absorptive capacity and cognitive proximity, however, to enable effective communication, and hence to ensure that knowledge can spill over (Breschi et al., 2003; Cohen & Levinthal, 1989).

This implies that diversification is a process in which existing cumulated capabilities are constantly broadened and developed further. In this way, firms leverage intertemporal economies of scope (Breschi, et al., 2003;

Helfat & Raubitschek, 2000) when they diversify into products that are technologically related to their current products. The process of product development and innovation is thus highly cumulative and dependent on the sequence of past choices, and innovative search outcomes at the firm level are likely to be serially correlated in time. This is consistent with recent work on the so-called 'product space' linking the observed path dependence in comparative advantages in trade in specific product lines to their relatedness to other products in which countries have already developed a comparative advantage (Hidalgo et al., 2007).

At the regional level, path dependence emerges because of 'untraded interdependencies' in the regional systems of innovation and production (Storper, 1995; Boschma et al, 2012). These are information and coordination externalities that arise from technological complementarities, untraded technological linkages, information flows, coordination externalities and knowledge spillovers across companies in a region. They are enforced and perpetuated through common infrastructures as well as economic, technical and educational institutions that have been developed to support the knowledge base underlying these interdependencies. They are therefore instrumental in generating the common experiences, knowledge and skills embodied in organisations and the people moving between them.

The better that firms are embedded in these information and coordination externalities present in an economy, the better they will be able to translate them into lower cost or higher quality products, and hence higher productivity that favours their competitiveness in international markets (cf. Tallman et al., 2004). They will also contribute to the collective asset and thereby strengthen the competitiveness of other companies active in related fields of economic activity. Hence, embedded firms are both a sink and a source for external effects.

Because of the positive feedback from dynamically increasing returns on competitiveness, some authors have argued that path dependence has a dual character. It is either a reflection of technological competence and competitiveness or is a source of structural inertia hampering economic adjustments and growth potential (Kogler et al., 2013). The variety of economic activities across regions will be lower than would be socially preferable (cf. Rodrik, 2004). Activities that are only weakly embedded in local economic activities and cannot benefit from 'untraded interdependencies' will be less competitive and will be sorted out by the global competition process. This will reduce the variety of economic activities at the regional level, and may also lead to development traps if regions are specialised economic domains that do not allow them to diversify into industries that have higher growth potentials (cf. Jankowska et al., 2012).

Given these considerations, S3 clearly must strike a balance between exploiting given capabilities to promote economic growth and development in the short run and exploring and developing new activities rooted in new capabilities that drive economic growth in the long run (Frenken et al., 2007; Saviotti & Frenken, 2008).

Another important aspect is that the economic structure, the embedding into global value chains and the level of economic development differ considerably across the European Union. S3, therefore, have to carefully consider, on the one hand, current specialisations and the underlying capabilities and 'untraded interdependencies' shaping them. On the other hand, they should develop an understanding about which knowledge generation and transmission activities are best suited to promote diversification, with the goal of strengthening regional employment and prosperity starting from current specialisation patterns. This is especially important for LFRs that are well known not to dispose of the same assets to pursue innovation strategies as more developed regions do (cf. Kroll, 2017).

Impact of knowledge generation and transmission on regional specialisation patterns

Regional economic ecosystems differ in their capacities to support the learning and innovation processes of companies. Leading regions that typically are also urban regions have greater capacities to support learning and innovation processes and also show a greater variety of economic activities than LFRs. For this reason, their economic development and structural transformation processes are often technology driven. This also finds a reflection in their overall innovation capability, which is systematically higher than in LFRs (cf. Howells, 2005). There is, therefore, nowadays a general agreement that the pursuit of 'best practice' development strategies copied from more advanced regions is not feasible for less advantaged ones (cf. Radosevic & Kaderabkova, 2011).

There are many channels of knowledge generation and transmission that are likely to affect regional industrial specialisations and contribute to either broaden or deepen the regional knowledge base. To develop adequate S3s, it is therefore necessary to assess how they affect regions, depending on their level of economic development. Given that LFRs tend to differ from more advanced regions in terms of their capacity to support learning and innovation processes, it should be expected that different channels of knowledge generation and transmission also unfold different effects on regional industrial specialisation. The remainder of this chapter will address this research question. Because of data availability, it will focus on research activities, human capital development and inward foreign direct investment (FDI). While this is a limited set of indicators, they capture different and important levers, considered by policymakers to promote economic development at the regional level.

Research activities (R&D) are an important channel of knowledge generation and absorption. Their impact on existing path dependencies in regional industrial specialisation is, however, ambiguous and depends on the breadth of technological search. In the presence of sunk costs and the irreversibilities of technological investments, research will focus on specific activities and deepen existing specialisations in industrial structure (Manez et al., 2009; Rodrik, 2004). However, research activities may also aim at the development of absorptive capacities (cf. Cohen & Levinthal, 1989), and this, in turn, may allow companies to engage in recombinant technical change (cf. Bresnahan, 2012). This may increase the variety of economic activities and favour industrial diversification across regions.

The key role of education and cognitive skills for growth and economic development is well established in the literature, but with regard to their impact on specialisation patterns, the evidence is mixed. Ciccone and Papaioannou (2007), for instance, show that there is a positive relationship between employment growth in skill-intensive industries and the educational expansion of countries. Krueger and Kumar (2004), however, argue that it is important to look at the quality of education measured in terms of cognitive skills, especially in mathematics, science and adult literacy. Mehta and Felipe (2014) show that these types of education also support industrial diversification. Skill-specific vocational education, on the other hand, supports the absorption of existing technologies and tends to deepen existing specialisations.

Inward FDI, finally, is an important channel of international knowledge diffusion (cf. Keller, 2009). The effects of FDI on exploration processes related to new export opportunities in destination countries are therefore ambiguous. The entry and presence of multinational companies in the regional business sector may affect local capabilities and the exploration and exploitation of export opportunities in many ways. On the one hand, it may widen the domestic technological capabilities of domestic firms through technology spillovers in domains that are new to the FDI destination. On the other hand, foreign firms may seek to tap into and absorb local capabilities and therefore invest in regions only if they themselves can benefit technologically and commercially from the entry. In the former case, FDI can contribute to the development of new specialisations by increasing the variety of capabilities in the country; in the latter case, it will harden existing specialisations rather, as foreign companies will be involved in the production and export of products that are closely related to local capabilities in the FDI destination.

Data and indicators

In order to analyse the impact of different channels of knowledge generation and transmission on regional industrial specialisation patterns, it is necessary to set up a database that comprises (i) industrial specialisation indicators at the regional level, (ii) indicators capturing the embeddedness of these industries in the regional 'untraded interdependencies' and (iii) indicators reflecting different knowledge generation and transmission mechanisms.

Regional industry structure matrix for NUTS 2-digit regions and NACE 4-digit industries and location coefficients

One of the key issues affecting the analysis of the specialisation patterns at the regional level for the European Union is that disaggregated industry-level data for NUTS 2 regions are not available. Eurostat's Structural Business Statistics are available at either the NUTS 2-NACE 2-digit level or the NUTS 0-NACE 4-digit level. These data are not granular enough to allow a satisfactory analysis of regional specialisation patterns. For this reason, a NACE 4-digit NUTS 2-digit industry structure matrix was constructed using Amadeus firm-level data provided by Bureau van Dijk. These were allocated to NACE Rev. 2 4-digit sectors. Amadeus contains comprehensive information on around 21 million companies for the EU-28, including company addresses (including postal codes, cities, etc.), current employment and value added. The coverage of firms in Amadeus does not depend on statistical considerations with respect to representativeness, but on data availability. Consequently, the data are biased towards larger firms, while small firms are strongly underrepresented. The following issues had therefore to be resolved:

- The information on the location of each firm (address, postal code or city) had to be assigned to a NUTS 2 region.
- Missing values in the data set had to be imputed to minimise potential bias due to lack of information.
- Based on the first two steps, regional aggregates were calculated for NACE 4-digit industries in NUTS 2 regions.
- Aggregates based on non-representative Amadeus data on the NUTS 2-NACE 4-digit level were adjusted to the official Structural Business Statistics available at Eurostat at either the NUTS 2-NACE 2-digit level or the NUTS 0-NACE 4-digit level using RAS techniques.[1]

As a detailed description of the construction of these data can be found in Unterlass et al. (2015), further details are omitted here. These data have been used to calculate location coefficients at the NUTS 2-digit and NACE 4-digit levels.

The location coefficient, $LC_{r,s}$, is a measure of regional industrial specialisation. It is the share of employment in a NACE 4-digit industry s in a specific NUTS 2 region r over the employment share of that industry across region r:

$$(1)\quad LC_{r,s} = \frac{x_{r,s}}{X_r} / \sum_r \frac{x_{r,s}}{X_r}, \text{with } LC \in \left[0;\infty\right[$$

The LCs provide a demarcation regarding whether a region is specialised in a specific industry relative to other regions in Europe, i.e. LC > 1 indicates that the region is specialised in a specific industry in terms of employment shares relative to other regions. Due to the unfavourable support of $LC_{r,s}$, with values lying between 0 and 1 indicating low specialisation and values lying between 1 and infinity indicating some level of specialisation, in the econometric analysis a transformed version is used:

$$(2)\quad SLC_{r,s} = \frac{\frac{LC-1}{LC+1}+1}{2}, \text{with } SLC \in [0;1[$$

The threshold for being specialised is 0.5 for *SLC*.

Table 10.1 presents descriptive statistics for the location coefficients obtained from this exercise using both value added and employment data. The table shows very small differences between the data basis (employment or value added) used to calculate the indicators. The average standardised *LC* value for the 245 NACE Rev. 2 4-digit industries is about 0.25. From an analytical point of view, value added-based location coefficients would be preferable. Due to the higher reliability of the employment variables in the Amadeus database, the remainder of the chapter focuses on results using the employment-based location coefficients.

It should be noted that due to data availability the sample was restricted to mining and quarrying (NACE Rev. 2, Section B) and manufacturing (NACE Rev. 2, Section C). The results for this chapter therefore focus on the manufacturing sector.

Relatedness and sophistication of productive activities across manufacturing sectors at the regional level

As has been argued earlier, regional-level path dependence in industrial specialisation patterns emerges because of 'untraded interdependencies'. Recent developments in the analysis of trade patterns (Hidalgo et al., 2007) make it possible to empirically assess the importance of these untraded interdependencies. These indicators define the *proximity* of products a country (or region) exports in terms of the conditional probability of countries having a comparative advantage in any two pairs of commodities at the same time. This is a measure of relatedness that is based on outcomes in international trade and is a global characteristic of each product class (in the HS 6-digit trade classification used for the present analysis).

This proximity measure is used to construct a country–product level indicator, referred to as product density, that measures how closely related a product is

Table 10.1 Summary statistics: specialisation patterns in NUTS 2 regions based on employment or value added (NACE Rev. 2 4-digit industries)

	Observations	*Mean*	*Std. dev.*	*Min.*	*Max.*
Location coefficient based on					
Employment	330 750	0.25	0.29	0.00	1.00
Value added	330 750	0.24	0.29	0.00	1.00

Source: WIFO calculations. Bureau van Dijk (Amadeus), Eurostat (Structural Business Statistics)

to all other products a country exports with comparative advantage. Hausmann and Klinger (2007) show that this indicator, referred to as 'product density', captures the factor substitutability between products, i.e. to what extent factors used to produce one type of goods can be used to produce another type of goods. It can therefore be interpreted, on the one hand, as a measure for joint cumulated capabilities and untraded interdependencies and, on the other hand, as a measure for the embeddedness of a product in the productive system of an economy.

For the present analysis, a regional variant of this indicator has been calculated. Knowing the relatedness of products at the level of HS 6-digit product groups, it is possible to calculate the proximity of NACE 4-digit industries at the NUTS 2 level by averaging the proximity of all products in the first sector to all products in the second sector, resulting in a proximity matrix for NACE 4-digit industries instead of HS 6-digit product groups. The proximity matrix of industry, which does not vary across countries by definition, is then used to calculate the product density for NACE 4-digit industries for each NUTS 2 region. Regional *SLC* values for NACE 4-digit industries required for calculating the neighbourhood density for NUTS 2 regions are calculated from the regional industry structure matrix.

For the S3 agenda, it is important to understand not only the impact of 'untraded interdependencies' on regional specialisation, but also the level of technological sophistication of the industries located in a region. To capture this aspect in our analysis, an indicator reflecting the depth and breadth of the knowledge base needed to produce a product proposed by Hidalgo and Hausmann (2009) is used and referred to as product complexity. The key assumption underlying the construction of this indicator is that complex products need a broader set of capabilities and that, for this reason, they tend to be produced by relatively fewer countries than less sophisticated products. This can be captured by an analysis of international trade flows. At the regional level, this implies that the more diversified a region is in terms of the products it produces and the more exclusive (or less ubiquitous) these products are in terms of the number of countries producing and exporting them, the more competitive and better performing its economy should be, as its product mix represents a unique source of competitive advantage.

This indicator has first been calculated and standardised for HS 6-digit trade data. Using HS-NACE correspondences and the share of exports of a product of the total exports in a NACE 4-digit industry at the country level as aggregation weights, the average product sophistication has been calculated for each 4-digit industry in EU Member States. Since no information is available as to which regions within a country produce which products within a 4-digit industry, this indicator has been used as a proxy for the product sophistication of a NACE 4-digit industry in a NUTS 2-digit region. Product sophistication at the 4-digit industry level therefore does not differ across regions within a country in the present analysis.

Table 10.2 Summary statistics: average product complexity and neighbourhood density in NUTS 2 regions (NACE Rev. 2 4-digit industries)

	Observations	*Mean*	*Std. dev.*	*Min.*	*Max.*
Product density	281 220	0.25	0.06	0.04	0.48
Product complexity	299 422	−0.01	0.72	−3.12	1.87

Source: authors' calculations. BACI data set (Gaulier & Zignago, 2010). Bureau van Dijk (Amadeus), Eurostat (Structural Business Statistics)

Table 10.2 summarises the indicators on product sophistication and neighbourhood density for NACE Rev. 2 4-digit industries in NUTS 2 regions. Average product sophistication at the NACE 4-digit industry level across NUTS 2 regions varies between −3.12 and +1.87. These are standard deviations from a mean sophistication normalised to be zero. The product-level density varies on the unit interval as the indicator is defined on this support, where 0 indicates that a product is not related to other products produced in a region, and 1 indicates that it is related to all other products in the region. The maximum is close to 0.5, which is very reasonable, as one should expect that strongly related products should also be assigned to the same 4-digit industries. At higher levels of aggregation, generally lower relatedness values are observed.

Regional indicators of knowledge creation, technological search and knowledge transfer

To establish how knowledge creation, technological search and knowledge transfer impact on industrial specialisation at the regional level in the dependence of a region's level of economic development, specific indicators capturing the three distinct dimensions of knowledge generation and transmission discussed earlier are used. Most of the indicators are available from Eurostat at the NUTS 2 level and also for some at the NACE 1-digit level (see Table 10.3 for summary statistics of all indicators). A few other indicators have been calculated from other data sources.

The standard indicator for the share of persons with tertiary education in total employment at the NUTS 2 level available from Eurostat is used to capture knowledge transfer from academia to a region's industry. To capture knowledge creation, two other Eurostat indicators of different stringency that reflect notions of the human resources in science and technology (HRST) concept are used. Relying on the combination of different employment and education characteristics of the labour force, the broad HRST concept captures the share of persons employed in science and technology-related activities of the total number employed in a NUTS 2 region. The narrower concept captures the share of persons with tertiary education that are also employed in science and technology-related activities of the total number employed.

Table 10.3 Summary statistics: education and skills in NUTS 2 regions

	Observations	*Mean*	*Std. dev.*	*Min.*	*Max.*
Persons with tertiary education (% of total employed)	2500	17.89	11.2	0.9	74.3
Persons with tertiary education AND employment in science/technology (% of total employed)	1955	8.79	6.15	0.6	46.9
Patent density	31 165	0.25	0.15	0	0.8
Share of foreign-owned companies in region (manufacturing), Amadeus		0.3	0.11	0.08	0.63

Source: authors' calculations. BACI data set (Gaulier & Zignago, 2010). Bureau van Dijk (Amadeus), Eurostat (Structural Business Statistics)

Both indicators have been tested as alternatives in different specifications, but yield similar results. Therefore, only results related to the narrow concept are reported here.

To capture technological search, a patent-based indicator identical to the product density indicator specified earlier has been calculated using patent data from the OECD's REGPAT database. It includes information on (i) technology fields (IPC classes) and (ii) the geographic origins of patent applications at the European Patent Office. This is used to calculate the patent density of a region's patenting activities. Applicants' addresses have been used to allocate patents to regions and a concordance table between IPC classes and NACE 2-digit industries (cf. Van Looy et al., 2015) to assign patents to industries. The resulting indicator covers 23 NACE 2-digit industries in 271 NUTS 2 regions for the period 2008–2012.[2] Analogously to product density, the patent density measures the average proximity of a patent to a region's current patenting activities (at the NACE 2-digit level). In other words, the patent neighbourhood density indicates how closely related the patenting activities in the respective industry are to the region's patenting activities, and therefore captures the strengths of the local search bias in inventive activities in a region.

To capture knowledge transfer through FDI, information contained in Bureau van Dijk's AMADEUS database has been used because FDI data at the regional level are not available. The share of foreign-owned firms in total employment has been calculated to measure the impact of inward FDI on regional industrial specialisation. This indicator has been harmonised with official SBS statistics from Eurostat.[3]

Research design

The key propositions of this chapter are that regions differ in their capacities to generate innovation, learning and promote structural change and that therefore the impact of different channels of knowledge generation and transmission on regional industrial specialisation patterns will differ as well. These differences will not only depend on the level of economic development, but also on the existing industrial specialisation and path dependencies that come with it. This will be examined econometrically. The econometric analysis relies on a dynamic fractional logit panel model to examine the impact of indicators for the relatedness of productive activities and their technological sophistication, as well as indicators for regional knowledge creation and transmission on regional location coefficients at the NUTS 2-digit NACE 4-digit level.

The choice of the econometric approach is determined by the nature of the data. The data are available as a panel spanning the period 2008–2012 for 271 NUTS 2 regions, which allows us to use a panel model. The dependent variable, the location coefficient *SLC*, is bound between 0 and 1 with a high probability mass across the region of zero. Papke and Wooldridge (2008) propose for this type of data the use of fractional logit models. Given the persistence of specialisation patterns across regions, dynamic panel models should be estimated. Following Wooldridge (2005) and Papke and Wooldridge (2008), this would require including time averages of all independent variables, a lagged dependent variable and the initial condition (i.e. the dependent variable at time $t = 0$) in the regression. As the period spanned by the panel is relatively short, however, the analysis sticks to a static panel, in which only time averages of all independent variables must be included.

The time averages account for the dependence of unit effects, i.e. they model individual heterogeneity across units of observation. By including them in the regression, the analysis accounts for cross-sectional variation. At the same time, the inclusion of the time averages allows estimating the effect of the explanatory variables holding time averages fixed, which amounts to effects resulting from variation of the explanatory variable within the units. Hence, the time averages of the independent variables represent long-run effects as they model essentially the effects of cross-sectional variation on the dependent variable, whereas the quantitative variables, given the inclusion of the time averages, model essentially the effects of variation within units, and therefore can be interpreted as short-run effects.

Finally, as the indicators of knowledge capabilities are more highly aggregated (region or sector NACE 2-digit vs. NACE 4-digit level) than the dependent and other independent variables, Moulton bias and serial correlation in the errors must be considered, and hence clustered standard errors have been used.

Given these methodological considerations, the empirical model is now specified as follows:

$$\begin{aligned} E[SLC_{r,s,t} \mid x_{r,s,t}] = G(&\alpha_{r,s,t} + \beta_0 SLC_{r,s,t-1} + \beta_1 DENS_{r,s,t} + \\ &\beta_2 CAP_{r,t} + \beta_3 [DENS_{r,s,t} \times CAP_{r,t}] + \beta_4 SOPH_{r,s,t} + \\ &\beta_5 [SOPH_{r,s,t} \times CAP_{r,t}] + \sum_t \lambda_t d_t + \sum_r \lambda_r d_r + \epsilon_{r,s,t}) \end{aligned}$$

where *SLC* is the location coefficient, *DENS* is the indicator for product relatedness, *SOPH* is the indicator for product sophistication and *CAP* is a summary acronym for all indicators of regional knowledge production and transmission as outlined in the previous section. The indices run over regions *r* and sectors *s*, and $\sum_r \lambda_r d_r$ are regional dummies capturing unobserved variation at the regional level. Alternative models have been run with country dummies and regional variables controlling for the employment share in industry, the degree of urbanisation (i.e. the share of households in densely populated areas) and whether the country's capital is in the region, which have led to qualitatively identical results. Therefore, in what follows, only regressions with regional dummies will be presented.

From the discussion above, the key hypotheses tested with this model are as follows:

Hypothesis 1: Comparative advantages (measured in terms of relative industry location) in a region are positively related to the relatedness of a product to other products the region produces (as expression of the path-dependent nature of regional industrial specialisations): i.e. $\partial G(\bullet) / \partial DENS_{c,p,t-1} > 0$, which is equivalent to $\beta_1 > 0$ for any given level of $CAP_{c,p,t-1}$. This should hold for both more advanced regions and LFRs.

Hypothesis 2: Comparative advantages (or relative industry location) in advanced regions increase with the level of sophistication of the products companies located in that region produce, i.e. $\partial G(\bullet) / \partial SOPH_{p,t-1} > 0$, or $\beta_4 > 0$, for any given level of $CAP_{c,p,t-1}$, reflecting the circumstance that more sophisticated products require high levels of specific technological knowledge, which are better supported by the institutional set-up and cumulated capabilities in advanced regions. In LFRs, the reverse should be true: given that these regions have less favourable institutions supporting knowledge and technology-intense activities, comparative advantages should be negatively related to product sophistication.

Hypothesis 3: Knowledge capabilities increase the likelihood of developing comparative advantages or strengthening industrial location patterns in a region, i.e. $\partial G(\bullet) / \partial CAP_{c,p,t-1} > 0$, or $\beta_2 > 0$, for any given level of $DENS_{c,p,t-1}$. While this hypothesis in this general form follows from human capital and endogenous growth theory, differences between more advanced regions and LFRs are likely to be observed, depending on the industrial specialisation and the functioning of knowledge transmission into the business sector.

Hypothesis 4: Knowledge capabilities allow escaping from existing specialisation patterns, i.e. $\partial^2 G(\bullet) / \partial DENS_{c,p,t-1} \partial CAP_{c,p,t-1} < 0$, or $\beta_3 < 0$. In this general form, the hypothesis follows from the literature on the impact of cognitive skills on economic performance. However, depending on both the depths and breadths of these knowledge capabilities, as well as the functioning of knowledge transmission into the business sector, the results may differ between advanced regions and LFRs.

Hypothesis 5: Knowledge capabilities facilitate the upgrading of the product portfolio, i.e. $\partial^2 G(\bullet) / \partial SOPH_{p,t-1} \partial CAP_{c,p,t-1} > 0$, or $\beta_5 > 0$. Similar qualifications as for Hypothesis 4 apply here as well.

Empirical results

Table 10.4 allows assessing the first three hypotheses for favoured and less favoured regions. The table shows the results for the panel regressions as outlined in the previous section. It presents results for the pooled set of regions (All) and for regions classified according to the Regional Innovation Scoreboard (RIS) of the European Commission. It shows both short-run effects and long-run effects. Short-run effects capture the impact of changes in the explanatory variables within regions over time, whereas long-run effects capture the impact of these changes on differences across regions. In the short run, basically no significant impact of any of the indicators on industry location is observed. This is due to the short period of observation covered by the panel. It is an expected outcome, as the industrial specialisation of a region is a structural parameter that changes and can be affected by policy measures only slowly in the long run. Consequently, policies targeting regional structural change, such as S3, should also target the long run. In what follows, our description will therefore focus on the long-run effects.

Table 10.5 allows assessing the fourth and fifth hypotheses. Given that short-run effects tend not to be significant, for better readability it shows only the long-run effects. Hypothesis 4 and 5 are assessed by means of interaction effects, where the different indicators of regional capabilities are interacted with both the indicator for product relatedness capturing regional 'untraded interdependencies' between products and path dependence and the indicator for product sophistication capturing the technological capabilities. The interpretation of the coefficients differs from that in Table 4, insofar as the total effect of an indicator is a combination of the coefficient estimated for the indicator and the coefficient estimated for the interaction effect. The coefficient for each indicator must be understood as the impact on the dependent variable, when the variable with which it is interacted takes on a value of zero or is absent. With regard to the interaction effect, it should be kept in mind that in a non-linear regression set-up, these interaction terms are difficult to interpret, and the regression coefficients for the interaction effects should therefore not be interpreted as a simple linear combination of the direct and the interaction effect of the variables of interest. However, Unterlass et al. (2015), presenting all of the analytical details underlying this report, show that, for the current analysis, the reported coefficients capture the general tendency of the impact of the interaction effect on the dependent variable reasonably well, and will therefore be interpreted accordingly.

Looking now at the long-run impact of relatedness, product sophistication and the indicators of knowledge creation, technological search and knowledge transfer, one can observe that across regional groups they tend to be highly significant, implying that these indicators explain some of the variation in industrial location patterns across regions. Turning to the first three hypotheses, one can see that existing industrial specialisations are strongly determined by the relatedness of the products of an industrial sector (at the NACE 4-digit level) to the products that other industrial sectors in the region already produce; there are no differences across regions. The impact seems to be even somewhat stronger in LFRs (moderate and modest innovators). This is proof of the importance of information and coordination externalities in the development of industrial specialisations across regions.

Looking at Hypothesis 2, one sees impact patterns that vary with the level of development of the regions. For the pooled sample, an insignificant negative coefficient is observed. For the LFRs (region types 3 and 4), the hypothesis is confirmed: in these regions, the likelihood of having a comparative advantage in an industry decreases with the level of sophistication of its products. The reverse is true, however, for the most favoured regions (region type 1), where the industry location coefficient increases with the level of sophistication. More innovative and economically more advanced regions have comparative advantages in industries producing sophisticated products. This shows that more favoured regions have developed specific knowledge bases that support industries with sophisticated, technologically complex products, whereas the reverse is true for LFRs. Given that a product sophistication indicator reflects the breadth and depth of the knowledge base needed to produce a product, this outcome may be interpreted to imply that LFRs have less variety in their knowledge base and also have less depth in their knowledge base, i.e. they also have more limited knowledge bases in the technological fields where they have their core competences, if compared with favoured regions.

Hypothesis 3 postulates that higher levels of regional capabilities in terms of knowledge creation, technological search and knowledge transfer will strengthen existing industrial specialisations. The hypothesis, as such, is of course relatively unspecific, as it does not differentiate between the different qualitative and quantitative aspects of how capabilities affect industrial specialisation. One should therefore expect rather heterogeneous results. Looking at the variables capturing different aspects of regional knowledge creation first, patent density represents a qualitative dimension of the breadth of technological search. With the employment share of persons in STI jobs with tertiary education, a quantitative dimension differentiating regions by means of the research intensity of the workforce in a region is captured, which to some extent reflects also the presence of research institutions or research-intensive businesses.

Looking at the patent density first, one sees that technological search activities in the neighbourhood of existing technological specialisations strengthen existing industrial specialisations in all types of regions except for LFRs, where the reverse holds. The likely reason for this is that LFRs are typically specialised in low-tech industries or have a strong rural character. These sectors typically do not engage in inventive activities. If industries in these regions engage in patenting, then these will typically be industries that do not have a comparative advantage. It should also be kept in mind that, in LFRs, formal technological research and development is generally limited, such that patent indicators provide only a partial view of the technological activities in these regions.

The interaction effects in Table 10.5 show that local technological search strengthens the positive impact of both product relatedness and product sophistication on industrial specialisation across all types of regions. The sign of the interaction term in turn suggests that the negative impact of industry location observed earlier holds only for industries that are weakly embedded in the product domain but that try to build on local technological competences. Most likely, these industries are new to the region and, as a consequence, have low location coefficients. In this case, they contribute to regional diversification. However, the stronger an industry is embedded in the local production system, and can benefit from local 'untraded capabilities' in production, the more local technological search will also strengthen its comparative advantage.

The second indicator reflecting regional capabilities for creating new knowledge is the employment share of persons with tertiary education active in STI jobs. In LFRs, it is positively related to local industrialisation patterns, whereas in all other regions, it is negatively associated with existing industrial specialisations. This means that in LFRs, if they exist, STI activities tend to support existing industries, whereas in all other regions, STI activities favour industrial diversification.

The interaction effects in Table 10.5 show that these impacts tend to be strengthened for products that are related to other products the region produces. In the LFRs, the positive impact is higher the higher the product relat edness of an industry, and in the other regions it weakens the dependence of the comparative advantages of an industry on local untraded interdependencies.

For the employment share of tertiary-educated persons, it is observed that the impact is inverted with regard to the evidence obtained for the STI employment share: for the most favoured regions, higher employment shares of people with tertiary education in total employment are positively correlated with location coefficients, indicating that they tend to strengthen the industrial base of the regions. One should expect this given that, in these regions, product sophistication is higher than in LFRs. For LFRs, a higher product sophistication goes with lower location coefficients instead, indicating that people with tertiary education are generally employed in sectors where the regions do not have a comparative advantage. This can be interpreted as tertiary education contributing to industrial diversification in the LFRs.

The interaction effects show that there is again a difference between the more favoured regions and the LFRs as to what concerns the impact of tertiary education on the impact of the factors causing path dependence in industrial specialisation. It mirrors what has been observed for the STI employment share.

Table 10.4 Determinants of industry location across regions with different levels of development (period 2008–2012)

Dependent variable – location coefficient (SLC)					
	FLogit (static panel)				
	Region type				
Variables	*All*	*1*	*2*	*3*	*4*
	Short-run effects				
Product density (*DENS*)	0.367**	0.190	0.387	0.694**	0.305
	(0.020)	(0.585)	(0.188)	(0.011)	(0.554)
Product complexity (*SOPH*)	–0.002	0.001	–0.006	–0.001	0.004
	(0.882)	(0.974)	(0.825)	(0.962)	(0.921)
Patent density (*CAP1*)	–0.009	–0.015	–0.002	0.010	0.008
	(0.707)	(0.775)	(0.964)	(0.831)	(0.924)
Employment share of jobs in STI with tertiary education	–0.000	–0.001	0.001	0.002	–0.003
(*CAP2*)	(0.892)	(0.701)	(0.806)	(0.687)	(0.814)
Employment share of tertiary education	0.000	0.000	–0.001	–0.002	0.002
(*CAP3*)	(0.872)	(0.846)	(0.714)	(0.612)	(0.836)
Share of foreign-owned companies in region (manufacturing)	0.067	0.084	–0.031	0.139	–0.061
(*CAP4*)	(0.687)	(0.820)	(0.901)	(0.715)	(0.901)

	Long-run effects				
Product density (*DENS*)	7.630***	3.261***	3.021***	7.356***	7.304***
	(0.000)	(0.000)	(0.000)	(0.000)	(0.000)
Product complexity (*SOPH*)	−0.003	0.117***	0.042	−0.076***	−0.076*
	(0.836)	(0.001)	(0.123)	(0.009)	(0.073)
Patent density (*CAP1*)	4.567***	7.051***	4.552***	3.250***	−3.120***
	(0.000)	(0.000)	(0.000)	(0.000)	(0.000)
Employment share of jobs in STI with tertiary education	0.015	−0.464***	−0.040**	−0.044*	0.233***
(*CAP2*)	(0.733)	(0.000)	(0.011)	(0.062)	(0.002)
Employment share of tertiary education	0.363***	0.241***	0.186***	−0.039*	−0.261***
(*CAP3*)	(0.000)	(0.000)	(0.000)	(0.070)	(0.000)
Share of foreign-owned companies in region (manufacturing)	0.270	3.472***	−0.509	−2.634	5.873**
(*CAP4*)	(0.430)	(0.000)	(0.195)	(0.768)	(0.043)
Constant	−12.406***	−4.862***	−6.377***	−1.836***	−2.421***
	(0.000)	(0.000)	(0.000)	(0.000)	(0.006)
Observations	259.92	53.278	95.283	71.56	28.559
Region-dummies	Yes	Yes	Yes	Yes	Yes
Time-dummies	Yes	Yes	Yes	Yes	Yes
Wald test – Regional dummies	0	0	0	0	0
Deviance	120 989	23 322	47 288	32 061	12 620
R^2	0.0686	0.0759	0.0476	0.0987	0.0757
Log pseudo-likelihood	−117 579	−24 213	−42 377	−32 324	−13 106

Robust p-values in parentheses: *** $p < 0.01$, ** $p < 0.05$, * $p < 0.1$

Region type (following RIS): 1. Innovation leaders; 2. Strong innovators; 3. Moderate innovators; 4. Modest innovators

Source: authors' calculations

Table 10.5 Determinants of industry location across regions with different levels of development: policy impact on specialisation and sophistication (long-run effects only)

Dependent variable – location coefficient (SLC)

Variables	*Interaction: Patent density (CAP1) * Product density (DENS)*					*STI employment with tertiary education (CAP2) * Product density (DENS)*					*Tertiary education (CAP3) * Product density (DENS)*					*Inward FDI (CAP4) * Product density (DENS)*				
	All	1	2	3	4	All	1	2	3	4	All	1	2	3	4	All	1	2	3	4
Product density	8.550***	3.758***	0.730	6.555***	5.687***	11.884***	5.102***	4.155***	7.319***	1.696	9.698***	7.883***	3.100***	7.397***	4.518**	7.182***	−3.045	1.687*	6.194***	2.280
(*DENS* – lr)	(0.000)	(0.000)	(0.363)	(0.000)	(0.000)	(0.000)	(0.006)	(0.001)	(0.000)	(0.417)	(0.000)	(0.000)	(0.000)	(0.000)	(0.015)	(0.000)	(0.101)	(0.071)	(0.000)	(0.337)
Product conplexity	−0.137***	0.036	−0.087**	−0.153***	−0.161***	−0.169***	0.260***	0.138***	−0.213***	−0.239*	−0.090***	0.169**	0.097**	−0.116***	−0.081	−0.086**	0.299**	−0.011	−0.148**	−0.154
(*SOPH* – lr)	(0.000)	(0.423)	(0.013)	(0.000)	(0.000)	(0.000)	(0.003)	(0.008)	(0.000)	(0.056)	(0.000)	(0.021)	(0.030)	(0.006)	(0.404)	(0.022)	(0.014)	(0.864)	(0.016)	(0.269)
Patent density	6.465***	7.555***	3.151***	2.654***	−7.109***	4.814***	7.201***	4.489***	3.405***	−3.210***	4.690***	7.272***	4.508***	3.331***	−3.020***	4.500***	7.123***	4.747***	3.133***	−3.081***
(*CAP1* – lr)	(0.000)	(0.000)	(0.000)	(0.000)	(0.000)	(0.000)	(0.000)	(0.000)	(0.000)	(0.000)	(0.000)	(0.000)	(0.000)	(0.000)	(0.000)	(0.000)	(0.000)	(0.000)	(0.000)	(0.000)
CAP1 (lr) *	5.924***	1.806	6.650***	3.213**	11.892** *															
DENS (lr)	(0.000)	(0.527)	(0.002)	(0.019)	(0.000)															
CAP1 (lr) *	0.501***	0.262***	0.424***	0.322***	0.759***															
SOPH (lr)	(0.000)	(0.007)	(0.000)	(0.000)	(0.000)															
Employment Share of jobs in STI with tertiary education	0.025	−0.467***	−0.091***	−0.071***	−0.360***	−0.121***	−0.415***	−0.056***	−0.061**	1.017***	−0.037	−0.345***	−0.041**	−0.049**	0.161**	0.001	−0.358***	−0.005	−0.035	−0.044
(*CAP2* –lr)	(0.586)	(0.000)	(0.000)	(0.003)	(0.000)	(0.009)	(0.000)	(0.001)	(0.041)	(0.000)	(0.423)	(0.000)	(0.011)	(0.039)	(0.031)	(0.979)	(0.000)	(0.744)	(0.376)	(0.565)
CAP2 (lr) *						−0.170***	−0.059	−0.031	0.001	0.277***										
DENS (lr)						(0.000)	(0.239)	(0.333)	(0.980)	(0.005)										
CAP2 (lr) * *SOPH* (lr)						0.006***	−0.004*	−0.003**	0.006***	0.008										
						(0.000)	(0.080)	(0.029)	(0.002)	(0.181)										
Employment share of tertiary education	0.378***	0.242***	0.144***	−0.020	0.305***	0.384***	0.226***	0.200***	−0.027	−1.116***	0.355***	0.210***	0.185***	−0.038	−0.230***	0.349***	0.175***	0.177***	−0.046	0.026
(*CAP3* – lr)	(0.000)	(0.000)	(0.000)	(0.366)	(0.000)	(0.000)	(0.000)	(0.000)	(0.347)	(0.000)	(0.000)	(0.000)	(0.000)	(0.107)	(0.000)	(0.000)	(0.000)	(0.000)	(0.190)	(0.433)

CAP3 (lr) * *DENS* (lr)											−0.123***	−0.195***	−0.004	0.007	0.208*					
											(0.000)	(0.002)	(0.916)	(0.826)	(0.093)					
CAP3 (lr) * *SOPH* (lr)											0.004***	−0.002	−0.002	0.003	0.000					
											(0.000)	(0.404)	(0.119)	(0.163)	(0.980)					
Share of foreign-owned companies in region (manuf.)	0.132	3.489***	−0.760*	−3.410	1.556	−0.335	3.024***	−0.528	−3.078	5.155*	−0.081	2.460***	−0.506	−2.821	5.762**	−0.006	−0.879	−1.186*	−3.460	0.916
(*CAP4* – lr)	(0.699)	(0.000)	(0.054)	(.)	(0.611)	(0.332)	(0.000)	(0.180)	(.)	(0.078)	(0.814)	(0.000)	(0.200)	(.)	(0.047)	(0.990)	(0.496)	(0.069)	(.)	(0.801)
CAP4 (lr) * *DENS* (lr)																0.506	16.890***	4.195	4.732	16.201**
																(0.745)	(0.000)	(0.153	(0.102)	(0.031)
CAP4 (lr) * *SOPH* (lr)																0.277**	−0.490	0.168	0.303	0.244
																(0.016)	(0.119)	(0.363)	(0.175)	(0.587)
Constant	−13.137***	−5.015***	−4.302***	−1.466***	−2.457**	−11.085***	−4.877***	−6.542***	−1.736***	0.880	−11.417***	−5.254***	−6.317***	−1.810***	−1.976**	−11.872***	−2.900***	−6.381***	−1.713***	−1.996*
	(0.000)	(0.000)	(0.000)	(0.000)	(0.013)	(0.000)	(0.000)	(0.000)	(0.000)	(0.324)	(0.000)	(0.000)	(0.000)	(0.000)	(0.040)	(0.000)	(0.000)	(0.000)	(0.000)	(0.052)
Observations	259 920	53 278	95 283	71 560	28 559	259 920	53 278	95 283	71 560	28 559	259 920	53 278	95 283	71 560	28 559	259 920	53 278	95 283	71 560	28 559
Region-dummies	Yes	Yes	Yes	Yes	Yes	Yes	Yes	Yes	Yes	Yes	Yes	Yes	Yes	Yes	Yes	Yes	Yes	Yes	Yes	Yes
Time-dummies	Yes	Yes	Yes	Yes	Yes	Yes	Yes	Yes	Yes	Yes	Yes	Yes	Yes	Yes	Yes	Yes	Yes	Yes	Yes	Yes
Wald test -- Country dummies	0	0	0	0	0	0	0	0	0	0	0	0	0	0	0	0	0	0	0	0
Deviance	120 729	23 316	47 258	32 034	12 602	120 692	23 306	47 281	32 021	12 612	120 847	23 304	47 281	32 050	12 613	120 899	23 309	47 265	32 047	12 614
R^2	0.0707	0.0763	0.0482	0.0992	0.0775	0.0712	0.0766	0.0477	0.0998	0.0763	0.0698	0.0764	0.0477	0.0990	0.0758	0.0692	0.0765	0.0480	0.0990	0.0760
Log pseudo-likelihood	−117 449	−24 210	−42 362	−32 310	−13 098	−117 431	−24 205	−42 374	−32 303	−13 102	−117 508	−24 204	−42 373	−32 318	−13 103	−117 534	−24 207	−42 365	−32 317	−13 104

*** $p < 0.01$, ** $p < 0.05$, * $p < 0.1$
Robust p-values in parentheses
Region type (following RIS): 1. Innovation leaders; 2. Strong innovators; 3. Moderate innovators; 4. Modest innovators
Source: authors' calculations

The share of tertiary-educated persons in total employment tends to increase the impact of product relatedness on industrial specialisation and therefore tends to deepen existing industrial specialisations. The reverse is true for the most favoured regions (and the pooled sample): in these regions, a higher share of tertiary-educated persons in the workforce tends to weaken path dependencies. The interaction effects with product sophistication are not significant across region types.

Looking at knowledge transfer from foreign companies, the impact on regional industrial comparative advantages is identical for the most favoured and the least favoured regions. For both types of regions, higher shares of foreign-owned companies also go along with higher location coefficients. This indicates that FDI tends to tap into existing capabilities and tries to benefit from existing comparative advantages. The interaction effects in Table 10.5 show that in the more advanced and less favoured regions, FDI strongly promotes existing path dependencies. This strengthens the view that FDI typically searches to exploit local capabilities for its own benefit. For the pooled sample, the interaction effects suggest that FDI tends to strengthen the impact of product sophistication on industrial location.

To summarise, the empirical findings presented in this section suggest that local technological search and knowledge generation reinforce existing specialisation patterns at the regional level since companies have an incentive to engage in research and innovation activities that are closely related to their core competences. The results also clearly show that educational investments may weaken path dependence reducing the importance of already existing local capabilities and allowing tapping into new technologies or industries fostering diversification. Furthermore, regions with higher educational attainment levels are in general more specialised in high-end niche markets. The educational system therefore plays a key role in diversification processes and should be a constitutive element of S3 policies, especially in LFRs.

Conclusions

Comparative advantages in the manufacturing sector at the regional level are strongly determined by 'untraded interdependencies' in production, which have been identified as a major source of path dependence. Path dependence in productive structures is therefore a reality; policymakers engaging in S3 have to consider path dependence irrespective of the level of economic development of the region.

More favoured regions generally have comparative advantages in products that are more sophisticated in terms of the breadth and depth of the knowledge base needed to produce them. LFRs are clearly disadvantaged in these types of products. They have less variety and also less depth in their industrial knowledge base.

R&D activities in these regions tend to support the deepening of the existing knowledge base, and therefore promote path dependence. The same can also be said for the different channels of knowledge transfer: a higher employment share of people with tertiary education supports existing industries as much as FDI does. In the more favoured regions, this is different, to some extent. Here, a higher employment share of people with tertiary education and of tertiary-educated persons in STI activities clearly supports the weakening of path dependences. Thus, a prime difficulty of LFRs seems to be the promotion of industrial diversity. The main purpose of S3 policies is to diversify the economy and generate new areas of industrial specialisation.

The results presented in this chapter indicate that the educational system can play a key role in industrial diversification processes in LFRs and should be a constitutive element of S3 policies to promote the diversification of the knowledge base. However, to achieve this goal, they should not predominantly target the support of existing industries.

For LFRs, more than for others, the challenge is to increase and leverage related variety in economic activities. This implies exploiting existing capabilities to develop new regional industrial specialisations and to promote the development of technologies that take existing capabilities as a starting point. Indeed, the results indicate that new industrial specialisations, where no comparative advantage (yet) exists, seem to be related to sectors that search locally in the knowledge space (patenting related to other patents in the region), but that have products that are weakly embedded in the regional production structures.

The first-best policy response in the domain of industrial policy in this case is to set incentives and promote investment as well as entrepreneurial activities in non-traditional industries. However, these industries should ideally engage in economic or technological activities that are related to, but not completely congruent with, the established knowledge base in the region. The goal must be to maximise information externalities and minimise coordination failures. In other words, regional policies should promote the development of new activities and technologies that can make the best use of the 'untraded interdependencies', as well as contribute to them. However, these activities need to go beyond existing capabilities and lead to the creation of new knowledge that will eventually lead to the development of new industrial specialisations. Thus, the key criterion for promoting such activities has to be their potential to spawn new areas of specialisation for the region. The results also show that attracting FDI seems not to be an adequate means to promote structural change. Rather, LFRs should try to fund efforts to identify, adapt and transfer technology from more advanced regions or from abroad.

The results presented in this chapter come with a number of limitations. On the one hand, some of the explanatory variables used in the empirical analysis are only available at high levels of aggregation, and therefore may not reflect the situation at more disaggregated levels adequately. On the other hand, the indicators used in this analysis may not capture all of the aspects that are relevant for the promotion of economic development of LFRs in Europe. These limitations are largely driven by data availability, and the results of this chapter should therefore be carefully reconsidered in further research for subsets of regions where better data may become available. Finally, there are also limitations from a methodological point of view that should be considered. While the choice of the quantitative approach is dictated by the nature of the data, the panel characteristics of the data, and also the non-linear regression approach, warrant some caution in the interpretation of the results.

Acknowledgement

The research underlying this paper has received funding from the European Commission under specific contract No. ENT-SME-14-F-S107-SI2-698839 in the framework contract ENTR/300/PP/2013/FC-WIFO.

Notes

1 RAS calculates row (in this case, the sum of a NACE 4-digit sector over regions within a country) and column sums (i.e. the sum of NACE 4-digit sectors within a NACE 2-digit sector in a NUTS 2 region) of a matrix and compares them with the correct counterparts taken from official statistics (i.e. SBS statistics). Using an iterative procedure that adjusts the row and column sums to the official statistics, the procedure allows the calculation of a refined matrix where the values within the matrix are consistent with the official statistics. Finally, employment and value-added shares, both at the country level and the EU 28, have been calculated for each NACE 4-digit industry active in a region.

2 See Unterlass et al. (2015) for details of how these indicators have been calculated.

3 See Unterlass et al. (2015) for details. The Amadeus-based FDI indicator suffers from a lack of representatives. Alternative specifications using country- and industry-level indicators from Eurostat's FATS statistics show that the indicator provides robust results.

References

Antonelli, C. (1998). The dynamics of localized technological change. The interaction between factor costs inducement, demand pull and Schumpeterian rivalry. *Economics of Innovation and New Technology*, *6*(1), 97–120.

Boschma, R., & Gianelle, C. (2014). Regional branching and smart specialisation policy. *S3 Policy Brief Series*, No. 06/2014.

Boschma, R., Minondo, A., & Navarro, M. (2012). The emergence of new industries at the regional level in Spain: a proximity approach based on product relatedness. *Economic Geography*, *89*(1), 29–51.

Breschi, S., Lissoni, F., & Malerba, F. (2003). Knowledge-relatedness in firm technological diversification. *Research Policy*, *32*, 69–87.

Bresnahan, T. F. (2012). Generality, recombination and reuse. In: J. Lerner & S. Stern (Eds.), *The rate and direction of inventive activity revisited* (pp. 611–656). Chicago: University of Chicago Press.

Ciccone, A., & Papaioannou, E. (2007). Red tape and delayed entry. *Journal of the European Economic Association*, *5*(2–3), 444–458.

Cohen, W.M., & Levinthal, D.A. (1989). Innovation and learning: the two faces of R&D. *The Economic Journal*, *99*, 569–596.

Dosi, G. (1988). Sources, procedures, and microeconomic effects of innovation. *Journal of Economic Literature, 26*(3), 1120–1171.

Dosi, G., Pavitt, K., & Soete, L. (1990). *The Economics of Technical Change and International Trade.* New York: Harvester Wheatsheaf.Foray, D., David, P.A., & Hall, B.H. (2011). Smart specialisation. *MTEI Working Paper No. 2011–001.*

Foray, D., & Goenaga, X. (2013). The goals of smart specialisation. *JRC S3 Policy Brief Series*, No. 01-2013.

Frenken, K., van Oort, F., & Verburg, T. (2007). Related variety, unrelated variety, and regional economic growth. *Regional Studies, 41*(5), 685–697.

Gaulier, G., & Zignago, S. (2010). BACI: international trade database at the product-level. *CEPII Working Paper*, No. 2010–23.

Hausmann, R., & Klinger, B. (2007). The structure of the product space and the evolution of comparative advantage. *CID Harvard University Working Paper*, No. 146.

Helfat, C.E., & Raubitschek, R.S. (2000). Product sequencing: co-evolution of knowledge, capabilities and products. *Strategic Management Journal, 21*, 961–979.

Hidalgo, C.A., & Hausmann, R. (2009). The building blocks of economic complexity. *PNAS*, 106(26), 10570–10575

Hidalgo, C.A., Klinger, B., Barabasi, L., & Hausmann, R. (2007). The product space conditions the development of nations. *Science, 317*(5837), 482–487.

Howells, J. (2005). Innovation and regional economic development: a matter of perspective? *Research Policy, 34*(8), 1220–1234.

Jankowska, A., Nagengast, A., & Perea, J.R. (2012). The product space and the middle-income trap: comparing Asian and Latin American experiences. *OECD DEVELOPMENT CENTRE Working Paper, 311.*

Keller, W. (2009). International trade, foreign direct investment, and technology spillovers. *Centre for Economic Policy Research Working Paper No. 7503.*

Kogler, D.F., Rigby, D.L., & Tucker, I. (2013). Mapping knowledge space and technological relatedness in US cities. *European Planning Studies, 21*(9), 1374–1391. http://dx.doi.org/10.1080/09654313.2012.755832

Kroll, H. (2017). The Challenge of Smart Specialisation in Less Favoured Regions. Working Paper Firms and Regions No. R1/2017, Fraunhofer Institute, Karlsruhe.

Krueger, D., & Kumar, K.B. (2004). Skill-specific rather than general education: a reason for US–Europe Growth Differences? *Journal of Economic Growth, 9*(2), 167–207. https://doi.org/10.1023/B:JOEG.0000031426.09886.bd

Manez, J.A., Rochina-Barrachina, M.E., Sanchis, A., & Sanchis, J.A. (2009). The role of sunk costs in the decision to invest in R&D. *Journal of Industrial Economics, 52*(4), 712–735.

March, J.G. (1991). Exploration and exploitation in organizational learning. *Organization Science, 2*(1), 71–87.

Mehta, A., & Felipe, J. (2014). Education and the journey to the core: path dependence or leapfrogging? (SSRN Scholarly Paper No. ID 2467895). Rochester, NY: Social Science Research Network. Retrieved from http://papers.ssrn.com/abstract=2467895

Nelson, R., & Winter, S. (1982). *An Evolutionary Theory of Economic Change*. Boston, MA: Belknap, Harvard University Press.

Papke, L.E., & Wooldridge, J.M. (2008). Panel data method for fractional response variables with an application to test pass rates. *Journal of Econometrics, 145*, 121–133.

Radosevic, S., & Kaderabkova, A. (Eds.) (2011). *Challenges for European Innovation Policy: Cohesion and Excellence from a Schumpeterian Perspective*. Cheltenham, UK: Edward Elgar.

Rodrik, D. (2004). Industrial policy for the twenty-first century. *KSG Faculty Research Working Paper Series, RWP04-047.*

Saviotti, P.P., & Frenken, K. (2008). Export variety and the economic performance of countries. *Journal of Evolutionary Economics, 18*(2), 201–218.

Storper, M., (1995). The resurgence of regional economies, ten years later: the region as a nexus of untraded interdependencies. *European Urban and Regional Studies, 2*(3), 191–221.

Tallman, S., Jenkins, M., Henry, N., & Pinch, S. (2004). Knowledge, clusters and competitive advantage. *Academy of Management Review, 29*, 258–271.

Unterlass, F., Reinstaller, A., Vogel, J., Reschenhofer, P., Unterlass, S., Weingärtner, S., . . . Charos, A. (2015). The relationship between export and technological specialisation profiles across EU Member States and regions and the identification of development potentials (Final Report carried out for the European Commission, Directorate-General Enterprise). Vienna: Austrian Institute of Economic Research.

Van Looy, B., Vereyen, C., & Schmoch, U. (2015). Patent statistics: concordance IPC V8 – Nace Rev. 2 (version 2.0). *EUROSTAT Working Paper.*

Wooldridge, J.M. (2005). Simple solutions to the initial conditions problem in dynamic, nonlinear panel data models with unobserved heterogeneity. *Journal of Applied Econometrics, 20*(1), 39–54.

11 The role of proximity in less-favoured regions

Smart experimentation between triple helix actors

Antti Mäenpää and Seija Virkkala

Introduction

Smart specialisation (Foray et al. 2012) is an academic concept that has been implemented in practice as the EU's latest research and innovation strategy for smart specialisation (RIS3). One of its central concepts is the entrepreneurial discovery process (EDP), the main idea of which is to define regional assets and utilise them for maximum effect to improve economic prosperity (Foray et al. 2012). The EDP is a challenging process, which demands a broad partnership of entrepreneurial agents, like relevant public and private stakeholders. The stakeholders should form a public–private partnership to make entrepreneurial discoveries and to prepare regional strategies based on these discoveries. However, in a less-favoured region (LFR), there might only be a few relevant stakeholders, who might be too distant from each other, which might lead to a partnership that is weak or short on interaction.

Less-favoured or peripheral regions have traditionally been defined as areas with low levels of accessibility to large-scale (national, continental, and global) interaction centres offering access to markets, production factors, private and public services, cultural facilities, sources of innovation systems, and to economic and political power (Lorentzen 2012: 16–17). They have high travel and transport costs and are remote from centres of economic activity. They also suffer from the absence of agglomeration advantages, which manifests as low rates of entrepreneurship and innovation. The category of LFR is a relative category, which should be studied in relation to the more-favoured regions. In a knowledge-based economy, accessibility to transport for physical goods has become less important, and other forms of accessibility, such as to business air travel and ICT, have become more important (Crone 2012).

The innovation systems in an LFR can often be characterised by a low level of interaction between knowledge producers and knowledge users, a lack of a critical mass of innovative firms, a weak connection with key organisations (e.g. universities, companies, and public actors), and by a low level of clustering (Tödtling and Trippl 2005). These characteristics can make the RIS3 process challenging in LFRs. A less-developed regional innovation system (RIS) has a weak capacity to support the renewal of the regional economy over time, which is important in the RIS3 targeting initiating regional transformation via the EDP (Blažek et al. 2014: 5). Moreover, the stakeholders in the LFRs might lack knowledge of innovation and might also have a low absorption capacity in terms of acquiring key knowledge.

This chapter discusses two challenges associated with the EDP: the low connectivity between stakeholders and the lack of a role for stakeholders/entrepreneurial agents, or a weak role for them. The chapter approaches the innovation system in LFRs by analysing the innovation cooperation between the triple helix (TH) actors and companies in particular. The chapter presents an analysis adopting two approaches: the proximity approach and the knowledge typology approach developed by Lundvall and Johnson (1994), which focuses on the role of codified and tacit knowledge. The chapter aims to advance understanding regarding networking preconditions, behaviour, and knowledge acquisition regarding companies in LFRs, and also to analyse the role of different proximities in their cooperation for innovation. This is also crucial for the EDP because companies are usually the main implementers or beneficiaries of innovation strategies and because new ideas leading to domains might emerge from these relationships and interactions. This also contributes to the proximity discussion from the perspective of the LFRs, and to that on how to overcome institutional barriers in peripheral regions.

The chapter aims to respond to the following research questions: what is the relationship between geographical and non-spatial proximity in companies in LFRs? What could be undertaken in LFRs to increase proximity between stakeholders?

These research questions are approached via the findings of a Finnish case study from the region of Ostrobothnia on various proximities and aspects of knowledge creation through innovation cooperation between TH actors. The Finnish region of Ostrobothnia and the country in general have managed to at least partly overcome the less-favoured conditions of being on the northern periphery of Europe. The innovation scoreboard of the EU ranks Finland as an innovation forerunner. This study also introduces a new way to measure social and cognitive proximity, and thus provides detailed information regarding the institutional, social, cognitive, and geographical proximities required for innovation cooperation among the various actors.

Conceptual background

Regional innovation system (RIS) and triple-helix models

Innovation is becoming an evermore complex, interactive, and open phenomenon, and different types of knowledge are combined in innovation processes. Strambach and Klement (2012) introduce the concept of the *combinatorial micro-dynamics of knowledge*, in which innovation relies on the combination of different types of knowledge. Within innovation processes, relevant knowledge is distributed, as a result of different actors in different places having elements of the necessary knowledge. Collaboration in formal and informal networks is one way for firms to acquire knowledge for innovation, and this chapter concentrates on that form. Other forms supporting knowledge acquisition include labour mobility, market links, monitoring, and knowledge spillovers.

Territorial innovation models, for example, RIS theories, emphasise the importance of regional knowledge for innovation. The RIS approach underlines the importance of interactive learning (i.e. networks): innovations are the outcome of interactive learning within and between two subsystems – knowledge generation (universities) and knowledge application (firms) – located in the region. The exchange of tacit knowledge is facilitated by geographical proximity and regional cultural contexts, that is, geographical and social proximity. However, external knowledge links are also important (Bathelt et al. 2004) and often complement regional knowledge. The combination of knowledge acquired from different spatial scales is the key to innovation. The term *local buzz* refers to free and automatic participation in often unintended knowledge circulation of actors in the same location. *Global pipelines* are seen as planned connections to distant partners and knowledge sources, which can provide new technologies and markets (Grillitsch and Trippl 2014).

LFRs usually have relatively few actors and limited local knowledge flows, only a few knowledge and support organisations, and no, or only weak, clusters. Isaksen and Trippl (2014) call them "organizationally thin regions". Regions with thin RISs are far less dynamic. They generally have fewer innovative new firms than thicker RIS regions, and the role of support organisations and extra-regional knowledge links might be more important to the EDP than in thick regions with their dense organisational network and rich local knowledge flows.

Jensen et al. (2007) introduce two modes of innovation: science, technology, and innovation (STI) and doing, using, and interacting (DUI). The STI mode of learning and innovation is based on the production and use of codified scientific and technical knowledge, whereas the DUI mode is an experience-based mode of learning that relies on informal processes. The STI mode prioritises the production of know-why, while the DUI mode typically prioritises know-how and know-who (Jensen et al. 2007). Know-how and know-who are typically tacit, while innovations focus mainly on incremental changes in existing products and processes. In the DUI mode, crucial knowledge of innovation processes is formed through a combination of the employees' training and working-life experience. The knowledge base is developed through in-house problem-solving by individuals and teams of workers, and this becomes evident, for example, when firms cooperate with customers who are facing new problems and when suppliers engage in innovation activity (Jensen et al. 2007; Virkkala 2013). The DUI mode is based on synthetic and symbolic knowledge (that is market/user-driven), emphasising competence-building and organisational innovations, but analytical knowledge is more important in the STI mode of innovation. The DUI mode depends more on implicit and local knowledge where know-how and know-who play an important role, but the STI mode of innovation is based on explicit and global knowledge, and emphasises know-why and know-what.

The TH model has been used as a framework of knowledge-based societies, and universities are at the core of the model. According to the model, universities, industry, and government are the key institutes whose interaction is necessary for innovations (Etzkowitz and Leydesdorff 2000). The TH approach has been criticised for conceptualising only three groups of actors (Carayannis and Campbell 2012) and neglecting the absorptive capacity of companies and government to engage with universities. Responses to the criticism include attempts to incorporate a wider set of actors and institutions, as in the *quadruple helix* that includes non-governmental knowledge production, utilisation, and renewal entities as well as other civil society entities, institutions, and stakeholders (Carayannis and Campbell 2012).

The concept of the TH has been applied in smart specialisation to form the basis for connectivity within regions. A connected region is a norm or vision where the three helices work in harmony, thereby mutually reinforcing each other (Goddard et al. 2013). The collaboration between TH actors in different helices is especially beneficial for many reasons, but usually the idea of different types of people, schools of thought, and varying overall objectives adds value to the innovation process (Ranga and Etzkowitz 2013). The public sector focuses on the public good, companies add market knowledge, and universities link the region to global research networks. This collaboration also provides a solid framework for the EDP, as various ideas intermingle.

In a disconnected region, there are no boundary spanners, the partnerships are ineffective or non-existent, and there is a lack of understanding about the required changes. Entrepreneurs are locked out of regional planning (Goddard et al., 2013), and the EDP cannot emerge properly. This applies especially to an LFR lacking important actors; however, RIS3 is based on the idea that if a region lacks some actors, it may use its existing knowledge to compensate for that lack; so, for example, if there are few companies, then universities and local development agencies may prove to be sources of market knowledge. Therefore, one can state that one important precondition for regional innovation is optimal proximity between the actors, and this can vary depending on whether the region contains all the necessary actors.

Proximity as a precondition of a relationship

The proximity approach was introduced by Boschma (2005) and by Torre and Rallet (2005) and is used mostly to understand which type of proximity produces innovation, and to what degree. The approach primarily focuses on dyadic relationships. Proximity is required to connect actors and to enable interactive learning and innovation. Geographical proximity promotes unique local competencies, skills, and new knowledge, which can diffuse spontaneously through personal contacts via the local buzz (Bathelt et al. 2004). However, geographical proximity alone is not sufficient to foster knowledge creation, but it does facilitate non-spatial forms of proximities and the sharing of tacit knowledge. In addition to geographical proximity, Boschma (2005) suggests four non-spatial dimensions of proximity: social, institutional, organisational, and cognitive proximity. Geographical proximity refers to physical distance measured in kilometres or time. Institutional proximity indicates shared formal and informal rules. Cognitive proximity refers to the similarity of the knowledge bases of the partners, and social proximity refers to the personal or professional relationships between partners. Organisational proximity refers to the same relational framework or share of common knowledge and capacities (Torre and Gilly 1999).

When actors get closer in one dimension, they also get closer in other dimensions. This means that the dimensions have somewhat overlapping boundaries. Geographical proximity tends to create an overlap between geographical and other (non-spatial) forms of proximity (Malmberg and Maskell 2006). For instance, geographical proximity stimulates the emergence of trustful relations through the possibility of the frequency of relationship, resulting in higher social proximity. Geographical proximity may also stimulate territorial specialisation and cluster formation, which may then turn into cognitive proximity as people work closely on related fields. The overlap of geographical and cognitive proximities depends on the degree of regional specialisation (Hansen 2015). In addition to the effect of overlap, the proximity literature emphasises the possibility of substitution of non-spatial proximities for geographical proximity. According to Boschma (2005), geographical proximity is neither a necessary nor a sufficient condition for learning. The lack of one proximity can be compensated for by the presence of another form of proximity. This is a very important statement as a precondition of innovation development in LFRs, since their actors might need to cooperate with partners in other regions to deliver innovation.

However, proximity between agents in networks does not always increase their innovative performance, and may even harm it; this is the so-called proximity paradox (Boschma and Frenken 2013). If two actors have a similar knowledge base, the cognitive distance between them is short, and their collaboration might not improve innovation performance because new ideas may require somewhat different views, and some level of recombination is usually central to innovation. Instead, the collaboration might even give rise to what are termed lock-ins (Boschma and Frenken 2013), where collaboration among actors is so strong that other partners cannot 'fit in'. Moreover, the strength of social ties between two actors can vary. Proximity may also hinder extra-regional collaboration and sometimes even local learning. This is especially true for institutional proximity, which in this chapter is operationalised as the proximity inside helices (companies, universities, or government), as high levels of institutional proximity mean less cross-sectoral knowledge transfer. In addition, geographical proximity can become a hindrance if collaboration occurs only on the local level. High social proximity might mean that new actors are not easily accepted. Optimal proximity varies region by region, and therefore should be studied in association with its regional background.

Innovation cooperation can also be dynamic: interaction between actors can contribute to various forms of proximity that can cut across organisational, institutional, and spatial boundaries. During interactions in the innovation process, the partners learn from each other, their knowledge bases will change, and their shared mental models will be adjusted, which leads to a reduction in their cognitive distance, which enhances the learning effects (Menzel 2016). The interaction can also create a common social context in which personal relations develop despite organisational, geographical, or institutional backgrounds or knowledge bases (Balland et al. 2015). In a similar way, it is possible to see the EDP as a process in which the different proximities are changing and new relationships will be created. In order to better understand social and cognitive proximity, in this chapter the proximity approach is linked to the knowledge typology.

Research design

Knowledge taxonomy as proximity

The literature review provided a framework on TH and proximity as theoretical concepts, but they can be operationalised in different ways. The authors think that the idea of institutional differentiation (as in the TH model) can offer a good point of departure for an empirical study. Whereas most firms specialise mainly in the exploitation of knowledge for economically useful purposes, universities are involved mainly in knowledge creation through research, followed by its dissemination through education. The TH concept provides ready-made empirical categories for studying relationships between different actors. Accordingly, data were collected on the basis of the described institutional spheres: companies, universities, and public government.

Geographical proximity normally refers to physical distance measured in kilometres or time, but in this chapter the concept refers to intra-regional as opposed to extra-regional proximity. Institutional proximity indicates the joint formal and informal rules, and, in this chapter, refers to the helices: universities, as scientific systems, communicate and function in accordance with the code of true/false, companies in accordance with the code of profit/loss, and the public sector in accordance with the code of right/wrong. Cognitive proximity refers to the similarity of the knowledge bases of the partners, and social proximity refers to the personal or professional relationships between partners (Virkkala et al. 2017). Our empirical analysis is based on the data on geographical, institutional, social, and cognitive proximities. There were insufficient data available on organisational proximity to be able to include it.

The authors illuminate the relationships between actors with the help of a knowledge taxonomy that takes account of the division between codified and tacit knowledge. Codified knowledge consists of information that can be written in an explicit form. Tacit knowledge is acquired through experience, demonstration, and practice, requiring personal physical interactions. The knowledge typology of Lundvall and Johnson (1994; Jensen et al. 2007) mixes codified and tacit elements and specifies functional types of knowledge with the help of four categories: *know-what* is knowledge about facts on regions, inhabitants, and industrial structure, and describes what is going on; *know-why* is knowledge that explains why things are done in a certain way (or theories on the reasons for development), the principles and laws of nature, in the human mind, and of society; *know-how* defines how things happen in practice (or how to perform skills), and is often tacit by nature; and *know-who* identifies the actors and partners, and also who is authorised to make decisions. It is knowledge regarding who knows what (Lundvall and Johnson 1994).

Knowledge taxonomy has been used in a survey to define the depth of the relationship with regard to a respondent's knowledge of his/her partner. The deeper the relationship, the more dimensions are covered by the respondent's knowledge about his/her partner's activities connected to innovation. Table 11.1. combines the knowledge taxonomy with the proximity dimensions. *Know-what* and *know-why* refer to cognitive proximity, *know-who* and *know-how* to social proximity.

The region of Ostrobothnia: data and methods

Ostrobothnia is a region in western Finland with a population of 181 000 people. The national capital, Helsinki, is situated over 400 kilometres away, and the largest regional city, Vaasa, has 67 000 inhabitants. The region is known for its industrial sector, which consists of the energy technology cluster in and around the regional capital Vaasa, a boat building cluster, and fur farming businesses in the surrounding countryside. Over 80% of the value of energy technology production was exported in 2017, and Ostrobothnia has been characterised as a globalised innovation system. Among the Ostrobothnian workforce in 2014, 6% earned their living from agriculture, 29% from industry, and 64% from the service sector (EnergyVaasa 2018; Regional Council of Ostrobothnia 2018).

Table 11.1 Knowledge taxonomy and proximity dimensions explaining the network relations between triple helix actors

Knowledge taxonomy	*Content*	*Proximity dimension*
Know-what	Knowledge about facts (often codified knowledge)	Cognitive
Know-why	Knowledge that explains why things are done in certain ways	Cognitive
Know-how	Practical knowledge about how to perform skills (often tacit knowledge)	Social
Know-who	Knowledge regarding who knows what: the actors and partners	Social

Source: authors' own analysis

The case study region has some characteristics of an LFR, in that it is relatively small and the agglomerative advantages are limited. In addition, its location is unfavourable relative to the main national and European centres of population and economic activity, which results in increased travel and transport costs. However, the case study region and Finland in general have managed to at least partly overcome the less-favoured conditions of Europe's northern periphery. In the innovation scoreboard of the EU, Finland has been classified as an innovation forerunner.

The Finnish innovation system is centralised and many important policy domains such as science, technology, innovation, and university policies are coordinated at the national level, with weak regional approaches. Regional Councils are responsible for regional development, including RIS3. This background has obviously affected the authors' view on regional innovation and needs to be addressed here. In Ostrobothnia, a 'connected region' was selected as a vision for RIS3, and a policy model was developed according to that vision.

The data used in this chapter were gathered during 2013 as part of an earlier study on overall regional connectivity (Mäenpää 2014). In total, there were 53 respondents representing various expert and leading positions in companies (21), the public sector (17), and universities (15); the group represents the three most important export sectors of the region: the energy technology cluster, boat building, and the fur industry. The actual data gathering was undertaken via surveys, but, due to the wide range of questions, was complemented by an interviewer helping the respondents to complete the survey sheets. The cooperation between the TH actors was studied via nine relations. First, there were the three types of organisations: universities, public organisations, and companies. Second, there were also three geographical levels: regional, national, and international. This created the nine connections that were focused upon. The respondents reported the number of partners and their importance by utilising simple tables into which they entered the (exact) number of partners and, in another table, their importance on a scale from 1 to 10 (from lowest to highest, and using 0 to denote no connection).

Different knowledge types were analysed by asking about experiences of cooperation according to the different aspects of knowledge typology (also on a scale from 1 to 10, and 0 if there was no connection) (Table 11.1). The questions were designed to elicit the extent to which the respondents knew the staff of their partners, or the ways in which their partners work (social aspects), or what their partners were working on, or why they were doing so (cognitive aspects). Questions were asked about the innovation partner, and there was a general description (actual dialogue, not just purchasing activities) for it, as the aim was to let the respondents themselves decide what they considered important aspects of collaboration. The method offered a route to identifying possible development challenges.

The same question sets were answered three times within a single helix, according to the chosen geographical division: first for the region, then for the other parts of Finland, and lastly for the international connections. The only exceptions were public organisations, as their connections to companies outside the region were not studied at all. This was because, in Finland, several of the public actors are regional entities, and they have no jurisdiction to act in other areas.

This chapter presents a new analysis investigating how different non-spatial (institutional, social, and cognitive) proximities substitute for and/or facilitate geographical proximity. The idea is to analyse data regarding the importance and number of different partners for the respondents and regarding a respondent's knowledge of their partners' innovation activities. The authors then evaluate how proximity affects the emergence and functioning of the innovation network among the TH actors.

Analysis and results

Geographical and institutional proximity

Taking account of the total number of partners (657) mentioned in the 53 interviews, only 38% of the relations are directed towards the respondents' own helices and 62% are directed towards the other helices. These figures can be interpreted as signifying quite low institutional proximity. However, low institutional proximity also implies high connectivity between the helices. Comparing the geographical proximity (67%) figure to this indication, it is clear that, overall, the region of Ostrobothnia has a good number of connections between helices, but they are mostly regionally embedded (Table 11.2).

With regard to the companies, most of their partners (70%) are based in Ostrobothnia, which indicates high geographical proximity. The institutional proximity of the companies is, however, even higher (87%), suggesting that they largely cooperate with other companies instead of the other two helices. The university sector has an average rate of geographical proximity (51%) and a low /average rate of institutional proximity (17%). However, in this case the low institutional proximity might mean that universities are not living in

Table 11.2 Geographical and institutional proximity in Ostrobothnia

Helix of respondents	*Geographical proximity: Ostrobothnia vs other regions*	*Institutional proximity: own helix vs other helices*
Companies	High (70%; 119/171)	High (87%; 148/171)
Universities	Average (51%; 91/179)	Low (17%; 31/179)
Public sector	High (75%; 231/307)	Low (22%; 68/307)
All	Average (67%; 441/657)	Average (38%; 247/657)

Low proximity: less than 30% of the number of partners in the helix or in the region.
Average proximity: 30–70% of the number the partners in the helix or in the region.
High proximity: More than 70% of the number of the partners in the helix or in the region.

Source: Virkkala et al. 2014a: 120

a closed academic world, but instead are open to other parts of society, and that they cooperate particularly with firms in Ostrobothnia. Public organisations display a high rate of geographical proximity (75%) and a low rate of institutional proximity (22%), meaning that their networks are mostly in the region of Ostrobothnia (as the legislation establishes) and also consist mainly of companies.

The data on the importance of partners (Table 11.3) reflect similar results, as regional companies are valued above all others in importance. This is especially relevant as the question was related to the innovation and actual collaboration of all respondents. Thus, simply buying products was not sufficient to justify the connection, which had to include innovation-related dialogue.

The data regarding the number and importance of partners highlight the fact that the Ostrobothnian region is business-oriented. The majority of respondents thought that their most important partners are regional companies, but the list of most important partners also includes national and international companies. It seems fair to say that the innovation system in Ostrobothnia is business-driven. The analysis of the structure of Ostrobothnia's innovation network helps to examine the social and cognitive aspects of companies' relationships to determine the degree to which they are embedded in the region. This analysis is also important owing to the significant role of companies in the EDP as custodians of market knowledge.

Social and cognitive proximity

The role of geographical proximity is especially relevant regarding LFRs. Might there be a scenario involving overlapping proximities so that when geographical proximity is high (i.e. the innovation partners of Ostrobothnian companies are located in the region of Ostrobothnia), social and/or cognitive proximities are also high? The scenario of overlapping proximities means that geographical proximity might facilitate either social or cognitive proximity or both. The second possibility is that the companies compensate for the absence or weak supply of innovation partners in the region (especially in an LFR) by cooperating with extra-regional (national and international) partners. In that case, firms might have developed high social and cognitive proximities with the extra-regional partners. It is also interesting to see if there are differences

Table 11.3 Importance of partners across spatial scales and helices for all respondents

How important are these partners? (avg)	*Companies (n = 21)*	*Public organisations (n = 17)*	*Universities (n = 15)*
Regional level	8.5	7.7	7.2
National level	7.4	7.0	6.9
International level	6.1	5.0	5.8

Source: authors' own analysis

across the helices in the social and cognitive proximities of the innovation partners of Ostrobothnian companies.

An inspection of the relationships between companies and public organisations (Table 11.4) reveals that both social (know-how/who) and cognitive (know-what/why) proximities are lower from the companies' view of cooperation at the regional level. Companies have weaker experiences of cooperation with public organisations overall on all spatial levels. The experiences are lowest for both companies and public organisations regarding their knowledge of their partners' reasons for their activity, and on the theories underpinning their activity (the know-why typology), as it requires a wealth of knowledge of the actual processes within the companies/public actors. Our analysis offers results only on the intra-regional connection from the public actors' side, as their legal status requires that they operate on a regional level only.

An examination of the relationships between companies and universities (Table 11.5) reveals that both social (know-how/who) proximity and cognitive (know-what/why) proximity are lower from the companies' than from the universities' perspective. Companies have weaker experiences regarding cooperation with universities on all scales. Universities seem to have quite strong experiences of cooperation with companies regarding social and cognitive proximities. This is interesting because companies' institutional proximity is high (Table 11.2.), so the knowledge residing within universities does not seem to be of interest to local companies. Indeed, institutional and geographical proximity seem to correlate, and it is probable that the explanation lies with the regional innovation structure.

Companies' experiences of cooperation with regional universities with regard to analytical knowledge that improves the innovation process (know-why) are lower than those with national and international university partners. This indicates that companies might substitute the knowledge production of regional universities with extra-regional cooperation. It also reflects the fact that innovations are complex and the knowledge necessary for production is often dispersed in different locations and on different scales (Strambach and Klement 2012). To acquire knowledge, companies must cooperate in innovation networks even with geographically distant university partners. According to our case study, this seems to be the situation for companies in the LFRs too. However, to acquire the distributed knowledge might be more challenging than to cooperate with the regional universities, and could also demand a higher absorptive capacity of the companies.

The Ostrobothnian companies knew the staff (know-who) of their regional partner universities better than the staff of their national and international partners. Even if the overall social proximity regarding innovation cooperation is higher on the regional level, the knowledge of partners' research and development methods (know-how) is higher at the national and international levels. On national and global levels, one can already see indications that companies do not know research staff (know-who), as these are the lowest figures. One explanation is also institutional proximity, as some previous results indicate

Table 11.4 Social and cognitive proximities in relations between companies and public organisations

Proximity type	Companies, experiences (avg)	*n*	⟷	*n*	Public organisations, experiences (avg)
Regional level					
Cognitive	7.1	15	Knows our work (know-what)	11	8.9
Cognitive	5.5	15	Helps us with our difficult problems (know-why)	10	7
Social	7.1	14	Contacts us (know-how)	12	8.4
Social	5.6	15	Knows our staff (know-who)	10	8.2
National level					
Proximity type	Companies, experiences (avg)	*n*	⟷	*n*	Public organisations*, experiences (avg)
Cognitive	6.3	12	Knows our work (know-what)	No data	No data
Cognitive	5.8	12	Helps us with our difficult problems (know-why)	No data	No data
Social	6.7	11	Contacts us (know-how)	No data	No data
Social	5.4	11	Knows our staff (know-who)	No data	No data
International level					
Proximity type	Companies, experiences (avg)	*n*	⟷	*n*	Public organisations*, experiences (avg)
Cognitive	5.8	4	Knows our work (know-what)	No data	No data
Cognitive	5.8	4	Helps us with our difficult problems (know-why)	No data	No data
Social	7.0	4	Contacts us (know-how)	No data	No data
Social	6.3	4	Knows our staff (know-who)	No data	No data

* Interviewed public actors only have jurisdiction on the regional level

Source: authors' own analysis

Table 11.5 Social and cognitive proximities in relations between companies and universities

Regional level					
Proximity type	Companies, experiences (avg)	*n*	↔	*n*	Universities, experiences (avg)
Cognitive	6.0	14	We know our most important partner's work (know-what)	12	8.4
Cognitive	5.5	14	Improves our innovation process (know-why)	12	8.2
Social	6.1	14	We know our most important partner's research and development methods (know-how)	12	7.5
Social	6.1	13	We know our most important partner's staff working in our field (know-who)	12	7.9
National level					
Proximity type	Companies, Experiences (avg)	*n*	↔	*n*	Universities, experiences (avg)
Cognitive	6.1	8	We know our most important partner's work (know-what)	9	7.7
Cognitive	6.9	7	Improves our innovation process (know-why)	9	7.3
Social	6.8	8	We know our most important partner's research and development methods (know-how)	9	6.8
Social	4.7	7	We know our most important partner's staff working in our field (know-who)	9	7.0

(continued)

Table 11.5 *(continued)*

International level					
Proximity type	Companies, experiences (avg)	*n*	↔	*n*	Universities, experiences (avg)
Cognitive	6.2	6	We know our most important partner's work (know-what)	5	7.6
Cognitive	6.2	6	Improves our innovation process (know-why)	4	7.8
Social	6.5	6	We know our most important partner's research and development methods (know-how)	4	7.0
Social	5.0	5	We know our most important partner's staff working in our field (know-who)	4	7.0

Source: authors' own analysis

that, for Ostrobothnian companies, other companies on any spatial scale are more preferable partners than universities (Table 11.2).

Social proximity (know-how and know-who) between the Ostrobothnian companies and their university partners seems to be little higher at the regional level than on the other spatial scales, which suggests that geographical proximity is facilitating social proximity. Spatial collocation increases the likelihood of accidental encounters, and trustful relations can emerge when the exchanges are regular and the people know each other (Storper and Venables 2004).

Companies' connections with other companies are intra-helix relationships according to the TH model, and that is the reason we have measurements from only one side regarding both social (know-how/who) and cognitive proximities (know-what/why) in Table 11.6. Both social and cognitive proximities are higher in the context of cooperation between regional companies than that between Ostrobothnian companies and extra-regional companies. However, the results still show that, on a regional level, social proximity between companies

Table 11.6 Social and cognitive proximities between companies

Regional level			
Proximity type		*n*	Companies, experiences (avg)
Cognitive	Knows the standards/concepts (know-what)	13	7.8
Cognitive	Helps us with our difficult problems (know-why)	14	8.0
Social	Knows our products/services (know-how)	14	8.2
Social	Knows our key staff (know-who)	15	9.3
National level			
Proximity type		n	Companies, experiences (avg)
Cognitive	Knows the standards/concepts (know-what)	12	7.1
Cognitive	Helps us with our difficult problems (know-why)	13	7.2
Social	Knows our products/services (know-how)	13	6.8
Social	Knows our key staff (know-who)	14	6.2
International level			
Proximity type		n	Companies, experiences (avg)
Cognitive	Knows the standards/concepts (know-what)	9	7.3
Cognitive	Helps us with our difficult problems (know-why)	9	6.9
Social	Knows our products/services (know-how)	9	7.6
Social	Knows our key staff (know-who)	9	6.3

Source: authors' own analysis

is higher than cognitive proximity, and a comparison of cognitive proximity between companies at the regional and extra-regional (i.e. national and international) levels shows that cognitive proximity is higher among regional companies. High levels of institutional proximity, as indicated by the finding that companies prefer to cooperate with other companies rather than with universities and public organisations, also affect social proximity between companies at the regional level. This is in line with the structural analysis and the fact that the RIS in Ostrobothnia is business-driven.

Summary of findings

An interesting question is whether geographical proximity explains the high rates of other proximities. If one looks at the companies' relations to universities (Table 11.5), one can see that they are generally more distant (i.e. the level of proximities is lower) than the relationships between companies, which may indicate that geographical proximity cannot totally explain the findings. Institutional proximity might be one indication, and companies are known for their focus on business-related matters (which directs cooperation with other companies), but one indicator in the company results might offer a more profound explanation. Social proximity, and especially the knowledge of partners' staff (know-who), seem to be quite high at the regional level. This result stands out in the analysis as a whole, as it is the only one near the maximum figure (9.3).

The findings of the analysis show that both social and cognitive proximities are highest at the regional level. However, the differences between cognitive proximity across spatial levels (regional, national, and international) are smaller than those of social proximity across spatial levels.

With regard to the proximities across helices, the findings indicate a clear pattern, according to which social and cognitive proximities are highest in relationships between companies at all spatial scales, but these proximities are especially high at the regional level. One can say that the findings indicate that companies' institutional, geographical, social, and cognitive proximities are overlapping, and it can also be inferred that regional proximity really does facilitate other forms of proximities (Table 11.7) However, this is verified only for innovation cooperation with other companies and public organisations because cooperation between companies and universities indicates generally higher social and cognitive proximities at the national and international levels than at the regional level.

This result is especially interesting in relation to LFRs, as they may lack intra-regional connections, and, in the case of Ostrobothnia, it would seem that regional cooperation has affected the overall TH collaboration, as the regional results for cooperation between companies and universities are low. Local companies, in particular, network among themselves, which might explain why there is high institutional proximity. Universities may not have been able to step into the business-driven networks, as the results indicate that companies' cognitive proximity with universities is lower than the other way around.

Table 11.7 Geographical proximity facilitating other proximities; other proximities substituting for geographical proximity

Geographical proximity vs other proximities	Facilitating/ overlapping with geographical proximity	Substituting for geographical proximity
Social proximity (know-how)	Yes (average proximities higher at regional than at other scales)	Yes (company–university relationship of higher proximity at national and international levels)
Social proximity (know-who)	Yes (higher at regional than at other scales)	No
Cognitive proximity (know-what)	Yes (company–company relationship)	Yes, slightly (company–university relationship)
Cognitive proximity (know-why)	Yes (company–company relationship)	Yes (company–university relationship and company–public organisation relationships)

Facilitating = Proximity between partners is higher in the region of Ostrobothnia than at other geographical scales (national, international).
Substituting = Proximity between the partners is higher at other geographical scales (national, international) than in the region of Ostrobothnia.

Source: authors' own analysis

This might indicate that universities are studying what companies do, but that companies have not invited universities to participate in their entrepreneurial initiatives. Or perhaps regional companies prefer extra-regional universities for collaboration more than regional ones.

Conclusions

This chapter has discussed the proximity dimension of innovation cooperation from the perspective of LFRs. Based on the literature on proximities, the innovation system, and the TH, the chapter used a Finnish case study to focus particularly on the role of geographical and non-spatial proximities as they affect innovation partners in LFRs. The chapter focused on companies because they are especially important to the EDP. It is important for actors in an LFR to understand the degree to which the possible weaknesses or lack of actors and knowledge suppliers can be improved via cooperation with extra-regional innovation partners. This means the substitution of geographical proximity with non-spatial proximities. The proximities are seen as preconditions for relationships and innovation cooperation between different TH actors across different spatial scales and helices. It seems valid to ask what actions could be undertaken in LFRs to enhance proximity between stakeholders.

The analysis of the Finnish case study leads to four major conclusions. First, different proximities overlap at the regional level, and geographical proximity slightly facilitates social proximity. This might not be surprising since collocation increases the likelihood of accidental encounters, and trustful relations can emerge when people familiar with each other have regular exchanges (Storper and Venables 2004).

Second, companies operating in LFRs might substitute the insufficient knowledge production of regional universities for extra-regional cooperation. We might even suppose that the companies of the case region have managed to overcome the limitations of the LFR, such as there being few actors and tiny knowledge resources, by undertaking extra-regional networking to acquire and utilise geographically dispersed knowledge in their production processes. Regarding LFRs in general, there seem to be opportunities for high levels of cognitive proximity (i.e. knowledge exchange) even in the absence of some regional connections or key enablers. If one considers this in the EDP setting, it might indicate that the idea of utilising universities or development organisations as substitutes for a lack of market knowledge may work, as has been suggested in the RIS3 guidebook (Foray et al. 2012).

Third, in the Finnish case, the level of social proximity was relatively high between regional companies and their international company partners, which might indicate that collaboration over distance is more likely between individuals and organisations with established social relationships. This would seem to indicate that dynamic changes are in play, but the issue should be studied further.

Fourth, and as a response to the research question of how to enhance proximity between stakeholders, the authors suggest that public government should promote and establish a successful EDP partnership between relevant stakeholders. By providing a tool for measuring and improving the connections between stakeholders, the connectivity model with its proximity analysis (developed by Virkkala et al. 2017; 2014b) could broaden the scope of the discussion and provide a proper scenario for possible entrepreneurial discovery. The EDP can be seen as a search process for new business areas, but it is also a process advancing an optimal proximity between actors. This example indicates there is an opportunity for regional developers to search for optimal proximities, which is a precondition for smart experimentation.

In the Finnish case study, one notion was the fact that companies and universities do not cooperate enough, because universities "lack projects and students" (Mäenpää 2014: 62). However, this dialogue continued and, finally, during 2017, the Regional Council, in cooperation with regional technology companies and the University of Vaasa, and with the help of European Regional Development Fund funding, managed to establish a fuel and engine laboratory, VEBIC (Vaasa Energy and Business Innovation Centre), in the region, which is specifically designed to help bridge the gap between company and university knowledge. This is one example of regional collaboration not offering a direct route to new domains and innovation, but one that will nurture a stronger region. This sort of smart experimentation may very well turn into a new specialisation.

The empirical case study has limitations. The data only reflect one region, are based on structured interviews, and come from a limited number of respondents. One research avenue would be to examine the dynamic aspects of the proximities and relationships. Proximities are constantly changing during interactions between partners in the innovation process. When the partners learn from each other, their knowledge bases will change, and their shared mental models will be adjusted, which will lead to the reduction of their cognitive distance, which in turn will enhance the learning effects (Menzel 2016). The interaction can also create a common social context in which personal relations develop despite differences in organisational, geographical, or institutional backgrounds or knowledge bases (Balland et al. 2015). One way to dynamise the proximity analysis would be to employ longitudinal data (Hansen 2015), but more qualitative data with in-depth analysis would also be required. The authors have tried to capture the dynamic aspects of innovation cooperation by measuring the gaps between the expectations and experiences of relationships (Virkkala et al. 2017).

To evaluate the proximities of partners with the help of knowledge typology is only one option. There could also be other measurements, including more statistical analysis (cf. Hansen 2015), but that would require more quantitative data. Furthermore, more case studies would illustrate how regions differ in their collaboration, and which types of proximities and balances between proximate and distant relationships are prominent in different types of LFRs, and how the proximities might be enhanced to mitigate the limitations of the peripheral regions. This knowledge could be used to develop more tools to encourage specific types of collaboration between various actors. In this way, the EDP could be enhanced and unique ideas for regional specialisation could be promoted. Regional comparison and transnational learning among LFRs would then become possible.

The actors in the LFRs may find new ideas within the region, and need not automatically be left behind in the innovation race owing to their potential lack of connections. Proximity analysis does not address all of the issues, but it does provide one viewpoint for regional analysis and serves as a discussion opener. The authors argue that sometimes it may be smart to focus on the relationships; the rest can then follow.

References

Balland, P.A., Boschma, R., & Frenken, K. (2015). Proximity and innovation: from statics to dynamics, *Regional Studies 49*(6), 907–920.

Bathelt, H., Malmberg, A., & Maskell, P. (2004). Clusters and knowledge: local buzz, global pipelines and the process of knowledge creation, *Progress in Human Geography 28*, 31–56.

Blažek, J., Healy, A., Wilson, J., Magro, E., Trippl, M., Grillitsch, M., Hansen, T., Goddard, J., &Vallance, P. (2014). Smart specialisation for regional innovation: regions with less developed research and innovation systems, Work Package 3, Reflection Paper. Available at: https://orca.cf.ac.uk/78219/1/Regions%20with%20Less%20Developed%20Research%20and%20Innovation%20Systems.pdf

Boschma, R. (2005). Proximity and innovation: a critical assessment, *Regional Studies 39*(1), 61–74.

Boschma, R., & Frenken, K. (2013). Technological relatedness and regional branching. In: Bathelt, H., Feldman, M.P., & Kogler, D.F. (Eds.) *Beyond territory: dynamic geographies of knowledge creation, diffusion, and innovation* (pp. 64–81). London: Routledge.

Carayannis, E., & Campbell, D. (2012). *Mode 3 knowledge production in quadruple helix innovation systems: 21st-century democracy, innovation, and entrepreneurship for development*. SpringerBriefs in Business 7. New York: Springer.

Crone, M. (2012). Rethinking peripherality in the context of knowledge-intensive service-dominated economy. In: Danson, M. & de Souza, P. (Eds.): *Regional development in northern Europe: peripherality, marginality and border issues* (pp. 49–64). London: Routledge.

EnergyVaasa (2018). EnergyVaasa shortly. Available at: http://energyvaasa.vaasanseutu.fi/energyvaasa-shortly/.

Etzkowitz, H., & Leydesdorff, L. (1998). The endless transition: a "triple helix" of university–industry–government relations, *Minerva 36*(3), 203–208.

Etzkowitz, H., &Leydesdorff, L. (2000). The dynamics of innovation: from national systems and "Mode 2" to a triple helix of university–industry–government relations, *Research Policy 29*(2), 109–123.

Foray, D., Goddard, J., Beldarrain, X., Landabaso, M., McCann, P., Morgan, K., . . . & Ortega-Argilés, R. (2012). *Guide to research and innovation strategies for smart specialisation (RIS3)*. Brussels: European Commission.

Goddard, J., Kempton, L., & Vallance, P. (2013). Universities and smart specialisation: challenges, tensions, and opportunities for the innovation strategies of European regions, *Ekonomiaz 2*, 83–102.

Grillitsch, M., & Trippl, M. (2014). Combining knowledge from different sources, channels and geographical scales, *European Planning Studies 22*(11), 2305–2325.

Hansen, T. (2015) Substitution or overlap? The relations between geographical and non-spatial proximity dimensions in collaborative innovation projects, *Regional Studies 49*(10), 1672–1684.

Isaksen, A., & Trippl, M. (2014). Regional industrial path development in different regional innovation systems: a conceptual analysis. Papers in Innovation Studies (Report No. 2014/17). CIRCLE, University of Lund.

Jensen, M.B., Johnson, B., Lorenz, E., & Lundvall, B.-Å. (2007). Forms of knowledge and modes of innovation. *Research Policy 36*, 1993–2008.

Lorentzen, A. (2012). The development of periphery in the experience economy. In: Danson, M., & de Souza, P. (Eds.) *Regional development in northern Europe: peripherality, marginality and border issues* (pp. 16–29). London: Routledge.

Lundvall, B.-Å., & Johnson, B. (1994). The learning economy, *Industry & Innovation 1*(2), 23–42.

Mäenpää, A. (2014). Methodology and research design. In: Virkkala, S., Mäenpää, A., & Mariussen, Å. (Eds.). The Ostrobothnian model of smart specialisation. Proceedings of the University of Vaasa. Reports 196.

Malmberg, A. & Maskell, P. (2006). Localized learning revisited, *Growth and Change 37*(1), 1–8.
Menzel, M.-P. (2016). Interrelating dynamic proximities by bridging, reducing and producing distances, *Regional Studies 49*(11): 1892–1907.
Ranga, M., & Etzkowitz, H. (2013). Triple helix systems: an analytical framework for innovation policy and practice in the knowledge society, *Industry & Higher Education 27*(3), 237–262.
Regional Council of Ostrobothnia (2018). 2016 Ostrobothnia in figures. Available at: http://www.pohjanmaalukuina.fi/assets/10/Uploads/Pohjanmaa-lukuina2016-valmis.pdf.
Strambach, S., & Klement, B. (2012). Cumulative and combinatorial micro-dynamics of knowledge: the role of space and place in knowledge integration, *European Planning Studies 20*(11), 1843–1866.
Storper, M., & Venables, A. (2004). Buzz: face-to-face contact and the urban economy, *Journal of Economic Geography 4*(4), 351–370.
Torre A., & Gilly, J.P. (1999). On the analytical dimension of proximity dynamics, *Regional Studies 34*(2), 169–180.
Torre, A., & Rallet, A. (2005). Proximity and localization, *Regional Studies 39*(1), 47–59.
Tödtling, F., & Trippl, M. (2005). One size fits all? Towards a differential regional innovation policy approach, *Research Policy 34*(8),1203–1219.
Virkkala, S. (2013). Geographical perspectives: regional development and transnational learning. In: Mariussen, Å., & Virkkala, S. (Eds.). *Learning Transnational Learning* (pp. 51–102). London: Routledge.
Virkkala, S., Johnson, J., & Mariussen, Å. (2014a). Summary and conclusion. In: Virkkala, S., Mäenpää, A., & Mariussen, Å. (Eds). The Ostrobothnian model of smart specialisation. Proceedings of the University of Vaasa. Reports 196.
Virkkala, S., Mäenpää, A., & Mariussen, Å. (2014b). The Ostrobothnian model of smart specialisation. Proceedings of the University of Vaasa, Reports 196.
Virkkala, S., Mäenpää, A., & Mariussen, Å. (2017). A connectivity model as a potential tool for smart specialization strategies, *European Planning Studies 25*(4), 661–679.

12 Relatedness, diversification and economic performance at the regional level

Differences between advantaged and less favoured regions

Johanna Vogel and Stefan Weingärtner

Introduction

With its smart specialisation approach, the European Union encourages regions to identify existing areas of economic strength as well as new, but related, areas that the existing regional set of capabilities allows 'branching' into. This is known as related diversification or related variety, and is considered a key driver of regional economic growth (Boschma and Frenken, 2011). The counterpart concept of unrelated diversification or unrelated variety has so far received less attention in the literature (Boschma, 2017). Spreading economic activity over a variety of unrelated areas may, however, be especially beneficial for less favoured regions, for example, since it provides a buffer against shocks affecting one economic activity and those directly related to it.

The analysis in this chapter tests the roles of related and unrelated variety in production and knowledge for regional employment growth using annual data on 250 NUTS-2 regions from the 28 (as of 2018) EU Member States between 2008 and 2011. The study thus aims to provide empirical evidence on the growth impact of a measure of smart specialisation for a broad range of regions, allowing for a differentiation between economically less favoured regions and more advantaged ones. The fact that the time period from 2008 to 2011 coincides with the most acute years of the financial and economic crisis in Europe adds an additional dimension to this differentiation. Although the time span considered is relatively short,[1] and precedes the introduction of smart specialisation into EU regional policy, it may be well suited to identifying the shock-absorbing role of unrelated variety for less favoured regions.

Three types of distinctions between regions emerge from the empirical set-up, yielding three economic definitions of 'less favoured regions' (LFR): first, between regions from countries that were most heavily affected by the economic crisis and those that were less affected; second, between regions that are closer to the technological frontier and those further away from it; and third, between highly urbanised regions and less urbanised or rural regions. The roles of related and unrelated variety for employment growth in each of these three types of LFR and for all regions combined lead to four econometrically testable hypotheses, which are formulated in the following section. The descriptions of variables and data as well as the estimation design employed to test the four hypotheses are presented and explained, followed by a discussion of the results and conclusions.

Conceptual background and hypotheses tested

The concepts of related and unrelated variety are concerned with the diversity of economic activities in terms of the industries and knowledge-generating capabilities present in a region and with their technological proximity. A key reason why the presence of a variety of economic activities in a region should be beneficial to growth are the advantages of *knowledge spillovers* between a diverse mix of industries, which provide opportunities for learning new ways to solve problems by recombining knowledge from different sources (Jacobs, 1969). Knowledge flows operate between industries, for example, through formal or informal networks and the mobility of employees or cooperation and exchange between firms. In particularly, new industries at an early stage of product development have been shown to benefit from access to a variety of local knowledge sources, while more mature industries should benefit more from a specialised environment offering access to industry-specific know-how (Duranton and Puga, 2001; Neffke et al., 2011).

Frenken, van Oort and Verburg (2007) argue that knowledge spills over more easily between industries that are technologically related than between unrelated ones sharing less-common knowledge. Hence, the presence of a *variety of related sectors* in a region should have a stronger growth-enhancing effect than a *variety of unrelated sectors*. Unrelated variety can, however, still play an important role for regional economic performance by moderating economic shocks. Regional diversification across a portfolio of (unrelated) industries provides a buffer against the contraction of a particular sector, which would hit those regions harder that specialise in it or in industries related to this sector *(portfolio effect)*. In our sample, this shock-moderating role of unrelated variety should be especially relevant for those *regions most heavily affected by the financial and economic crisis* that began in late 2008 – our first definition of less favoured regions.

Variety is relevant not only regarding the regional production structure, but also in terms of the knowledge-generating or innovative capabilities that a region possesses, captured, for instance, by patenting activities (Castaldi et al., 2015). Similar to the argument for industries, a greater technological diversity of regional innovative activities should positively affect economic performance, as variety creates opportunities for cross-fertilisation and recombinations of diverse knowledge into innovations. Again, a variety of *related knowledge capabilities* facilitates the *absorption of knowledge spillovers*, and hence innovation and growth in general, since innovators in related fields share a common cognitive framework. Related variety is thus thought to contribute to growth by fostering incremental innovation within narrower technological domains. *Unrelated variety*, on the other hand, has the potential to give rise to radical or *breakthrough innovations* through the combination of previously unrelated technological approaches. If successful, this can create entire new industries and generate employment growth in the long term (Saviotti and Frenken, 2008).

From this discussion, the following two hypotheses emerge, which are tested econometrically:

> *Hypothesis 1: Related and unrelated variety in production and knowledge are positively related to regional employment growth across all regions.*
>
> *Hypothesis 2: Unrelated variety in production has a stronger positive impact on employment growth in the regions that were most affected by the economic crisis (LFR type 1).*

The European regions differ in terms of their level of technological development and hence their industrial structure. In particular, the Central and Eastern European Member States (EU-12) have undergone substantial structural change since the mid-1990s, with their transition from the planned communist to a market-based economic system and EU accession in the 2000s. Their catching-up process involved the decline of old monopolies and the emergence of a multitude of new firms in new sectors (e.g. services). By means of large inflows of foreign direct investment (FDI), the EU-12 also established themselves as suppliers of intermediate inputs in European and global production chains. Hence, their industries are likely younger and less technologically advanced. By comparison, industries in the Member States from Western Europe (EU-15) are more mature and closer to the technological frontier. *Diversification into less related industries* could therefore be a stronger growth driver in the regions of the EU-12 – or, more generally, in *regions further from the technological frontier*, our second definition of less favoured regions – where industries are at an earlier stage of their life cycle than in Western Europe and therefore benefit from spillovers from unrelated industries (cf. Neffke et al., 2011). Regions closer to the frontier, on the other hand, which are at a later stage of their life cycle, would benefit from *diversification into related industries*. Alternatively, as argued by Saviotti and Frenken (2008), long-term growth stems from the *recombination of previously unrelated knowledge* creating entirely new goods and industries, which is likely to be more effective closer to the technological frontier where the required advanced cognitive and technological capabilities are available (Krueger and Kumar, 2004). Thus, unrelated variety could also be a growth driver for regions closer to the frontier. This leads to the following testable hypothesis:

> *Hypothesis 3: The effects of related and unrelated variety on employment growth differ by regional distance to the technological frontier, with a stronger role for unrelated variety in regions further from the frontier (LFR type 2).*

Our final regional differentiation is by degree of urbanisation. Highly urbanised areas tend to be characterised by greater sectoral diversity, inspiring Jacobs (1969) to formulate her original hypothesis on the *growth benefits of local variety in cities*. Combined with the life cycle view of industrial development, this implies that industries at an early stage of their life cycle benefit from locating in diverse cities, while at later stages, firms benefit from locating in more specialised cities, which are often smaller and located more peripherally than the dominant metropolitan agglomerations (Duranton and Puga, 2001; Neffke et al., 2011). Hence, employment growth in more urbanised regions could be expected to be driven by *unrelated variety*, while in *less urbanised or rural regions* – our third definition of less favoured regions – *related variety* should play a stronger role. Van Oort, de Geus and Dogaru (2015) indeed find a significant positive effect of related variety on employment growth for small and medium-sized EU city regions and no significant effect of either related or unrelated variety for large and capital regions. On the other hand, more mature industries also need to locate close to potential customers to sustain sales, which would favour related variety as a growth driver in more urbanised areas. In line with this explanation, Firgo and Mayerhofer (2017) find that unrelated variety has a stronger positive effect for rural and industrialised NUTS-3 regions in Austria, while related variety matters more for employment growth in urban regions.

> *Hypothesis 4: The effects of related and unrelated variety on employment growth differ by the regions' degree of urbanisation, with a stronger role for related variety in less urbanised or rural regions (LFR type 3).*

Variables and data

Measuring 'less favoured regions'

Following the conceptual discussion above, our three types of economically less favoured regions are defined and measured as follows. The *first type (LFR type 1)*, comprising the regions most heavily affected by the financial and economic crisis, uses *economic performance* as an indicator to distinguish between advantaged and less favoured regions. To measure regional economic performance, employment growth is used, which is also the dependent variable in the empirical analysis. The data are taken from the Cambridge Econometrics European Regional Database (2014 update). Figure 12.1 maps the average annual growth rate of regional employment between 2008 and 2011 for the NUTS-2 regions in the sample. During this time, employment in several countries contracted. Most affected were regions of Greece, Ireland, Portugal, Spain, Estonia, Latvia, Lithuania and Bulgaria, where employment shrank by more than 2% per year on average. Latvia registered the largest annual decline, at an average of 8.8% per year, followed by south-eastern Bulgaria and Galicia in Spain.

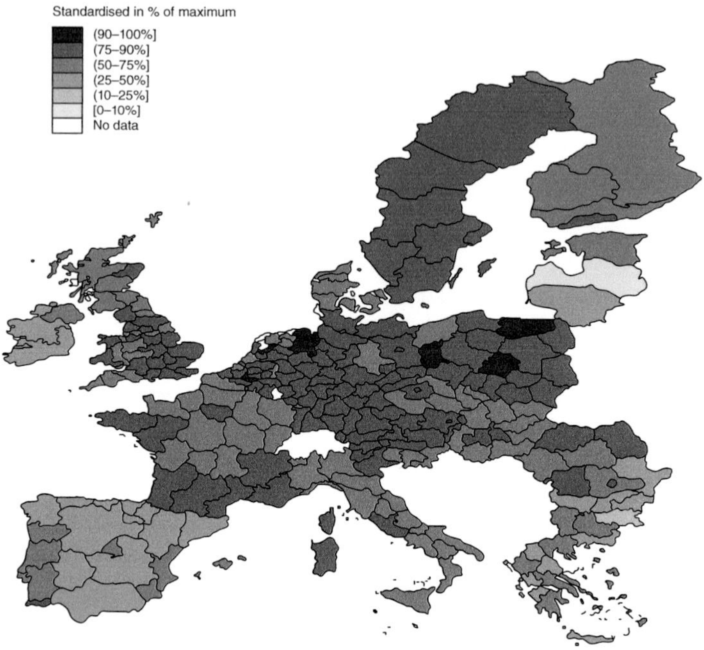

Figure 12.1 Regional employment growth: annual average 2008–2011

Source: own calculations based on data by Cambridge Econometrics. Values standardised between 0 (min.) and 1 (max. in sample)

Our definition of the *second type of less favoured region*, those further from the technological frontier, is based on the *regional level of technological development*, which is proxied with innovative capacity. To construct an indicator of regional distance to the frontier, information from the Regional Innovation Scoreboard 2014 is used, which groups the NUTS-2 regions into innovation leaders, innovation followers, moderate and modest innovators for the years 2008 and 2010. We assign the value zero to the innovation leaders (regions at the frontier), one to the innovation followers, and two and three to the moderate and modest innovators (regions furthest from the frontier). Regions in the last two categories are designated as *LFR type 2*. These regions are from the Czech Republic, Greece, Spain, Hungary, Italy, Portugal, Slovakia, Poland, Bulgaria and Romania. Regions at the frontier are from Germany, Denmark, Finland, Sweden and the UK.

The *third type of less favoured region*, those less urbanised or rural, uses the *regional degree of urbanisation* as an indicator to distinguish between advantaged and less favoured regions. Degree of urbanisation is approximated using Eurostat data on the share of households per region living in densely populated or urbanised areas, intermediately populated/urbanised areas and thinly populated or rural areas. This latter category – the group of regions where the share of households living in thinly populated or rural areas is high – is designated as *LFR type 3*.

Measuring related and unrelated variety in regional production and knowledge

To measure *related and unrelated variety in regional production structures*, we follow Frenken, van Oort and Verburg (2007) who identify relatedness by using the structure of the NACE classification.[2] While the 2-digit NACE sectors are assumed to be unrelated to each other, the 4-digit industries within each 2-digit sector are assumed to be related. Variety for each NUTS-2 region is then measured using the distribution of economic activity – proxied by employment in this chapter – across and within NACE 2-digit sectors using Shannon's index of information entropy. Box 12.1 below explains this approach in more detail.

Box 12.1 Related and unrelated variety in production

Let $E_{s,r}$ denote employment in NACE 2-digit sector *s* in NUTS-2 region *r*, so that the share of 2-digit sector *s* in total regional employment is given by $E_{s,r} / E_r$. Unrelated variety in production in region *r* is then measured by the Shannon entropy over the region's employment shares in the 2-digit sectors:

$$UV_r^P = \sum_{s=1}^{S} \frac{E_{s,r}}{E_r} \log_2\left(\frac{E_r}{E_{s,r}}\right)$$

where *S* is the total number of 2-digit sectors.

This measure reaches its minimum value of zero when all regional employment is concentrated in one 2-digit sector and its theoretical maximum value of $\log_2(S)$ when a region's employment is equally distributed across all 2-digit sectors.

Further, let $E_{i,s,r}$ denote employment in NACE 4-digit industry *i* belonging to sector *s* in region *r*, so that the regional employment share of industry *i* in sector *s* is given by $E_{i,s,r} / E_{s,r}$. Related variety in production in region *r* is then measured by the weighted sum of the entropy of employment shares across the 4-digit industries within each 2-digit sector:

$$RV_r^P = \sum_{s=1}^{S} \frac{E_{s,r}}{E_r} \bullet H_{s,r}^P$$

(continued)

(continued)

where $H^{P}_{s,r} = \sum_{i=1}^{I} \frac{E_{i,s,r}}{E_{s.r}} \log_2\left(\frac{E_{s,r}}{E_{i,s,r}}\right)$ and I is the number of 4-digit industries within each 2-digit sector.

This measure takes on its minimum value of zero if regional employment within each 2-digit sector is entirely concentrated in one 4-digit industry and its theoretical maximum value if employment is equally distributed across the 4-digit industries of that 2-digit sector with the largest number of 4-digit industries. The theoretical maximum value is equal to $\log_2(I_{max})$, where I_{max} is the maximum number of 4-digit industries within 2-digit sectors.

The data on regional employment in 2- and 4-digit industries (NACE Rev. 2) required to construct *UVP* and *RVP* are constructed from Bureau van Dijk's Amadeus database as well as Eurostat. For this project, they were available from 2008 onwards, so the analysis is constrained to begin in that year.

Figure 12.2 depicts the distributions of related and unrelated variety in production across the NUTS-2 regions of the EU. Related production variety is particularly high in the EU-15 regions of Lombardy, Emilia-Romagna and Veneto (IT), Brittany (FR) and Catalonia (ES). For unrelated production variety, the maxima are attained by the Polish regions of Lesser Poland and Lower Silesia, followed by Tuscany (IT), Bucharest-Ilfov (RO) and Madrid (ES). In general, regions in the Central and Eastern European Member States score highly on unrelated variety.

To measure *related and unrelated variety in knowledge-generating capabilities* for the NUTS-2 regions, the approach for sectors of production is applied to regional patent applications to the European Patent Office using the structure of the International Patent Classification (IPC). The 3-digit technology classes in the IPC are assumed to be unrelated to each other, while the 7-digit subclasses within each 3-digit class are assumed to be related. In choosing these disaggregation levels, the aim was to keep the approach comparable to that for sectors of production using the NACE classification.[3] Since observations on regional patent applications are low and variable from year to year for some regions, especially at the 7-digit disaggregation level of technology fields, a discounted sum of patent applications as far back as 1990 was constructed as a first step for each region. This reflects the continued, but declining, value of past innovations for the regional knowledge base (a discount factor of 0.8 is assumed).[4] Box 12.2 below outlines the construction of measures of related and unrelated variety in knowledge capabilities based on the patent or knowledge stocks thus constructed.

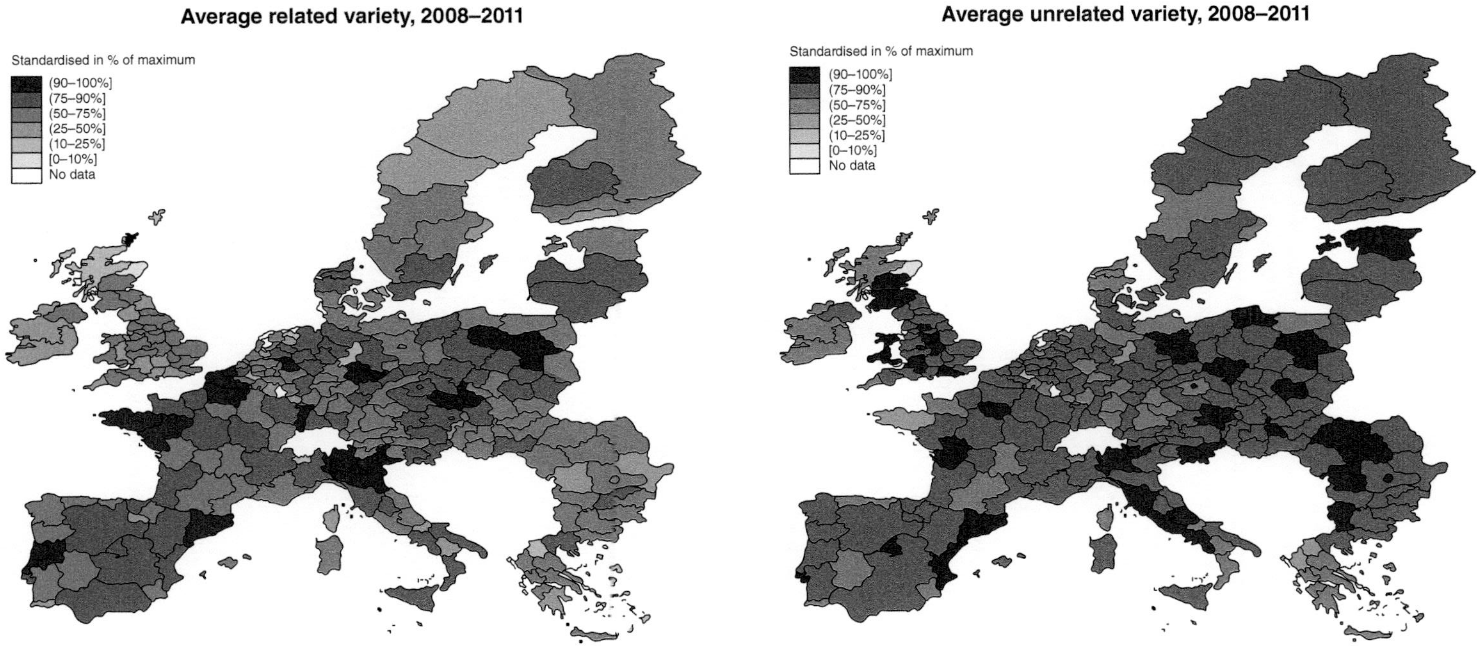

Figure 12.2 Regional related and unrelated variety in production

Source: own calculations based on data by BvD (Amadeus) and Eurostat (SBS). Values standardised between 0 (min.) and 1 (max. in sample)

Box 12.2 Related and unrelated variety in knowledge generation

Let $P_{c,r}$ denote the stock of patents filed by NUTS-2 region *r* in 3-digit IPC class *c*, and $P_{s,c,r}$ the stock of patents in 7-digit subclass *s* belonging to 3-digit class *c*. If P_r is the total stock of patents in all IPC classes in region *r*, unrelated variety in knowledge generation in region *r* is measured by the entropy over the region's patent shares in the 3-digit IPC classes:

$$UV_r^K = \sum_{c=1}^{C} \frac{P_{c,r}}{P_r} \log_2 \left(\frac{P_r}{P_{c,r}} \right)$$

where *C* is the total number of 3-digit IPC classes.

This measure reaches its minimum value of zero when all regional patenting is concentrated in one 3-digit class and its theoretical maximum value of $\log_2(C)$ when a region's patents are equally distributed across all 3-digit technology classes.

Related variety in knowledge generation in region *r* is measured by the weighted sum of the entropy of the region's patent shares over the 7-digit subclasses within each 3-digit IPC class:

$$RV_r^K = \sum_{c=1}^{C} \frac{P_{c,r}}{P_r} \bullet H_{c,r}^K$$

where $H_{c,r}^K = \sum_{j=1}^{J} \frac{P_{s,c,r}}{P_{c,r}} \log_2 \left(\frac{P_{c,r}}{P_{s,c,r}} \right)$ and *J* is the number of 7-digit subclasses within each 3-digit IPC class.

This measure takes on its minimum value of zero if regional patenting within each 3-digit class is entirely concentrated in one 7-digit subclass and its theoretical maximum value if patents are equally distributed across the 7-digit subclasses of that 3-digit class with the largest number of 7-digit subclasses. The theoretical maximum is equal to $\log_2(J_{max})$, where J_{max} is the maximum number of 7-digit subclasses within 3-digit IPC classes.

UVK and *RVK* are computed using data on regional patent applications to the European Patent Office taken from the OECD REGPAT database. The patent applications are counted by priority year and allocated to the regions according to the place of residence of the applicant.[5] Patents with applicants from several regions are divided equally among these (fractional counts).

Other control variables

Following the empirical literature on related and unrelated variety, we control for several additional determinants of regional employment growth. First among these are indicators of *localisation and urbanisation economies*. In addition to the benefits of the presence of a variety of economic activities in a region for employment growth – whether in related or unrelated industries – there are also advantages to the specialisation of a region in a particular industry. The localisation of many firms of the same industry in one region facilitates access to specialised labour and intermediate input suppliers as well as intra-sectoral knowledge spillovers. To control for such localisation economies, a measure of regional specialisation in NACE 2-digit sectors, relative to the EU as a whole, is constructed from the location quotients of 2-digit sectoral employment.[6] Urbanisation economies, on the other hand, are available to firms of all sectors and result from the concentration of economic activity independent of its sectoral composition. They may arise from the existence of superior infrastructure, universities, government institutions or trade associations and networks. To control for this, the population density of a region, i.e. total regional population divided by regional land area, is included. The data are taken from Eurostat.

In addition, we include the *regional hourly wage rate, investment per worker* and *the share of manufacturing in total employment*, the latter accounting for differences in the sectoral composition of regional economies. The data on these variables also come from the Cambridge Econometrics European Regional Database (2014 update).

Estimation design

To test Hypotheses 1 to 4 described in the section on conceptual background above, *three empirical specifications* are estimated using panel data for 250 NUTS-2 regions for the period from 2008 to 2011. The baseline equation takes the following form:

$$\Delta \ln E_{r,t} = \alpha + \beta_1 \ln RV_{r,t-1} + \beta_2 \ln UV_{r,t-1} + \gamma_i X_{i,r,t-1} + \mu_r + \eta_t + \epsilon_{r,t}, \qquad (12.1)$$

where the dependent variable is annual employment growth in region r and RV_r and UV_r denote related and unrelated variety. $X_{i,r}$ contains the control variables for regional specialisation, population density, the regional wage rate, investment per worker and the share of manufacturing employment. All explanatory variables are lagged by one period to reduce endogeneity concerns and all variables are included in logarithmic form to ease interpretation. The estimated coefficients on related and unrelated variety can thus be read as the percentage point increase in regional employment growth induced by a 1% increase in variety. The terms μ_r and η_t denote region- and time-specific fixed effects and $\varepsilon_{r,t}$ is the error term.

Equation (12.2) is used to test Hypotheses 1 and 2 discussed above. It is estimated to investigate the effects of related and unrelated variety, first in production and then also in knowledge. For both types of variety, separate regimes are then estimated for regions strongly affected by the economic crisis in terms of employment growth and those less affected. This is implemented by interacting all explanatory variables with a dummy variable taking the value 1 for crisis regions and zero for non-crisis regions. Crisis regions are defined as those where employment contracted by more than 2% per year on average between 2008 and 2011.

To test Hypotheses 3 and 4, that is, whether the effects of related and unrelated variety differ by distance to the frontier and degree of urbanisation, the following specifications are estimated:

$$\Delta \ln E_{r,t} = \alpha + \beta_1 \ln RV_{r,t-1} + \beta_2 \ln UV_{r,t-1} + \beta_3 \left[\ln RV_{r,t-1} \times DTF_{r,t-1} \right] + \beta_4 \left[\ln UV_{r,t-1} \times DTF_{r,t-1} \right] + \beta_5 DTF_{r,t-1} + \gamma_i X_{i,r,t-1} + \mu_r + \eta_t + \epsilon_{r,t} \quad (12.2)$$

$$\Delta \ln E_{r,t} = \alpha + \beta_1 \ln RV_{r,t-1} + \beta_2 \ln UV_{r,t-1} + \beta_3 \left[\ln RV_{r,t-1} \times DOU^i_{r,t-1} \right] + \beta_4 \left[\ln UV_{r,t-1} \times DOU^i_{r,t-1} \right] + \beta_5 DOU^i_{r,t-1} + \gamma_i X_{i,r,t-1} + \mu_r + \eta_t + \epsilon_{r,t} \quad (12.3)$$

where DTF_r stands for distance to the frontier and takes on (integer) values between 0 and 3, and DOU^i_r stands for degree of urbanisation *i*, i.e. the share of households living in densely/intermediate/thinly populated areas, per region.

All equations are estimated using the *fixed-effects estimator* for panel data in order to account for unobserved variables that can be assumed to remain constant for each region during the sample period. These include region-specific factors such as differences in institutional quality and geographical location. Time-varying effects that affect all regions equally, on the other hand, are controlled for by the time-specific fixed effects.

The hypotheses tested in this chapter can be restated using the estimation equations, Eqs. (12.1), (12.2) and (12.3), as in Box 12.3:

Box 12.3 Hypotheses tested in Chapter 12

H1: Related and unrelated variety in production and knowledge are positively related to employment growth across all regions: using Equation (12.1), this corresponds to $\beta_1>0$ and $\beta_2>0$.

H2: Unrelated variety in production has a stronger positive impact on employment growth in the regions that were most affected by the economic crisis (LFR type 1): using Eq. (12.1), this implies that β_2 is larger in the regime estimated for crisis regions than in that for non-crisis regions.

H3: The effects of related and unrelated variety differ by regional distance to the technological frontier, with a stronger role for unrelated variety in regions further from the frontier (LFR type 2): using Eq. (12.2), this implies that the marginal effects of related and unrelated variety on employment growth vary for different realisations of the variable DTF_r, and the marginal effect of unrelated variety rises with distance to the frontier.

H4: The effects of related and unrelated variety differ by regional degree of urbanisation: using Eq. (12.3), this implies that the marginal effects of related and unrelated variety on employment growth vary for different realisations of the variable DOU_r, and the marginal effect of related variety rises the lower the degree of urbanisation (LFR type 3).

Empirical results

Table 12.1 illustrates the empirical findings for the first part of Hypothesis 1 on related and unrelated variety in production across all regions, as well as for Hypothesis 2 regarding their role in LFR type 1. In the first two columns, the variables in Eq. (12.1) are added group-wise to examine their effects on employment growth for the full sample of regions. Related variety is insignificant, but unrelated variety in production has a statistically significant positive effect that is robust to the inclusion of all control variables considered in Eq. (12.1).[7] Its estimated coefficient in column 2 suggests that regions with 1% higher unrelated variety register on average 0.15 percentage points more employment growth per year. To better judge the size of this estimate, Eq. (12.1) is re-estimated with the variety variables entering in levels rather than logs (not shown), which yields a coefficient estimate of unrelated variety of 0.05. Using the summary statistics provided in Table 12.A1 in the Appendix, this implies that an increase in unrelated variety by one sample standard deviation is associated with an increase in employment growth by 1.7 percentage points, which is a sizeable effect.

When estimating separate regimes for crisis and non-crisis regions by interacting all explanatory variables with a dummy for the crisis countries, it becomes clear that the aggregate effect of unrelated variety in columns 1 and 2 is driven by the importance of this variable in the regions of the crisis countries. The effect of unrelated variety in the latter is more than twice as high as that on aggregate (compare column 4 with column 2). A 1% increase in unrelated variety is now associated with a 0.35 percentage point increase in annual employment growth. Alternatively, when estimated with levels of the variety variables, an increase by one standard deviation (in the crisis subsample) goes along with 4 percentage points of higher employment growth, which illustrates just how important the portfolio effect seems to be for the crisis regions (*LFR type 1*) according to the estimates. In the non-crisis regions, unrelated variety is not significantly different from zero, while related variety has a comparatively small positive effect on employment growth (1 percentage point higher growth for one standard deviation increase in the non-crisis subsample).

Table 12.1 Employment growth and related and unrelated variety in production

	NUTS 2 regions			
	Panel fixed effects estimator			
Model	*(1)*	*(2)*	*(3)*	*(4)*
Dependent variable:	*Baseline*		*Country regimes*	
Annual employment growth	*Coeff. (p-value)*	*Coeff. (p-value)*	*Non-crisis*	*Crisis*
Lagged ln (related variety)	0.004	0.010	0.047**	0.04
	(0.886)	(0.734)	(0.032)	(0.504)
Lagged ln (unrelated variety)	0.169***	0.148***	−0.032	0.352***
	(0.001)	(0.007)	(0.415)	(0.008)
Lagged ln (specialisation)		−0.012	−0.001	−0.013
		(0.233)	(0.882)	(0.696)
Lagged ln (population density)		0.093	0.078	0.334
		(0.622)	(0.504)	(0.518)
Lagged ln (wage rate)		0.035	0.038*	−0.082
		(0.139)	(0.052)	(0.470)
Lagged ln (investment per worker)		0.008	0.015	0.015
		(0.699)	(0.293)	(0.756)
Lagged ln (manufacturing employment share)		−0.228	−0.148	−1.257
		(0.246)	(0.398)	(0.195)
Time dummies	Yes	Yes	Yes	Yes
Region dummies	Yes	Yes	Yes	Yes
Number of observations	750	750	750	750
Number of regions	250	250	250	250
R^2	0.295	0.312	0.366	0.366

Source: own calculations. Robust p-values in parentheses. ***, ** and * indicate significance at the 1%, 5% and 10% levels, respectively.

Therefore, the first key result emerging from the econometric analysis is that unrelated variety in production was a dominant driver of aggregate regional employment growth between 2008 and 2011, and this can largely be explained by its importance in those regions that were most strongly affected by the economic crisis. Given the time period examined, this can be interpreted as evidence in favour of the *portfolio effect* for LFRs – that is, the importance of a diverse regional portfolio of weakly related industries for absorbing asymmetric shocks affecting particular sectors. Related variety, on the other hand, has a small positive effect on employment growth only in the non-crisis regions, hinting at the growth-enhancing role of diversification into related economic activities during more normal economic times and for less disadvantaged regions.

Table 12.2 presents the results of introducing measures of related and unrelated knowledge variety in addition to variety in production (the second part of Hypothesis 1). They provide further evidence of the importance of unrelated variety, especially for the crisis regions. For the full sample of regions, unrelated variety in knowledge-generating capabilities has a small but significant positive effect, while unrelated production variety drops in size and becomes insignificant. A joint F-test, however, reveals that the two measures of unrelated variety are jointly significantly different from zero,[8] indicating that collinearity between them may make it difficult to identify their effects separately. In any case, estimating regimes for crisis and non-crisis countries, a pattern similar to Table 12.1 is found: related variety in production matters in non-crisis regions, while unrelated variety in production has a large and significant positive effect on employment growth in crisis regions. In addition, there is a comparatively small but significant positive effect of unrelated knowledge variety in crisis regions, while related knowledge variety does not matter across all specifications.

Table 12.3 presents the estimation results testing Hypotheses 3 and 4 using Eqs. (12.2) and (12.3).[9] For comparison, column 1 reproduces the estimates of Eq. (12.1) in column 2 of Table 12.1 above. Next, to examine whether the effects of related and unrelated variety differ by regional distance to the technological frontier (Hypothesis 3), the variable DTF_r as well as its interactions with the variety variables are included in column 2. They are all statistically significant, but for their proper interpretation, the marginal effects of related and unrelated variety on employment growth must be computed for different values of distance to the frontier. These are shown in the top panel of Figure 12.3: related variety has a positive and significant effect for regions at the frontier (for which DTF_r takes the value zero), but less so further away from it. The estimated coefficients in column 2 imply that an increase in related variety by one standard deviation for regions at the frontier is associated with an increase in employment growth by 1.3 percentage points. Unrelated variety has the strongest positive effect on employment growth for regions furthest behind

Table 12.2 Employment growth and related and unrelated variety in production and knowledge

	NUTS 2 regions				
	Panel fixed effects estimator				
Model	*(1)*	*(2)*	*(3)*	*(4)*	*(5)*
Dependent variable:	*Baseline*			*Country regimes*	
Annual employment growth	*Coeff. (p-value)*	*Coeff. (p-value)*	*Coeff. (p-value)*	*Non-crisis*	*Crisis*
Lagged ln (related variety)	0.004	0.024	0.024	0.046**	0.041
	(0.886)	(0.447)	(0.440)	(0.049)	(0.742)
Lagged ln (unrelated variety)	0.169***	0.050	0.042	−0.037	0.623***
	(0.001)	(0.475)	(0.557)	(0.360)	(0.003)
Lagged ln (related knowledge variety)		0.002	0.002	0.002	0.002
		(0.432)	(0.532)	(0.471)	(0.576)
Lagged ln (unrelated knowledge variety)		0.012**	0.011**	0.002	0.058***
		(0.016)	(0.025)	(0.583)	(0.001)
Lagged ln (specialisation)			0.001	−0.003	−0.022
			(0.947)	(0.716)	(0.449)
Lagged ln (population density)			−0.024	0.086	−0.373
			(0.894)	(0.480)	(0.365)
Lagged ln (wage rate)			0.041	0.026	−0.101
			(0.192)	(0.321)	(0.532)
Lagged ln (investment per worker)			−0.022	0.030*	−0.070
			(0.416)	(0.064)	(0.181)
Lagged ln (manufacturing employment share)			−0.263	−0.128	−0.939
			(0.232)	(0.505)	(0.276)
Time dummies	Yes	Yes	Yes	Yes	Yes
Region dummies	Yes	Yes	Yes	Yes	Yes
Number of observations	750	677	677	677	677
Number of regions	250	241	241	241	241
R^2	0.295	0.374	0.382	0.496	0.496

the frontier (for which DTF_r takes on the value three), and a weaker but still significant effect for those regions that are just ahead of the most distant group. The estimated marginal effect of a one standard-deviation increase in unrelated variety for regions furthest from the frontier is a 1.6 percentage point increase in annual employment growth.

In summary, a second key result of the empirical analysis is that when distinguishing regions by distance to the frontier, employment growth in the most technologically advanced regions benefits from related variety, while the benefits of unrelated variety increase the LFRs in terms of their technological development. Hence also for LFR type 2, unrelated variety matters.[10] This implies that one way for less technologically advanced regions to generate employment is through diversification into unrelated industries. Since most of the regions that fall into this category are from the EU-12, while regions at the frontier are from the EU-15, this evidence is consistent with the life-cycle view on industrial development, whereby more mature industries benefit from related knowledge spillovers, while industries at earlier stages of product development benefit from unrelated spillovers. The recent economic history of the regions from Central and Eastern Europe – characterised by highly dynamic structural change, FDI inflows and integration into the intermediate stages of European and global value chains – offers some intuitive understanding for this result.

Columns 3 to 5 of Table 12.3 investigate whether the effects of related and unrelated variety differ by degree of urbanisation (Hypothesis 4). To this end, the variable DOU_r^i, which is measured, respectively, by the share of households per region that live in densely populated or urbanised areas, intermediately populated/urbanised areas and thinly populated or rural areas, as well as their interactions with the variety variables, are included in each column.[11] Related variety turns out not to be significantly associated with employment growth at different levels of urbanisation. Unrelated variety is positively associated with employment growth in regions with intermediate and low levels of urban density, and the marginal effect increases the less densely populated a region is. This can perhaps best be seen from the bottom panel of Figure 12.3: roughly from the median level of population density onwards, unrelated variety starts to have a significant positive relationship with employment growth that reaches its maximum for the least densely populated regions. At the median level of urbanisation, an increase in unrelated variety by one sample standard deviation is associated with approximately 1.6 percentage points higher employment growth.

In the sample of European regions considered here, the intermediately urbanised and rural regions have, on average, higher levels of related and lower levels of unrelated variety.[12] Diminishing returns to spillovers from related industries could therefore be a reason why, according to the results, these regions stand to gain the most from diversifying their production structures into unrelated areas. While these results differ from what would be expected

Table 12.3 Employment growth and related and unrelated variety in production: region-type interactions

	NUTS 2 regions				
	Panel fixed effects estimator				
Model	*(1)*	*(2)*	*(3)*	*(4)*	*(5)*
Dependent variable: *Annual employment growth*	*Coeff.* *(p-value)*	*Coeff.* *(p-value)*	*Coeff.* *(p-value)*	*Coeff.* *(p-value)*	*Coeff.* *(p-value)*
Lagged ln (related variety)	0.010	0.061***	−0.007	−0.009	0.032
	(0.734)	(0.008)	(0.825)	(0.818)	(0.205)
Lagged ln (unrelated variety)	0.148***	−0.104	0.298***	0.199**	−0.012
	(0.007)	(0.137)	(0.000)	(0.020)	(0.851)
Interaction related variety × distance to frontier		−0.025**			
		(0.041)			
Interaction unrelated variety × distance to frontier		0.159***			
		(0.000)			
Distance to frontier		−0.196***			
		(0.000)			
Interaction related variety × urbanised			0.048		
			(0.240)		
Interaction unrelated variety × urbanised			−0.407***		
			(0.001)		
Urbanised			0.478***		

			(0.001)		
Interaction related variety × intermediately urbanised				0.069	
				(0.485)	
Interaction unrelated variety × intermediately urbanised				−0.145	
				(0.393)	
Intermediately urbanised				0.157	
				(0.470)	
Interaction related variety × rural					−0.022
					(0.490)
Interaction unrelated variety × rural					0.283***
					(0.002)
Rural					−0.364***
					(0.002)
Other control variables	Yes	Yes	Yes	Yes	Yes
Time dummies	Yes	Yes	Yes	Yes	Yes
Region dummies	Yes	Yes	Yes	Yes	Yes
Number of observations	750	741	750	750	750
Number of regions	250	247	250	250	250
R^2	0.312	0.387	0.330	0.315	0.331

Source: own calculations. Robust p-values in parentheses. ***, ** and * indicate significance at the 1%, 5% and 10% levels, respectively

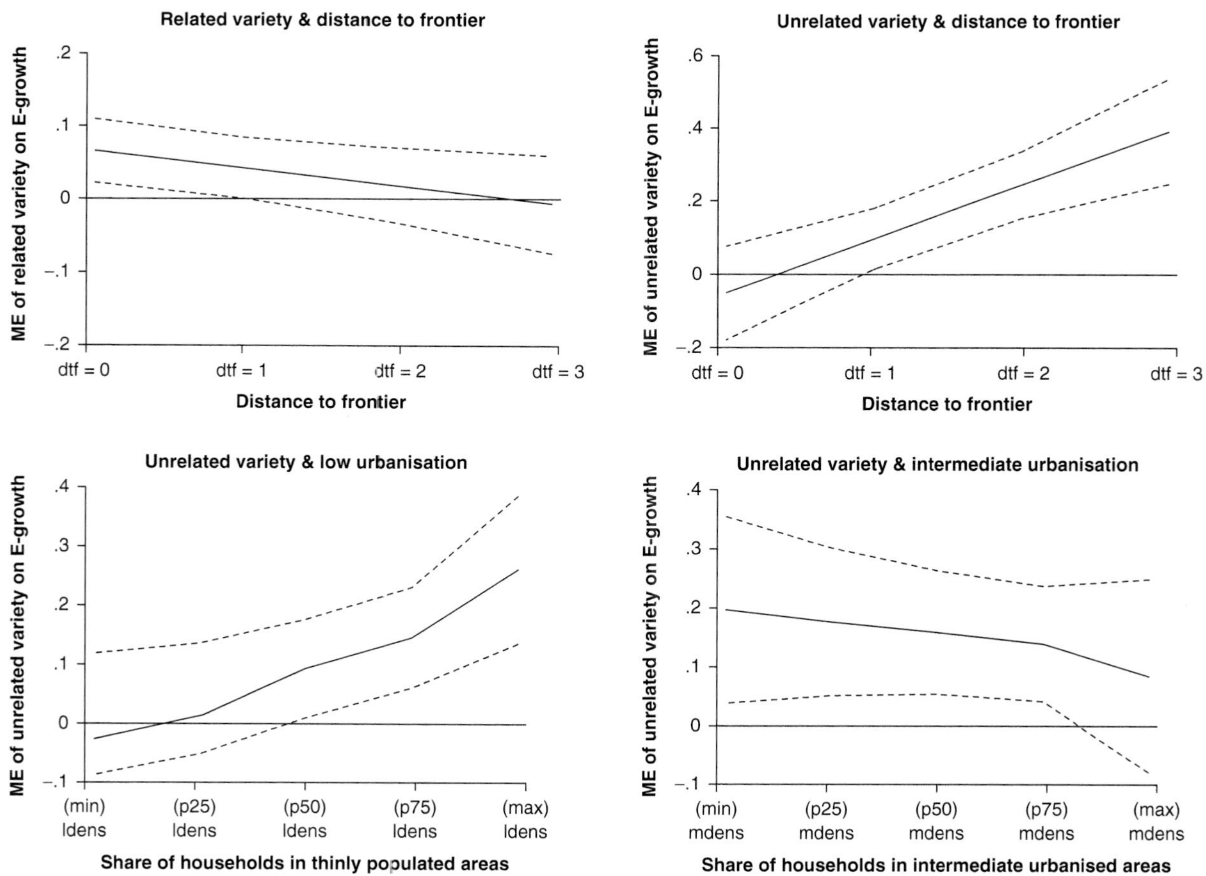

Figure 12.3 Marginal effects of production variety by distance to frontier and degree of urbanisation

Source: own calculations

from the product life cycle view on industrial location and our Hypothesis 4, they are consistent with the results of Firgo and Mayerhofer (2017), who investigate urbanised versus rural and industrial regions in Austria and find strong positive effects of unrelated variety for the latter group. The intermediate urban and the rural regions (LFR type 3) especially, which constitute the large majority of regions in Europe, should therefore benefit from diversification into unrelated economic activities.

Summary and conclusions

This chapter has analysed the roles of related and unrelated variety in production and knowledge for employment growth in European regions that can be considered more or less favoured according to the following dimensions: the strength of the impact of the economic crisis in the late 2000s, their level of technological development and, hence, their distance to the technological frontier, and their degree of urbanisation.

The theme that becomes evident throughout the empirical analysis is the strong role that unrelated variety – both in production and knowledge generation – can play in mitigating the disadvantages characterising regions that are less favoured, be they as a result of the economic crisis, an earlier stage of technological development or low population density. While related variety is significantly and positively associated with employment growth only for regions less affected by the crisis as well as for regions at the technological frontier, unrelated variety drives growth in those regions heavily affected by the crisis, those further behind the technological frontier and in less densely populated or rural regions.

The results presented in this chapter therefore highlight the importance of diversification into new economic activities and knowledge in fields that are unrelated to existing local structures as a portfolio strategy for LFRs to generate employment and strengthen their resilience to economic shocks. More generally, branching into new industrial sectors and recombining diverse fields of technological knowledge can be considered a key driver of long-run economic growth. Although relatedness may help gain product and industry market shares in the short run, it can lead to structural lock-in, and it is diversification into less related areas that drives economies forward (Saviotti and Frenken, 2008).

Because the time period analysed in this chapter coincides with the recent economic crisis and is relatively short, however, further research is needed to substantiate these conclusions. In particular, given the sample period studied, the shock-absorbing role of unrelated diversification probably matters more than would be the case in calmer economic times. The small but positive and statistically significant effect of related variety for the non-crisis regions is an indication of this. One fruitful avenue for future research would therefore be to analyse the impact of related and unrelated variety on economic performance in different types of LFRs over a longer time period. This would also allow dealing more robustly with endogeneity. In addition, a combination of quantitative and qualitative research, such as case studies, would be useful for drawing conclusions about the impact of smart specialisation on regional economic performance in the EU.

On the whole, therefore, this chapter provides a first empirical indication that both related and unrelated diversification matter for economic performance for different types of regions. Accordingly, it is important for regional policy to be appropriately tailored. Especially given its role in the development of LFRs found in this chapter, unrelated variety should not be neglected in the smart specialisation strategies of the European Union.

Acknowledgements

The authors would like to thank Andreas Reinstaller and Fabian Unterlass for insightful conceptual and empirical discussions; Peter Reschenhofer and Sebastian Unterlass for data and programming support; Peter Mayerhofer for comments on an earlier draft of this chapter; the participants of the September 2017 Nordregio book meeting in Stockholm for useful suggestions; and the editors for helping to get the chapter in shape for book publication. Financial support by the European Commission under Contract No. ENT/SMEI14IFISI07/SI2.698839 is gratefully acknowledged.

Appendix

Table 12A.1 Summary statistics: data used in Chapter 12 (period 2008–2011)

	Observations	*Mean*	*Std. dev.*	*Min.*	*Max.*
Employment growth	750	−0.008	0.022	−0.141	0.067
Related variety – Production	1000	1.890	0.422	0.331	2.728
Unrelated variety – Production	1000	3.847	0.333	1.593	4.390
Related variety – Knowledge	957	1.625	0.975	0	4.437
Unrelated variety – Knowledge	957	3.779	1.360	0	5.744
Specialisation	1000	0.919	0.525	0.350	4.042
Population density	1000	0.357	0.902	0.003	9.752
Compensation per hour worked	1000	14.93	7.731	1.083	37.52
Investment per person employed	1000	9.845	4.818	0.499	36.74
Manufacturing employment share	1000	0.165	0.069	0.018	0.383

Source: own calculations based on data by Cambridge Econometrics, BvD (Amadeus) and Eurostat (SBS and Regional Statistics)

Notes

1 The time period 2008–2011 was chosen due to data restrictions (see Section 12.3). Precautions were taken in the econometric analysis to control for the influence of short-term factors, such as the use of time dummies and lagged variables.
2 NACEstandsforNomenclaturestatistiquedesactivitéséconomiquesdanslaCommunauté Européenne and denotes the EU's statistical classification of economic activities. See alsohttp://ec.europa.eu/eurostat/ramon/nomenclatures/index.cfm?TargetUrl=LST_NOM_DTL&StrNom=NACE_REV2&StrLanguageCode=EN.
3 The top level in the IPC consists of eight technology fields, from human necessities via chemistry and textiles to engineering and physics. The next level below is the 3-digit level, similar to the 2-digit level in the NACE. Two levels below the 3-digit level in the IPC is the 7-digit level, thus resembling the 4-digit level in the NACE.
4 The patent stock at time t is calculated as $P_t = \sum_{s=0}^{S_{MAX}} \delta^s P_{t-s}$, where s denotes observations on patent applications dating from before the current period t back to 1990, so its maximum (S_{MAX}) ranges between 29 for $t = 2008$ and 32 ($t = 2011$), and δ is a discount factor assumed to equal 0.8.
5 The drawback to allocating patents to regions by place of residence of the applicant (which may be company headquarters) rather than of the inventor is that this may not accurately reflect the region in which the knowledge was produced or used.
6 The location quotient of relative specialisation of region r in sector s is defined as $LQ_{s,r} = (E_{s,r} / E_r) / (E_s / E)$, which measures the share of regional employment in 2-digit sector s relative to the share of this sector in total EU employment E. The location quotients for all sectors in region r are then summed and averaged to obtain a measure of regional specialisation (more, equally or less specialised in sector s than the EU as a whole).
7 The statistical insignificance of most control variables in Table 12.1 can plausibly be explained by their structural nature, implying that they are unlikely to vary much over the short time period available. It is difficult to identify the effects of variables with little time variation using the fixed-effects estimator.
8 The p-value of this test equals 0.03.
9 The focus is on related and unrelated variety in production rather than on knowledge, given that stronger effects were found for the former in the previous part of the analysis.
10 Note that the typology for regional distance to the technological frontier differs enough from that for regions most affected by the crisis to interpret these as separate transmission mechanisms. The correlation between the categorical variables for distance to the frontier and crisis regions is 0.35. Of the crisis countries, the Baltic Member States drop out of the regressions on distance to the frontier because the Regional Innovation Scoreboard 2014 contains no data for them.
11 In these specifications, the control variable for urbanisation economies, population density on aggregate, is omitted. In most regressions estimated in this chapter, it is not significantly different from zero.
12 The opposite holds the more densely populated regions are.

References

Boschma, R. (2017). Relatedness as driver of regional diversification: a research agenda, *Regional Studies 51*(3), 351–364.

Boschma, R., & Frenken, K. (2011). Technological relatedness and regional branching. In: Bathelt, H., Feldman, M., & Kogler, D.F. (Eds.) *Beyond Territory: Dynamic Geographies of Innovation and Knowledge Creation*. London: Routledge.

Castaldi, C., Frenken, K., & Los, B. (2015). Related variety, unrelated variety and technological breakthroughs: an analysis of US state-level patenting, *Regional Studies 49*(5), 67–781.

Duranton, G., & Puga, D. (2001). Nursery cities: urban diversity, process innovation, and the life cycle of products, *American Economic Review 91*(5), 1454–1477.

Firgo, M., & Mayerhofer, P. (2017). (Un)Related variety and employment growth at the sub-regional level, *Papers in Regional Science 97*(3), 519–547. doi.org/10.1111/pirs.12276.

Frenken, K., van Oort, F., & Verburg, T. (2007). Related variety, unrelated variety and regional economic growth, *Regional Studies 41*(5), 685–697.

Jacobs, J. (1969). *The Economy of Cities*. New York: Random House.

Krueger, D., & Kumar, K.B. (2004). Skill-specific rather than general education: a reason for US–Europe growth differences?, *Journal of Economic Growth 9*(2), 167–207.

Neffke, F., Henning, M., Boschma, R., Lundquist, K.-J., & Olander, L.-O. (2011). The dynamics of agglomeration externalities along the life cycle of industries, *Regional Studies 45*(1), 49–65.

Saviotti, P.P., & Frenken, K. (2008). Export variety and the economic performance of countries, *Journal of Evolutionary Economics 18*(2), 201–218.

Van Oort, F., de Geus, S., & Dogaru, T. (2015). Related variety and regional economic growth in a cross-section of European urban regions, *European Planning Studies 23*(6), 1110–1127.

13 Regional structural policies and industrial evolution

Evidence from three European case study regions

Klaus S. Friesenbichler

Introduction

This chapter compares the evolution of the industrial structures of three regions in the European Union (EU) from a smart specialisation perspective. Each region analysed was confronted with structural challenges, i.e. faced declining competitive advantages at some stage in recent history. Two of the three regions were able to overcome their issues by transforming and diversifying their economies.

This contribution asks why some regions were able to escape their structural problems, while others were not. The guiding question puts 'smart specialisation' into a slightly different light, concerning 'smart diversification' rather than specialisation. These insights give important inputs to the design of smart specialisation policies.[1]

The rest of the chapter is roughly structured into three parts. First, the methodological approach and its limitations are presented, also discussing the selection process of the regions. Second, empirical evidence from three case study regions is presented. Third, the observations are reflected against a conceptual background. On the one hand, the discussion draws on the evolutionary economics of structural change, path dependence and diversification. On the other hand, linkages to economic growth theory are also highlighted.

Methodology, data and selection of regions

This chapter relies on a case study approach, which is chosen because data are not sufficiently available to implement statistical methods, and the analysed experiences may largely depend on idiosyncratic environments. Quantitative methods are able to identify stylised development patterns and facilitating factors, but struggle to capture the role of softer, policy-related factors. These include the interplay of different policy fields that are difficult to quantify, yet have contributed to the emergence of different specialisation patterns. Several information sources are used to depict the structural change dynamics, such as publicly available economic data and secondary literature. The focus of the discussion lies on the cornerstones of economic structures, the attributes of institutions and policy fields. Considering the scope of this research, neither a granular policy discussion nor the underlying political economy will be analysed.

Certainly, there are limitations to this study. Even though the mechanisms proposed are based on the economics literature and supported by empirical observations, the case studies observe only the cornerstones of economic dynamics. Future research may explore the interplay of the policy fields portrayed in greater detail. Like any case study, there remain concerns with respect to the generalisability of the results. In spite of these concerns, this chapter makes several interesting contributions relevant to both researchers and policymakers.

Selection process

The wealth of European regions forms our sampling universe, which is obtained from the Nomenclature of Territorial Units for Statistics (NUTS 2010),[2] a geocode standard developed by the EU for referencing the subdivisions of countries for statistical purposes. The NUTS 2 classification is used, which is a subnational level of regional disaggregation. A qualitative, stepwise approach is implemented to identify the regions to be studied. First, the regions are meant to cover the EU geographically, and are therefore located in northern/western, southern and eastern Europe. This criterion not only reflects different histories and development paths, but also illustrates differences in socio-demographic characteristics. Regions are also required to be sufficiently large so that industrial evolution patterns become visible. This is why regions with fewer than 500,000 inhabitants are not considered.

Second, European regions differ in their innovation capabilities, which is why information from the Regional Innovation Scoreboard is used. It groups regions into different and distinct performance clusters: (i) Regional Innovation Leaders, (ii) Innovation Followers, (iii) Regional Moderate Innovators and (iv) Regional Modest Innovators (European Commission 2014). Regions that changed their relative position in the ranking over time were preferred in the selection, because these are likely to be particularly policy-relevant (information is available for the period between 2004 and 2014). The category of 'innovation leaders' is excluded to avoid the best performing regions, and thereby reflect on environments that are typically relevant for less-favoured regions.[3]

Third, regions with energy-intensive and carbon leakage-affected industries were explicitly considered. In regions with a high share of carbon leakage-affected industries, the industrial base is typically dominated by large, scale-intensive firms. Cost competitiveness might be offset by little flexibility to adjust production structures due to high fixed costs, increasing a region's vulnerability to the adverse effects of structural change. When a region suffers from a drop in competitiveness in its core industry, policymakers are typically required to implement industrial rejuvenation policies that may or may not be successful. This is reflected by the policymaking in the chosen regions, which can be interpreted against the background of a smart specialisation strategy.

Overview of selected regions

Implementing these selection criteria identified three distinctive regions – the NUTS 2 codes and the English names used henceforth are provided in parentheses:

- Bucureşti-Ilfov (RO32; Bucharest)
- Steiermark (AT22; Styria)
- Communidad Valenciana (ES52; Valencia).

Valencia and Bucharest, in particular, can be classified as 'less favoured'. Both regions were eligible for EU structural funds under 'Objective 1', which seeks to promote the development and adjustment of regions whose development is lagging. These areas are defined as those with a gross domestic product (GDP) of less than 75% of the EU average. Bucharest was an 'Objective 1' region in 2007–2013 and Valencia in 2000–2006. Styria was not an EU Member State and, by definition, not eligible when it underwent its economic challenges.[4]

The chosen regions offer a mix of regions with regard to regional characteristics. Located in Spain, Valencia is a region in southern Europe. Styria is in Austria, Central Europe, and thus represents an area in the north-west of Europe. Bucharest is the capital region of Romania, in eastern Europe. Styria and Valencia are in Old Member States, while Bucharest in Romania is in a New Member State. Table 13.1 shows selected structural indicators across the selected regions and for the countries in which the regions are located. The gross regional product per capita, a proxy for average economic activity, finds Styria relatively wealthier than the other regions. Bucharest's regional product per capita is lower, but the region is catching up fast. More generally, the growth figures follow the expected patterns: regions with lower per capita income levels grew faster than more developed regions. The impact of the economic crisis on growth rates differs substantially across these regions. While growth dropped only marginally in Styria after 2008, Bucharest experienced a sharp decline in economic growth. The growth rate for Valencia turned negative, mirroring Spain's macroeconomic performance in the crisis.

The unemployment rates indicate that Valencia, compared with Bucharest and Styria, struggles with labour market issues. When one compares these figures with the country-specific levels of unemployment, Styria is below the national average, whereas the unemployment figures for Bucharest and Valencia are higher than the national average. The share of trade- and energy-intensive industries at significant risk of carbon leakage and the share of energy-intensive industries serve as indicators of the degree of industrialisation. While Styria and Valencia exhibit vulnerability with respect to this indicator, there are hardly any emission-intensive industries in Bucharest.

Table 13.1 Regional characteristics

Region/country	*Valencia*	*Spain*	*Styria*	*Austria*	*Bucharest*	*Romania*
GDP/Total population 1990[1]	14,897	15,165	18,749	22,548	3,858	2,963
GDP/Total population 2011[1]	18,161	20,414	27,696	31,953	10,786	4,342
Mean GDP growth 1990–2008[1]	1.60%	2.00%	2.20%	2.00%	6.20%	2.40%
Mean GDP growth 2009–2011[1]	−0.60%	−0.70%	1.90%	1.90%	3.40%	0.80%
Unemployment rate by NUTS 2 regions[2]	28.00%	26.10%	4.00%	4.90%	7.80%	7.10%
Population at 1 January by NUTS 2 regions 2014 in millions[2]	4,956,427	46,512,199	1,214,927	8,506,889	2,282,968 [e]	19,947,311[e]
Population aged 25–64 with tertiary education attainment[2]	30.80%	33.7%	17.50%	20.6%	33.10%	15.6%
Carbon leakage share[3,cl]	50.60%		62.80%		43.90%	
Energy intensive industries (carbon leakage Types A and/or B)[3,cl]	12.80%		5.20%		2.30%	

Note: e = estimated; all data retrieved on 10 March 2015; cl = refers to carbon leakage (share of trade- and energy-intensive industries at significant risk of carbon leakage) and cof carbon leakage).

Source: [1)] Cambridge Econometrics, [2)] Eurostat (data for 2013), [3)] WIFO calculations, Eurostat (Structural Business Statistics). Bureau van Dijk (Amadeus database, 2011).

Empirical evidence

The development of each region is depicted in two steps. The initial part briefly explains the country-specific setting and the key indicators of the regional economic performance. Information provided by the Structural Business Statistics of Eurostat is used to describe changes in the industry structure over time.[5] It also includes information from the Regional Innovation Monitor, an initiative of the European Commission's Directorate General for Enterprise and Industry, whose objective is to describe and analyse innovation policy and performance trends across EU regions. The second part will focus on a qualitative assessment of the idiosyncratic regional developments. These parts offer a sketch of structural challenges and developments, as well as the reaction of regional policymakers.

Styria (Austria)

Styria is located in the south-east of Austria and borders Slovenia and other Austrian provinces. With a regional domestic per capita product of €27,696, its economic activity is approximately 15% below the Austrian average. Between 1990 and 2011, the regional per capita product in constant prices grew by 48% (reference year: 2005). With population density of merely 75 inhabitants per square kilometre, the region is rather rural. At 4%, the region's unemployment rate was below the national average of 4.9% in 2013, which indicates a labour market that matches supply with demand relatively well. The economic growth after the crisis remained relatively high – the post-crisis growth rate of +1.9% is marginally below the long-run average growth of +2.2%.

The region's sector composition shifted towards the service sector. Employment data are available for the years 1995 and 2007. Despite its increase in absolute employment figures, manufacturing declined as a share of total employment from 36% in 1995 to 31% in 2007. In the same period, the employment shares of real estate, renting and business activities increased from 8% to 16%. The other subsectors of the private sector remained quite constant in the overall sector composition. In 2007, construction accounted for 10% of total employment (1995: 11%); wholesale and retail trade, repair of motor vehicles, motorcycles and personal and household goods for 24% (1995: 25%); hotels and restaurants for 8% (1995: 9%); and transport and storage and communications for 9% (1995: 8%). The number of establishments reflects this growth performance and points towards a deepening of activities, especially in services. There were 2,145 establishments in real estate in 2007, which is more than five times that in 1995. There were 113 establishments in R&D (1995: 27; +319%), 1,501 in computer and related activities (1995: 364; +312%), 365 in the renting of machinery and equipment (1995: 226; +62%), and 7,380 establishments were assigned to other business activities (1995: 2946; +151%). At the same time, the region remained heavily industrialised. In 2007, the largest employment sectors within the manufacturing sector were the manufacture of machinery and equipment (13%), the manufacture of fabricated metal products (13%) and the manufacture of motor vehicles, trailers and semi-trailers (12%), which had an average establishment size of 178.

The Regional Innovation Monitor classifies Styria as an Innovation Follower, the second highest category. Even though the regional innovation performance has improved substantially since 2004, the sub-indicators paint a mixed picture. On the one hand, the share of people with tertiary education and government R&D expenditures is below the EU average. On the other hand, R&D financed by both private businesses and higher education facilities are above the EU mean, as was the number of patents per million inhabitants. The business environment is stable and reliable, and innovation promotion has a long tradition in manufacturing, but falls short in services as well as non-traditional sectors. This is surprising insofar as the Styrian economy diversified into (manufacturing-related) knowledge-intensive business services, which takes a more prominent position in economic structures than in other manufacturing-dominated regions in Europe (SBS data). Styria's strengths in (medium-tech) manufacturing expanded towards related services, which may serve as a basis for smart manufacturing (Industry 4.0). Over and above industrial path dependence, this policy focus might hamper the diversification of the regional economy. Policy measures often hinge on cluster initiatives, and instruments focus on human capital building and internationalisation (Leo and Seon 2011).

Styrian innovation policies rely on continuity. The region's 'smart regional specialisation' strategy focuses on three broad sectors: mobility, eco tech and health tech. The means adopted are typical innovation policy instruments, including business location development and business location management, supporting innovation and R&D, entrepreneurship and growth of young companies, skills development and the internationalisation processes.[6]

Legacy of the steel industry

The Styrian economy used to be dominated by largely state-owned manufacturing firms in the iron and steel industry. These highly vertically integrated firms already lost their headquarter functions in the 1960s and 1970s to the advantage of Vienna. The sector faced severe structural crisis when oil prices surged in the 1970s and there was a drop in demand that revealed operative inefficiencies. The exposure to a new economic situation in the 1990s due to the fall of the Iron Curtain on its border aggravated structural challenges. At the end of the 1980s, large firms were (re)privatised and downsized, which set the basis for corporate transformations. After the restructuring, a new firm base could exploit growing demand from the mid-1990s onwards. Wide parts of the economic activities could be maintained, even though planning functions, R&D and marketing/distribution functions had largely been lost. This led to poor economic growth until the 1990s, an unbalanced labour market and little economic dynamism, expressed by a low rate of innovation and firm entry. In particular, the problems of heavy industry located mainly in the northern part of Styria were affected by the structural crisis (Marchese and Potter 2010). These issues were overcome by a series of structural changes that facilitated the shift away from a Fordist system to a collaborative, SME-based cluster structure. Change already occurred in the 1980s, and is therefore not reflected in the present data series that begin in 1995. As large firms were broken up and a decentralised firm base emerged, firms were required to focus on niche markets and to specialise.

Innovation and diversification

The regional innovation pattern shifted away from firm-specific technologies towards a regional innovation system in the 1990s, when collaborations with universities and colleges started to play a crucial role. New industries were established through cluster policies, which often met strong political support. For instance, a car cluster was established by foreign direct investment (FDI) by a Tier 1 car supplier, also drawing on the 'endogenous roots' of the industry. Further investments by international manufacturers followed (Kaufmann and Tödtling 2000).

Knowledge-intensive functions such as R&D or marketing were outsourced, which led to the emergence of a knowledge-intensive service industry that is tightly linked to the region's manufacturing base. While the decentralisation reduced the product range at the firm level, it allowed for diversification at the regional level. There is evidence that some firms conducting R&D have shifted away from a demand-pull to a science-push business model. This was facilitated by regional policies, which promoted cooperation, networks and new institutions of knowledge generation. Yet, there remains a rather high concentration of economic activity in a relatively small range of technology fields (Marchese and Potter 2010).

Structural change was enabled by the relatively strong R&D capabilities in the region. There are several universities, such as the Technical University of Graz, the University of Graz and the University of Leoben, a university for mining, metallurgy and materials. In addition, applied colleges were established (e.g. FH Joanneum). Even though the education system has continuously adjusted to provide adequately skilled human capital, there are constant reports of skills shortages in certain knowledge fields. Matching labour demand to labour supply will continue to remain a challenge for local policymakers (Leo and Seon 2011). In addition, the region's manufacturing base has benefitted from Austria's dual education system. The long-established system combines apprenticeships in companies with compulsory training at a vocational school. This helped prevent human capital shortages by allowing larger firms especially to create the knowledge that they require.

Bucharest (Romania)

Romania's capital region consists of Bucharest, the capital city that is the national political and administrative centre, and Ilfov County, the surrounding area. The region exhibited a remarkable catching-up process. Between

1990 and 2011, the regional per capita product in constant prices grew by a total of 180% (base year: 2005). The regional domestic product per capita amounted to €10,786 in 2011. Economic growth declined with the crisis, but was still positive at +3.4%, amounting to approximately 6% before the crisis. These figures should be interpreted with caution, however. The Romanian currency was devalued sharply against the euro between 1999 and 2005, and the exchange rate became somewhat stable only from 2009 onwards. The unemployment rate amounted to 7.8% in 2013, which is only slightly above the national average.

In 2007, manufacturing accounted for 20% of the total economy. Wholesale and retail trade, repair of motor vehicles, motorcycles and personal and household goods accounted for 28%; real estate, renting and business activities for 24%; transport storage and communications for 11%; construction for 12%; hotels and restaurants for 3%; and electricity, gas and water supply for 2%. Total employment in the manufacturing sector decreased by 26.9%, from 260,930 employees in 1995 to 190,728 employees in 2007. Since unemployment rates remain relatively low, these dynamics in manufacturing point to a structural change towards the service industries, which is in line with observations for many transition economies (Friesenbichler et al. 2014). In 2007, the largest manufacturing industries were the manufacture of food products and beverages, with an employment share in the sector of 17.2%, followed by publishing, printing and reproduction of recorded media (10.2%) and the manufacture of wearing apparel, dressing and the dyeing of fur (9.4%).

The Regional Innovation Monitor classifies the Bucharest region as a Moderate Innovator with an increasing composite innovation score. As a region in a catching-up country, it pursues mainly an investment-driven growth strategy and imitates existing technologies (Acemoglu et al. 2006). It still struggles with the establishment of an efficient public administration, which imposes economic, social, political and structural challenges. Poor institutions have been identified as the single biggest challenge to innovation and diversification. Regional innovation policies and formal institutions are lacking (Ranga 2012). However, accession to the EU has not only opened markets but has also facilitated institutional reform that facilitated the provision of a level playing field for entrepreneurs (Böheim and Friesenbichler 2015).

A series of policy challenges have been identified, such as improvement of the region's connectivity via expansion of transport infrastructure and solving social and environmental issues (Ranga 2012). In 2012, the share of the population aged 25–64 with tertiary education attainment was 32%. This reflects a substantial increase over the previous decade – in 2003 the share was 22.6% (Eurostat data). The smart specialisation strategies of Bucharest-Ilfov are embedded in the country's overall strategies, which mainly focus on cohesion by attracting investments and cooperating with other EU regions.[7]

Managing the transition

The regional economic structure is the result of economic transformations that began in December 1989 with the collapse of the socialist economic system. After macroeconomic adjustments in the 1990s, Romania experienced rapid economic growth in the 2000s. Bucharest, and Romania as a whole, shared the experiences of other countries with a communist legacy. The transition process changed the economic system to private-sector allocation, which replaced the command economy. This occurred mainly through restructuring of the formerly state-owned enterprises and the establishment of a new firm base through facilitating firm entry and trade openness (Böheim and Friesenbichler 2015; Friesenbichler et al. 2014; Ranga 2012).

The establishment of a new allocation system implied that economic inefficiencies were being addressed, and 'labour hording' in inefficient firms became more difficult (Ferrari 1999). The restructuring – particularly of the mechanical, metallurgic and chemical industries in the period 1990–1995 – set labour free, which led to high unemployment rates and the shift of a large part of the industrial labour force to the services sector (Ranga 2012).

The average establishment size in machinery and equipment fell from 103 to 25 employees between the years 2000 and 2007. Transition policies led to a firm-level productivity distribution, which indicates higher efficiency levels (Friesenbichler et al. 2014). In 2010, employment in manufacturing accounted for 20%, construction for 10% and services for approximately 70% of the economy, with ICT, telecommunications and finance as the largest industries (Pen and Hoogerbrugge 2012).

Structural change affected the two subregions differently. Bucharest as the urban centre turned into a "re-construction city" (Pen and Hoogerbrugge 2012), and Ilfov experienced a transformation away from agriculture (Ianoş et al., 2010). This had a massive socio-economic impact on both areas, but especially on Ilfov. Its economic activities changed from subsistence farming as the starting point in the 1990s. The workforce became increasingly oriented toward the service sector, and the land was reclassified from agrarian to residential areas. This transformed large parts of Ilfov into suburbs of Bucharest. Hence, structural change not only required labour market adjustments, but also substantially altered the city's physical structure (Ianoş et al. 2010).

EU membership

Changes in economic policy were to a large degree driven by the European Union. Romania became an acceding country to the EU in 2004, and a full member in 2007. The EU accession process facilitated economic openness and institutional reforms (Böheim and Friesenbichler 2015), even though corruption remains an issue and the creation of a metropolitan area is still in its infancy.

The driver of change and productivity increases was the implementation of a better technology base (Friesenbichler and Peneder 2016). Foreign technologies were adapted, especially from EU-15 countries. This was made possible by incoming FDI. While this has driven the catching-up process of Romania as a whole, it was particularly pronounced in Bucharest, which is the country's foremost attractor region for FDI. Between 2003 and 2006, Bucharest recorded approximately 60% of the country's total FDI (Pen and Hoogerbrugge 2012). The industries that FDI targeted most were mainly food and drink in Ilfov County and real estate and financial intermediation in Bucharest itself (Ranga 2012). However, the strong linkages to the EU also imply that the region's economy depends on external economic developments. This not only holds due to its exposure to the business cycles of the EU and the need for FDI, but is also reflected by the region's reliance on structural funds (Pen and Hoogerbrugge 2012).

Even though the region struggles with a brain drain of the highly skilled, improvements in the knowledge base were driving structural change. The human capital base has been constantly evolving and adjusting to market needs. Bucharest's labour market is characterised by a pool of well-trained human capital. The majority of the employees have a university degree, and the wages of the work force are relatively low (Pen and Hoogerbrugge 2012).

The EU has also been a key driver of the formulation of economic policies, which also concerns smart specialisation. Since policies are hardly set at the regional due to the lack of functional regions in Romania, there is no document discussing Bucharest separately. However, Romania has chosen a bottom-up approach using an extensive consultation approach to identify fields that are relevant for specialisation policies. This reflects the fact that smart specialisation thinking is still in its infancy.[8]

Valencia (Spain)

The province of Valencia is an autonomous community located in the south-eastern part of the Iberian Peninsula. It is divided into the provinces of Castellon, Valencia and Alicante. The region is densely populated, with a population of almost five million and a population density of 217 inhabitants per square kilometre. The regional domestic product amounted to €18,161 in 2011, which was below the national average of €20,414. Between 1990 and 2011, the regional per capita product in constant prices grew by 22% (base year: 2005; +1.6% per annum). Like other regions in Spain, Valencia experienced a sharp decline in economic growth rates after the global financial crisis of 2008. The mean growth rate between 2009 and 2011 was negative at −0.6%. The region faces severe labour market issues, with an unemployment rate of 28%.

The sector wholesale and retail trade, repair of motor vehicles, motorcycles and personal and household goods accounted for 29% of the private sector's total employment; manufacturing for 21%; and construction for 20%. This high share mirrors the construction boom that became a structural issue in the later years of the crisis. Hotels and restaurants accounted for 8% of employment, showing the relevance of tourism to the region. Real estate, renting and business activities accounted for 6%. Within this sector, real estate activities accounted for 27%; and knowledge-intensive business services accounted for 64%.

Total employment in manufacturing and mining and quarrying increased from 210,022 in 1995 to 265,720 in 2007 (+27%). The largest industry in the region was the manufacture of other non-metallic mineral products, with an employment share of 19% in 2007 (1995: 18%). Other main industries were: the manufacture of fabricated metal products (13%) and the manufacture of furniture and other manufacturing (12%). This list indicates a structural change in industry composition. In 1995, the tanning industry and the dressing of leather, the manufacture of luggage, handbags, saddlery, harness and footwear accounted for 15% and the manufacture of textiles for 11%. The decline in the employment share of textiles exemplifies especially the structural issues that are common in Spain.

The Regional Innovation Monitor classifies Valencia as a Moderate Innovator. Since 2004, its composite innovation index has been falling marginally. Compared to the EU average, the Valencian community shows relative strengths with respect to public funding, such as the share of graduates with tertiary education, lifelong learning and public R&D expenditures. However, private-sector activities perform poorly, which is mirrored by low employment shares in medium–high and high technology manufacturing and the services sector, or low private R&D expenditures. Innovation policies have tried to address these shortcomings and have set up a sector-oriented network of research centres whose main objective is to bring R&D to private companies. Yet, the poor cooperation culture persists, and firms are often reluctant to cooperate due to a perceived insufficient appropriability of innovation rents (Etxaleku and Girbés 2011). In 2012, the share of the population aged 25–64 with tertiary education attainment was 30.1%, which lies significantly above the share of 21.7% (Eurostat data) in 2003.

Scale intensity and lack of diversification

Valencia is home to one of Spain's most important ports. Since 1985, the Port Authority has gradually expanded and developed the port's infrastructure. Maritime trade through Valencia has grown exponentially, increasing shipment volumes from 6.6 million tons in 1993 to more than 40 million tons in 2006. This has attracted major shipping and transport companies and has facilitated the region's connectedness with global value chains (Prytherch and Boira Maiques 2009). However, the port activities have generated few spin-offs, and the industrial structure of the region is still dominated by agriculture and, to a lesser extent, the manufacture of ceramic tiles, which continues to be a major source of income for the countryside.

Due to fierce international competition from Asia, the once prominent leather industry and the manufacture of textiles have been on the decline since the end of the quota system of multi-fibre agreements. In 1976, a car assembly plant of a major US car manufacturer opened in Almussafes in the southern part of the province. In 2006, approximately 7,000 employees were employed at the plant. However, the site could not generate a cluster and is exposed to fierce competition from different production sites of the car manufacturing industry.

Tourism is another major source of income. The municipal government of the city of Valencia planned to convert the city into a major destination for cultural entertainment tourism. This is most evident on lands to the east of the city, where a massive exhibition centre has been built – the Ciutat de les Arts i de les Ciències, where croplands and light manufacturing used to be (Prytherch and Boira Maiques 2009). However, the tourism industry frequently reaches infrastructure boundaries in the summertime, especially when hydrological demand is high.

Policy coordination issues

Given the structural issues and the need for diversification, the region is searching for sources for diversification. For instance, tertiary education might provide a growth impulse that leads to industrial diversification. Valencia is home to several universities, which are not linked to regional development goals, however. Involving the tertiary education sector is difficult, because Valencia's higher education institutions are highly autonomous (Zepeda et al. 2006). This is problematic, since policy documents perceive human capital as the central means to promote structural change. For instance, the Regional Innovation Monitor highlights the need to improve the training of human resources to suit the needs of business and the knowledge society in general. This reflects wider issues, however, such as underdeveloped coordination mechanisms of training and education facilities, or low degrees of collaboration between the private sector and education (Etxaleku and Girbés 2011). Innovation policies continue to search for diversification approaches, e.g. by policy-learning from other regions with respect to cluster formation. The recent smart specialisation strategy lists a series of priority sectors and corresponding innovation policy instruments.[9] However, it remains unclear how the region's smart specialisation strategy seeks to address the institutional coordination issues effectively.[10]

Results

The following analysis discusses the commonalities and differences of the regional developments against three guiding questions: how did the challenged and less-favoured regions overcome their structural issues? How do their experiences contrast with diversification concepts? Do the findings correspond to economic growth theory?

Overcoming path dependence

Economic structures are certainly not independent of their past, i.e. they are 'path dependent'. Structures are the outcomes of established decisions and routines, implying self-enforcing processes. While such path dependence tends to reinforce existing strengths and competitive advantages, it may also lead to lock-in situations, which is particularly challenging when existing structures cannot cope effectively with the economic environment. This was observable in all three regions, even if the evidence revealed different developmental challenges. Bucharest was challenged to establish a market economy after the collapse of communism, leading to substantial structural challenges, especially after overcoming the most pressing macroeconomic imbalances. Styria's metal industry, the region's formerly dominant sector, was confronted with a structural crisis in the 1970s and 1980s. Valencia had to compensate for the declining textile and leather industry. Two regions, Bucharest and Styria, overcame their structural issues, which were driven by diversification processes, especially towards more knowledge-intensive business services. In both regions, the initial base was challenged by inefficiencies linked to public ownership. These were eventually overcome by the fragmentation and decentralisation of troubled firms and industries. The number of firms increased, and the average establishment size decreased. This indicates a deepening of the industry structure and an increase in related variety. This 'industrial rejuvenation' seems to have been essential for the survival of the troubled industries. The fragmentation of the industrial structure facilitated the restructuring of the regional technology base.

In both Bucharest and Styria there was a shift away from manufacturing towards services. The declining manufacturing share was accompanied by an increase in the employment share of knowledge-intensive business services. It seems that activities that used to be conducted in manufacturing have shifted to specialised segments of the service sector, especially to knowledge-intensive business services. This suggests that the service sector is not independent of the manufacturing base.

Economic diversification occurred hardly at all in Valencia's economy, for various reasons. It lacked an external impetus, such as FDI. It suffers from substantial economies of scale, preventing the fragmentation of structures and making it difficult to react to structural shocks due to their relative inflexibility to adjust supply. This seems to be a key difference between Valencia and Styria. While the port in Valencia cannot be disintegrated into smaller parts, Styria's various steel plants allowed for a higher degree of fragmentation, which enabled restructuring processes.

Table 13.2 provides an overview of the regional developments of the regions discussed. The synopsis table includes the innovation capabilities according to the Regional Innovation Scoreboard, the industrial evolutions, the impetus to diversify and the challenges that remain.

Different diversification patterns

The development of comparative advantages tends to be driven by the diversification into more weakly related product varieties. It has been argued that closely related products drive export growth and export performance in the

Table 13.2 Overview of regional developments

	Styria	*Bucharest*	*Valencia*
Innovation Scoreboard (2014)	Innovation Follower	Moderate Innovator	Moderate Innovator
Industrial evolution	Shift from scale-intensive, medium-tech manufacturing industries to related (knowledge-intensive) services in the 1990s; strong manufacturing base remains	Communist legacy, emergence of the service sector and diversification into unrelated activities in the late 1990s and 2000s	Little diversification over time; structures dominated by low-tech industries such as tourism and scale-intensive activities (e.g. port)
Impetus to diversify	Privatisation of heavy industry, emergence of SMEs leading to a more fragmented knowledge base, which facilitated structural change, inward FDI, increase in R&D and skills development	Economic transition (privatisation of state-owned enterprises and establishment of a market economy, institution building), FDI, EU accession and technology inflow	Diversification dynamics are largely lacking; initiatives undermined by coordination failures
Challenges	Need to continue innovation-driven growth pattern; cluster policies rely on existing strengths; diversification into unrelated areas hardly occurs	Switch from an investment-driven to an innovation-based economy; need for better infrastructure, institution building, fighting corruption, brain drain	Overcoming structural lock-in; resolving coordination issues involving private-sector, R&D institutions, universities, government

Source: author's own analysis

short run, while weakly related products drive performance in the long run (Saviotti and Frenken 2008). The diversification of the economy of Bucharest (Romania) occurred through an increase in the overall industrial mix, the unrelated variety. New industries emerged, diversifying into areas that were not considered by Romania's command economy. The once underdeveloped service industry flourished and turned into a driver for economic growth. In Styria (Austria), diversification occurred after a deepening of industries and an increase in the related variety, within the boundaries of related technology fields. Styria diversified into both machinery and equipment and the relatively new automobile industry. This can be interpreted as a phoenix industry, a special case of the cluster literature, where the concentration of an industry in a region supports linkages between firms, improving the labour market pooling and creating specialised suppliers (Marshall and Guillebaud 1961; Porter 1998).

The evidence for both regions is in line with the entrepreneurship literature, which argues that diversification into new activities is typically driven by new firms (Dunne et al., 1988; Malerba 2002). Valencia (Spain) has not recovered from the decline of the textile industry, and its entrepreneurial base is largely centred around the rather low-tech tourism industry and scale-intensive transport and shipment firms that rely on the port of Valencia.

Economic performance and smart diversification are contingent on the specific regional and temporal context (Firgo and Mayerhofer 2017). This directionality can be interpreted from a 'varieties of capitalism' perspective. In 'liberal market economies', relations between firms and other actors are coordinated mainly by competitive markets and price mechanisms. In 'coordinated market economies', firms engage in more strategic interactions with trade unions, suppliers of finance and other actors (Hall and Soskice 2001). Styria in Austria can be classified as a coordinated market economy where existing actors and institutions interact strategically to channel and direct allocation processes. Bucharest does not have that degree of coordination among its actors due to its past as a command economy. Actors are required to rely on a more market-based economy. Valencia in Spain can be seen as a 'Mediterranean' hybrid. The move of Styria's economy towards related fields and Bucharest's economy towards unrelated structures support previous findings (Boschma et al. 2015), suggesting that relatedness is a stronger driver of diversification into new products in coordinated market economies, while liberal market economies show a higher probability of moving into more unrelated industries (Boschma and Capone 2014).

The regions also differ in their origins of diversification. In Bucharest, industrial diversification was predominantly caused by FDI, which served as a vehicle for technology transfer. While other inputs (e.g. education, infrastructure) were necessary (and improved) to maintain economic growth, the main stimulus was FDI investment from other EU countries. Industrial diversification in Styria was by and large a generic process, driven mainly by regional industrial policies. This is plausible if one assumes that rents from FDI spillovers decrease with regional capacities. Yet, FDI also played a role in Styria's diversification into relatively unrelated industries, which occurred at a time when its economic capabilities were lower than today's.

The experiences of both regions are line with insights from evolutionary economics, arguing that diversification into related activities tends to originate from existing structures and are often achieved by spin-offs from large firms. Diversification into more unrelated activities requires other kinds of start-ups, which are, for instance, FDI-driven, and is made possible by other externalities (Buenstorf and Klepper 2010).

The technological frontier and human capital

A technological frontier argument became evident also (Acemoglu et al. 2002). Technologically more advanced regions seek to promote R&D and establish an environment conducive to firms or networks of firms that generate innovations (e.g. Styria). A catching-up region like Bucharest seeks to foster a more encompassing business environment. For example, a more widely available skill base may facilitate overcoming the lopsided productivity structure in which less productive firms have poor access to adequately skilled human capital. Bucharest seems to be at a switching point, where an FDI-driven catching-up process is required to turn into a growth process driven by more innovation and domestic investment.

The case of Valencia shows that escaping path dependence is difficult. Policy documents often refer to the formation of human capital as a potential remedy for overcoming a lack of diversification dynamics.The provision of higher education, especially, often cited as a growth driver from endogenous growth theory, seems to have been a necessary input for diversification. Regions that do not achieve industrial diversification may perform well in education indicators. The regions in which substantial structural change occurred have shown themselves to continuously adjust the human capital base demanded by firms and have achieved a relatively efficient skill matching on the labour market. This may be reflected in higher shares of tertiary-educated people, but increasing the shares alone seems to be insufficient to generate growth and diversification processes. The case studies indicate rather that the human capital base needs to co-evolve with a region's technological base and firms' absorptive capacities.

Conclusions

This contribution compared three 'less-favoured' regions in Europe that faced structural challenges at some stage in recent history: Styria (Austria), Bucharest (Romania) and Valencia (Spain). The latter two were eligible for the EU's structural funds for lagging regions (Objective 1). Styria struggled economically before Austria's EU accession.

The transformation of Styria's economy after the decline of the steel industry can be interpreted against a phoenix industry background, where large firms were split into smaller units allowing for an industrial rejuvenation. This was accompanied by a permanently adjusting human capital base and a shift of economic activities towards knowledge-intensive services. Bucharest underwent a transition process from a command economy to a market-based allocation system, which changed both the city and its rural surroundings. It shifted economic activities to the service industry and restructured existing industries substantially. Valencia is struggling with a poor diversification performance. While the port of Valencia along with tourism and a relatively small manufacturing base generate some income, unemployment remains high and diversification into other sectors was hardly successful.

The case studies suggest a series of conclusions for smart specialisation policies. Certainly, there is no one-size-fits-all approach. Nevertheless, some commonalities between the regions became evident. For instance, regions where structures are dominated by substantial sunk costs struggle with diversifying the existing firm base. These regions also tend to be carbon leakage-intensive. Smaller organisational units are less burdened by sunk costs and are therefore less likely to lead to industrial structures that suffer from lock-ins, which again facilitates diversification processes. Hence, a policy conclusion is to foster the establishment of a firm base that is dominated by smaller firms and thereby facilitating diversification dynamics. This notion is also linked to a green industrial policy. If new activities cannot be generated locally – which is typically the case in less-favoured regions that are distant from the technological frontier – an impetus to diversify may originate from external sources such as FDI. Hence, policies that attract inward FDI and also technologies are an important driver to overcome lock-ins. Finally, local smart specialisation (or rather diversification) policies need to be linked to the local demand structures to be effective. As evidence from Valencia has shown, top-down policy instruments and fragmented initiatives are insufficient to generate structural change. The experiences in Styria have shown how a multitude of policy dimensions interact to eventually promote structural change. Such policies included human capital formation (e.g. via apprenticeships, universities and applied colleges) and thematic R&D promotion programmes, and reached beyond insular targets such as increasing the proportion of the population with tertiary education.

Notes

1 Parts of this chapter were published in an EU-funded project entitled The Relationship Between Export and Technological Specialisation Profiles Across EU Countries and Regions and the Identification of Development Potentials, Specific Contract ENT-SME-14-F-S107-SI2-698839 (Unterlass et al. 2015).

2 For more information, see http://database.espon.eu/db2/jsf/DicoSpatialUnits/DicoSpatialUnits_html/ch01s01.html (accessed on 23 October 2018).

3 The Regional Innovation Scoreboard is a regional extension of the Innovation Union Scoreboard (IUS), which replicates the methodology of the IUS at the regional level. The IUS gives a comparative assessment of the innovation performance at the country level of the EU Member States and other European countries. Innovation performance is measured by a composite indicator – the Summary Innovation Index – which

summarises the performance of a variety of different indicators. The IUS distinguishes between three types of indicators – Enablers, Firm activities and Outputs – and eight innovation dimensions, capturing, in total, 25 indicators that are used to construct the composite index (European Commission 2014). See http://ec.europa.eu/growth/industry/innovation/facts-figures/regional_en (accessed on 9 October 2018).

4 See http://ec.europa.eu/regional_policy/archive/policy/object/index_en.htm and https://de.wikipedia.org/wiki/Ziel-1-Region#/media/File:European_union_erdf_map_de.png (accessed on 23 October 2018).

5 Value added figures are not available at the industry (NACE Rev. 1) and NUTS 2-digit level, which is why employment data ("Number of persons employed" (V16110)) is used instead. As an indicator of the number of firms, a count of the number of local units active during at least a part of the reference period is used. These data allow for the computation of the average establishment size at the industry level. Information on the service sector is available for Styria only, which is why the sections on Bucharest and Valencia focus on the mining and quarrying and manufacturing industries (i.e. 2-digit Nace Rev. 1.1. data for the sectors C + D).

6 See https://www.sfg.at/cms/3724/Economic-Strategy/ (accessed on 9 October 2018).

7 See http://ec.europa.eu/regional_policy/en/atlas/romania/ro3 (accessed on 9 October 2018).

8 See http://s3platform.jrc.ec.europa.eu/documents/20182/89935/Web_DUBLIN_Romania_background_19June2014.pdf/e98a3f94-327f-4ee4-b1b7-61f5183ed7ed (accessed on 9 October 2018).

9 See http://s3platform.jrc.ec.europa.eu/documents/20182/224535/EN_RIS3_CValenciana_Final.pdf/0accb2d4-9990-4cb7-85dc-54b90d032ef5 (accessed on 9 October 2018).

10 For further information (in Spanish), see http://s3platform.jrc.ec.europa.eu/documents/20182/224535/ES_RIS3_CValenciana_Final.pdf/0accb2d4-9990-4cb7-85dc-54b90d032ef5 (accessed on 23 October 2018).

References

Acemoglu, D., Aghion, P., & Zilibotti, F. (2006). Distance to frontier, selection, and economic growth. *Journal of the European Economic Association 4*(1): 37–74.

Böheim, M.H., & Friesenbichler, K.S. (2015). Exporting the competition policy regime of the European Union: success or failure? Empirical evidence for acceding countries. *Journal of Common Market Studies*. doi:10.1111/jcms.12321.

Boschma, R., Balland, P.-A., & Kogler, D.F. (2015). Relatedness and technological change in cities: the rise and fall of technological knowledge in US metropolitan areas from 1981 to 2010. *Industrial and Corporate Change 24*(1): 223–50. doi:10.1093/icc/dtu012.

Boschma, R., & Capone, G. (2014). Relatedness and diversification in the EU-27 and ENP countries. *Papers in Evolutionary Economic Geography 14*(7): 1–43.

Buenstorf, G., & Klepper, S. (2010). Why does entry cluster geographically? Evidence from the US tire industry. *Journal of Urban Economics 68*(2): 103–14. doi:10.1016/j.jue.2010.03.005.

Dunne, T., Roberts, M.J., & Samuelson, L. (1988). Patterns of firm entry and exit in US manufacturing industries. *The RAND Journal of Economics 19*(4): 495–515.

Etxaleku, N., & Girbés, S. (2011). Regional Innovation Report (Valencian Community). Regional Innovation Monitor. Technopolis Group, UNU-Merit Maastricht University, Fraunhofer ISI.

European Commission (2014). Regional Innovation Scoreboard 2014. Brussels: DG Enterprise and Industry, European Commission.

Ferrari, M.R. (1999). Small enterprise clusters for local development in transition context: the case of Romania. Milan: Bocconi University.

Firgo, M., & Mayerhofer, P. (2017) (Un)Related variety and employment growth at the sub-regional level. *Papers in Regional Science* 97(3): 519–547. doi.org/10.1111/pirs.12276.

Friesenbichler, K.S., Böheim, M., & Laster, D.C. (2014). Market competition in transition economies: a literature review. *WIFO Working Papers*, No. 477 (August). http://www.wifo.ac.at/wwa/pubid/47443.

Friesenbichler, K.S., & Peneder, M. (2016). Innovation, competition and productivity. *Economics of Transition* 24(3): 535–580.

Hall, P.A., & Soskice, D. (2001). *Varieties of Capitalism: The Institutional Foundations of Comparative Advantage*. Oxford: Oxford University Press.

Ianoş, I., Cercleux, A.-L., & Pintilii, R.-D. (2010). Remarks on identity building of rural and urban communities in the Bucharest metropolitan area. Analele Universităţii din Oradea, Seria Geografie, *XX*(2): 173–183. http://istgeorelint.uoradea.ro/Reviste/Anale/Art/2010-2/03_OK_AUOG-504-Ianos+.pdf.

Kaufmann, A., & Tödtling, F. (2000). Systems of innovation in traditional industrial regions: the case of Styria in a comparative perspective. *Regional Studies* 34(1): 29–40.

Leo, H., & Seon, P. (2011). Regional Innovation Report (Styria). Regional Innovation Monitor. Technopolis Group, UNU-Merit Maastricht University, Fraunhofer ISI.

Malerba, F. (2002). Sectoral systems of innovation and production. *Research Policy* 31(2): 247–264.

Marchese, M., & Potter, J. (2010). A review of local economic and employment development policy approaches in OECD Countries. Part III: Case studies of regional economic development approaches, 2010. OECD Local Economic and Employment Development (LEED) Programme.

Marshall, A., & Guillebaud, C.W. (1961). *Principles of Economics*. London and New York: Macmillan for the Royal Economic Society.

Pen, C.-J., & Hoogerbrugge, M. (2012). Economic vitality of Bucharest. The Hague: European Metropolitan Network Institute.

Porter, M. (1998). Clusters and the new economics of competition. *Harvard Business Review* Reprint 98609 (December): 77–90.

Prytherch, D.L., & Boira Maiques, J.V. (2009). City profile: Valencia. *Cities* 26(2): 103–15. doi:10.1016/j.cities.2008.11.004.

Ranga, M. (2012). Regional Innovation Report (RO32 Bucharest - Ilfov). Regional Innovation Monitor. Technopolis Group, UNU-Merit Maastricht University, Fraunhofer ISI.

Saviotti, P.P., & Frenken, K. (2008). Export variety and the economic performance of countries. *Journal of Evolutionary Economics* 18(2): 201–218.

Unterlass, F., Reinstaller, A., Vogel, J., & Friesenbichler, K.S. (2015). The relationship between export and technological specialisation profiles across EU Member States and regions and the identification of development potentials. Final report carried out for the European Commission, Directorate-General Internal Market, Industry, Entrepreneurship within Framework Service Contract No. ENTR/2009/033. Vienna: Austrian Institute of Economic Research (WIFO).

Zepeda, E.A., Marmolejo, F., Dewayne, M., & Parellada, M. (2006). Supporting the contribution of higher education institutions to regional development. Paris: OECD, October.

14 A concluding note

Future prospects of entrepreneurship and innovation policy

Håkan Ylinenpää, Iryna Kristensen, Alexandre Dubois and Jukka Teräs

'Smart' regional innovation policies: a retrospective view

The core competence concept, originally coined by C. K. Prahalad and Gary Hamel in 1990, significantly changed our understanding of how to develop organisational competitive advantage, meaning the

> collective learning in the organization, especially how to coordinate diverse production skills and integrate multiple streams of technologies . . . The real sources of advantage are to be found in management's ability to consolidate corporate wide technologies and production skills into competencies that empower individual businesses to adapt quickly into changing opportunities.
>
> (Prahalad and Hamel 1990, pp. 81–82)

Using an analogy to *trees*, Prahalad and Hamel saw core competencies as the roots of a tree enabling a company to develop core products or services (*the tree's trunk*), which in turn created businesses (*the tree's branches*) and eventually products and services offered on a market (*the leaves on a tree*).

The analogy to trees has also been used more recently by a group of researchers at Harvard University in the USA (Hausmann 2016) for addressing the significant actors who enable the development of core competencies. Utilising this analogy, Hausmann talks about "*monkeys*" (*entrepreneurs*) who successfully serve markets by developing and exploiting new technologies and *knowledge areas* (*trees*). Underlining also the importance of quickly adapting to changing opportunities, Hausmann points out the importance of clever entrepreneurs moving their businesses upwards on the tree (further in the value chain) or transforming their businesses to operate on other 'trees' located close to the knowledge area/tree already familiar to the companies. In such transformation processes, serial entrepreneurs are especially important. This relates to classic contributions from Schumpeter (1934) who pinpointed the dynamic and transformative role of entrepreneurs forcing other economic actors into actions that imply continuous transformation and development.

Both research on core competencies and the roles played by entrepreneurial actors have then also been used at meso and macro levels to address the development of regional and national economies. Michael Porter (1980, 1998, 2003) illustrated the importance of entrepreneurs and their companies possessing specific and preferably discrete competencies forming the base for competitive clusters in dynamic regions and national economies. The understanding that entrepreneurial competencies form an important base for dynamic competition and competitiveness agrees with other studies on both the regional (see, for example, Marshall 1916; Dahmén 1984; Saxenian 1994) and national (see, for example, Freeman 1987; Freeman & Lundvall 1988; Nelson 1993) levels.

Evident from the argumentation above is the fact that specialisation per se is not any new or juvenile concept. As is often the case regarding issues of an epistemological or ontological nature, the discussion on the benefits of specialisation has its roots way back in history. Plato (429–348 BC) in his book *The Republic* denoted the division of labour and specialisation as a route to increased wealth and growth of a society's common good. His disciple Aristotle (384–322 BC) developed this understanding by pointing out the importance of securing private property and the use of currency payments instead of bartering on functional markets. Adding more recent historical contributions to our current understanding, Adam Smith (1723–1790) in his classic book *The Wealth of Nations*, published in 1776, demonstrated the importance of a developed market economy based on free trade and a division of labour based on national natural assets, the work force and production costs, a theme further developed by David Ricardo (1772–1823) in his book *On the Principles of Political Economy and Taxation*, published in 1817.

Diversification in related specialisations

From the argumentation above, we may understand human and organisational development as a historically steady and harmonic journey from general knowledge and a broad, but not especially deep, competence towards more and more sophisticated forms of specialisation. This is not the case, however. If we scrutinise history, we instead find an interplay where specialisation works as an overall paradigm for development during some phases of our development while diversification dominates other phases of our history.

Diversification is defined by Investopedia as a technique for managing risks that mixes a wide variety of investments within a portfolio. The rationale behind this technique contends that mixing different kinds of investments and different knowledge areas will, on average, yield higher returns and pose a lower risk than any individual investment found within the portfolio. In academic management research, diversification as a generic corporate strategy was an honoured strategy measure for growth. Several decades ago, Igor Ansoff (1965) pointed out that a diversification strategy stands apart from other management strategies since it usually requires a company to acquire new skills and knowledge in product development as well as new insights into market behaviour simultaneously. This not only requires the acquisition of new skills and knowledge, but also requires the company to acquire new resources, including new technologies and new facilities, which exposes the organisation to higher levels of risk.

As noted above, diversification may be seen as a strategy for both increasing and reducing risks. A key concept that at least partly resolves this contradiction is the degree to which a new product/service/activity is related to an already existing core competence. From a risk perspective, unrelated diversification requiring totally new resources and competencies to be implemented is thus a far more risky business than a diversification that is related to resources and competencies already present in an organisation. Here Boschma and Gianelle (2014) coined the concept of "related variety" to characterise functional diversification based on an existing knowledge and resource base – a concept also adopted and advocated in the S3 platform. In business management literature, this kind of diversification is characterised as concentric (as opposed to conglomerate) diversification (Amit and Livnat 1989).

Diversification as a generic strategy is thus known to be a strategy for risk reduction that in fact often involves considerable risk. Despite (or due to) this inbuilt tension, diversification during different phases in our history has been an honoured corporate strategy. Japanese conglomerates such as Mitsubishi and Sony, Philip Morris's acquisition of Miller Brewing in the USA, as well as the history of Finnish Nokia, are well-known examples. Swedish Volvo, under their then-CEO, Pehr Gustaf Gyllenhammar, diversified during the 1970s and the early 1980s from their core car manufacturing industry into food production (ABBA's fish balls) and sports equipment (Jofa). A common route to diversification is to join forces with or buy in another company (mergers and acquisitions, M&A). M&A are transactions in which the ownership of companies, other business organisations or their operating units are transferred or combined, allowing enterprises to grow, shrink and change the nature of their business or competitive position. Thereby, they also improve their organisational flexibility to adapt to new competitive requirements.

On the regional and national levels, similar, but perhaps more discrete, strategic shifts may be noted. Professor Jan-Evert Nilsson, in a report for the Swedish national agency Growth Analysis published in 2012, describes how a national policy evident during the 1960s and 1970s geared towards influencing companies to locate units to specific parts of the country, thereby creating equal national conditions, was substituted by a policy aimed at maximising national growth – a policy shift also obvious in most European countries. In practice, this shift often implied that a policy ambition aimed at creating similar conditions for people living in different parts of a country, by attracting new companies and new business sectors to locate to regions in the need to diversify their job market, was transformed into a policy aiming for maximal economic growth stimulating regional actors to develop its regions' specific potentials (if any) to contribute to this economic growth.

Shifting between specialisation and diversification, however, also implies other strategic priorities. While specialisation benefits from scaling up existing activities, and thereby reducing costs per unit produced, diversification relies more on economy of scope, where different target markets with different needs and preferences are served. This also implies a need for different organisational structures where very different organisational and regional cultures evolve. One such difference relates to a preference for standardisation versus a preference for maximising flexibility. Another difference refers to an appreciation for organisational and individual expert skills versus appreciating multi-skilled capabilities. Related to this in turn is that professional managers and management practices are highly appreciated in specialised regions/organisations, while their diversified counterparts normally prefer entrepreneurial talents and serial entrepreneurs. Taken together, these differences imply a preference for different regional innovation and business systems where regions/organisations geared towards specialisation tend to prefer systems that Cooke and Leydesdorff (2004) denote as institutional regional innovation systems (IRIS), and regions/organisations geared towards diversification prefer entrepreneurial regional innovation systems (ERIS). This and the overall discussion above is summarised in Table 14.1 below.

While conceptual analyses based on identifying dichotomies and other basic differences may be intellectually stimulating, they seldom appear in their extreme forms in practice. Instead, we may normally observe development strategies and practices that borrow elements from different schools of thought and mix different operational practices. Evident from many contributions in this book, this is also the case when we try to address regional and firm development strategies with a specific interest in regions outside our metropolitan areas. Most regions today try to develop economies of scale and economies of scope simultaneously, where traditional and often large-scale companies coexist with new and often small firms operating on new business/knowledge sectors. It may therefore be suggested that regions employing a successful smart specialisation strategy borrow elements de facto from diversification by identifying and advocating diversification based on related variety as a gateway for development. In this specific respect, smart

Table 14.1 Specialisation and diversification: some differences

Elements for comparison	*Specialisation*	*Diversification*
Main efficiency	Economies of scale	Economies of scope
Market preference	Large and standardised market	Different markets with specific needs
Organisation	Geared towards standardisation	Geared towards enabling flexibility
Critical resources	Management skills	Entrepreneurial skills
Preferred skills	Focused expert skills	Skills in multiple areas
Preferred innovation system structure	Institutional regional innovation system (IRIS)	Entrepreneurial regional innovation system (ERIS)

Source: author's own elaboration

specialisation may be regarded as a strategic alternative positioned in between specialisation and diversification.

Another issue raised by this book is whether different development strategies and cognitive models may benefit or hamper development in non-metropolitan regions, which is in fact the main subject addressed in this book. In many European countries, we may witness today a new-born interest in regional issues, an interest that is normally manifested in Europe as a revival of a regional development policy debate on national arenas often sliding into more political domains seeking more regional autonomy like in Spain, Italy or the UK.

Building on the understanding that regional issues and regional development policies are becoming more debated and higher on the political agenda, one may contemplate whether specialisation or diversification benefits central or more peripheral regions. Obviously, the characteristics of specialisation given in Table 14.1 above indicate a competitive advantage for regions hosting numerous actors with competencies and other resources enabling large-scale production of standardised products and services. On the other hand, dense regions with multiple actors normally also have the advantage of hosting actors possessing multiple and different resources and competence bases, enabling such regions to diversify into new and different knowledge areas. It should be noted, however, that this refers to the meso and macro levels of analysis. If we instead address the individual actor level, we find that individuals and companies in non-metropolitan and peripheral regions, due to lack or shortage of actors offering different kinds or competencies, tend to develop such capabilities in non-core, but complementary, areas themselves. This implies that the shortage of diverse local and regional competencies stimulates/enforces individuals and organisations, such as commercial firms, to become more multi-competent in order to survive. Sometimes, this kind of enforced diversification also results in firms operating very different business areas, such as when traditional farms develop farm stands selling home-grown as well as other farm produce and combine this with offering tourist activities.

In this specific respect, the diversity of regions that we have characterised as less favoured regions (see Chapter 1) may actually have a better territorial readiness for a diversification-oriented development strategy preferring flexibility, multi-competent (serial) entrepreneurs and ERIS-based innovation and business systems exploiting economy of scope more than economy of scale. Building on the understanding that the future will include more diversified market needs in need of multiple competencies and maximal flexibility, this should be good news for businesses and regions located outside our main metropolitan areas.

What have we learned from smart experimentation in less favoured regions?

This book has turned over a few stones to unpack complex and multifaceted challenges related to the implementation of innovation-based regional development strategies in less favoured regions. It demonstrates that the term *less favoured* is multifaceted and the choice of a smart, understood as 'appropriate', policy approach requires consideration of many aspects, such as the nature, function and composition of regional innovation systems, governance structures, proximity linkages, entrepreneurial ecosystems, industrial structures etc. The complex nature of the ongoing EU policy debates on regional disparities and cohesion calls attention to the question of *territoriality* and *place-basedness* in promoting regional economic growth and wellbeing based on existing knowledge dynamics and specific socio-economic, institutional and geographical conditions. Building on classic theories of comparative advantages, smart specialisation has emerged as an adequate space-neutral policy instrument to reduce the gap between the *reality* of livelihoods in the periphery and the *potentiality* for enhanced added value and innovation that these regions may generate. Hence, concentration of efforts and investments on developing regional competitive advantage (as proposed by the smart specialisation concept) is not a mere question of expanding regional economies; it refers directly to the policy's efficiency in using regional assets and (custom-built) tools to generate growth and innovation.

As some contributions in this book point out, this matter can be viewed from another angle, regional *less favouredness* can serve as a catalyst for creating technological and innovation *interdependencies* between sectors and/or regions (see Chapters 5, 7 & 8). Innovation is created via a process of learning and knowledge-building where the key role is assigned to knowledge transmission between economic agents. Adopting an industry perspective on knowledge interflow would imply that a transfer occurs within a specific industry or between related industries. This implies that each industry acts as a generator (a source of knowledge and innovation) or implementer (a targeted field for knowledge transmission) of innovation. From a place-based perspective, leading sectors and regions are usually first-movers in generating innovation, while other, related, sectors, as well as more peripheral regions, are more likely to create their competitive advantage through adopting this generic innovation and applying it to a specific set of activities, thereby enhancing the synergetic use of public investments and inter-industry and inter-regional flows of knowledge. As several authors in this book remark, *urban–rural linkages* play (or should play) a fundamental role in such development, as they stimulate spatial dynamics and knowledge interaction (see, for example, Chapters 2 & 4). Synergies and complementarities between regions and sectors are crucial elements in successful place-based transformations.

The question of the relationship between the *entrepreneurial ecosystems* of urban and less favoured territories remains open for further research. From a systemic perspective, "entrepreneurs are seen as social agents that learn by interacting and develop their entrepreneurial identities only within an appropriate supporting system because interdependence shapes and limits the innovative capabilities and competitive dynamics of local companies" (Kristensen and Scherrer 2016). Consequently, regional (innovation) actors need to seek out opportunities for collaboration with partners that have "a competitive advantage in particular aspects of an entrepreneurial ecosystem" (ibid.). As pointed out already, *SMEs* are *important change agents* in less favoured territorial settings, where business ecosystems are less dynamic and less diverse compared to urban ones. This implies that entrepreneurship and diversification of regional economic activities (see, for example, Chapters 10 & 12) strongly depend on the innovative pursuits of local SMEs or entrepreneurial actors that Hausmann (2016) characterised as monkeys. However, a region's institutional legacy and policy context (see, for example, Chapter 3) influence the entrepreneurial climate as well as cooperation and network dynamics among local agents. This highlights the challenge of developing the efficiency of institutions (in terms of both organisations and rules) in generating specific (often non-transferable) complex governance configurations and tailoring policies to local specificities and demand structures (see, for example, Chapters 6 & 13).

The advancement of the *systemic perspective* to structural change has widened the scope both for understanding the interactions between agents of the innovation process without intermediation of an organised market (i.e. the increasing importance of non-market coordination due to the systemic nature of innovation) and for developing new patterns of governance where public participation is initially motivated by the presence of systemic problems and not by market failures (Galli and Teubal 2002; Chaminade and Edquist 2010). This emphasises the coordinating function of heterogeneous agents required to ensure efficient communication between innovation agents with diverse backgrounds and institutional settings, as well as the alignment of multiple policy dimensions to promote regional transformation (Smits and Kuhlmann 2004). This allows diverse actors to exploit complementarities while maintaining sufficient diversity and increasing the capacity of the innovation system. Greater emphasis on coordination efficiency discloses the importance of different *proximity linkages* (see, for example, Chapter 11) in optimising synergies and spillovers combined with intensified cooperation and networking for innovation (Almeida et al. 2008). Proximity enables the formation of collaboration and enhances knowledge exchange – beyond physical borders (i.e. organised proximity) – by providing an institutional infrastructure and the linkages required for innovation processes. This increases the role of *intermediaries* and *innovation hubs* in strengthening the extra-regional links between diverse actors and resources and thereby filling gaps in the knowledge infrastructure (see, for example, Chapter 9).

While this book has provided empirical material to support a wide and in-depth understanding of the development trajectories of less favoured regions, the future work lying ahead for researchers and policymakers alike will need to focus on designing new development models at the regional level and new types of policy instruments at the European level able to cater for the diversity and richness of the territorial assets of less favoured regions and to promote truly place- and innovation-based development strategies enabling territorial cohesion and the achievement of sustainable development goals at all geographical levels.

References

Almeida, A., Santos, C. and Silva, M. R. (2008). Bridging science to economy: the role of science and technology parks in innovation strategies in "following" regions. *FEP* Working Papers 302, Universidade do Porto.

Amit, R. and Livnat, J. (1989). Efficient corporate diversification: methods and implications, *Management Science* 7, 879–98.

Ansoff, H.I. (1965). *Corporate strategy: an analytic approach to business policy for growth and expansion*. New York: McGraw-Hill.

Boschma, R. and Gianelle, C. (2014). Regional branching and smart specialization policy. JRC Technical Reports, S3 Policy Brief Series No 06/2014.

Cooke, P. and Leydesdorff, L. (2004). Regional development in the knowledge-based economy: the construction of advantage. *Journal of Technology Transfer 31*, 5–15.

Chaminade, C. and Edquist, C. (2010). Rationales for public policy intervention in the innovation process: systems of innovation approach. In: Smits, R., Kuhlmann, S. and Shapira, P. (Eds.) *The Theory and Practice of Innovation Policy, an International Research Handbook*, (pp. 95–114). Cheltenham, UK: Edward Elgar.

Dahmén, E. (1984). Schumpeterian dynamics. Some methodological notes, *Journal of Economic Behavior and Organization 5*(1), 25–34.

Freeman, C. and Lundvall, B-Å. (1988). *Small Countries Facing the Technological Revolution*. London: Pinter.

Freeman, C. (1987). *Technology Policy and Economic Performance: Lessons from Japan*. London: Pinter.

Galli, R. and Teubal, M. (2002). Paradigmatic shifts in national innovation systems. In: Edquist, C. (Ed.) *Systems of Innovation. Technologies, Institutions and Organizations*, (pp. 342–364). London and Washington, DC: Pinter.

Hausmann, R. (2016). Economic development and the accumulation of know-how, *Welsh Economic Review 24*, 13–16.

Kristensen, I. and Scherrer, W. (2016). Public private partnerships as a systemic instrument of governance in regional innovation policy. *International Public Administration Review 14*(1), 37–54.

Marshall, A. (1916). *Principles of Economics*. London: MacMillan.

Nelson, R. (1993). *National Innovation Systems: A Comparative Analysis*. New York and Oxford: Oxford University Press.

Porter, M. (1998). Clusters and the new economics of competition. *Harvard Business Review* Nov–Dec, 77–90.

Porter, M. (2003). The economic performance of regions, *Regional Studies 37*(6–7), 549–578.

Porter, M. (1980). *Competitive Strategy: Techniques for Analyzing Industries and Competitors*. New York: The Free Press.

Prahalad, C.K. and Hamel, G. (1990). The core competence of the corporation, *Harvard Business Review* May–June, 79–91.

Saxenian, A. (1994). *Regional Advantage: Culture and Competition in Silicon Valley and Route 128*. Cambridge, MA: Harvard University Press.

Schumpeter, J.A. (1934). *The Theory of Economic Development*. Cambridge, MA: Harvard University Press.

Smits, R. and Kuhlmann, S. (2004). The rise of systemic instruments in innovation policy, *International Journal of Foresight and Innovation Policy 1*, 4–32.

Index

Page numbers in *italics* refer to figures. Page numbers in **bold** refer to tables.